Foster Barham Zincke

Swiss Allmends and a Walk to See Them,

Being a Second Month in Switzerland

Foster Barham Zincke

Swiss Allmends and a Walk to See Them,
Being a Second Month in Switzerland

ISBN/EAN: 9783337152093

Printed in Europe, USA, Canada, Australia, Japan

Cover: Foto ©Andreas Hilbeck / pixelio.de

More available books at **www.hansebooks.com**

A SECOND MONTH
IN
SWITZERLAND

BY THE SAME AUTHOR.

*THE DUTY AND DISCIPLINE OF
EXTEMPORARY PREACHING.*
Second Edition.
NEW YORK: C. SCRIBNER & CO.

A WINTER IN THE UNITED STATES.
Being Table-Talk collected during a Tour through the Southern Confederation, the Far West, the Rocky Mountains, &c.
LONDON: JOHN MURRAY.

*EGYPT OF
THE PHARAOHS AND OF THE KHEDIVÉ.*
Second Edition.

A MONTH IN SWITZERLAND.
LONDON: SMITH, ELDER, & CO.

SWISS ALLMENDS

AND A WALK TO SEE THEM

BEING

A SECOND MONTH IN SWITZERLAND

BY

F. BARHAM ZINCKE

VICAR OF WHERSTEAD

CHAPLAIN IN ORDINARY TO THE QUEEN

Naturam, optimam ducem, tanquam Deum, sequimur

LONDON
SMITH, ELDER, & CO., 15 WATERLOO PLACE
1874

PREFACE.

WHILE I was engaged in writing my 'Month in Switzerland' of last year, there was in my mind a half-formed thought, that it might be the first of two or three sketches of the country and of the people. This, notwithstanding that 1 forbad its growing into anything so visionary as a common expectation, did yet, though somewhat illogically, dispose me to acquiesce in publishing what might have been regarded as the commencement only of a series, which would require time and opportunities for advancing towards anything at all approaching to completeness.

One of the omissions of that first 'Month,' the Swiss Allmends, or commonable land, I studied this year with some attention, and, too, with some assistance, for which I was indebted both to the Government, and to several Swiss investigators of the history and present action of the system. The results of this study will be found in the following pages.

As to the excursion itself: the ground it covered was greater in extent, and of more varied interest, than that of the excursion of the previous year. The narrative of its work, objects, and occurrences I give unbroken by digressions. To this the chapter on Einsiedln is not an exception, for it is a contribution to the study of that form of religion which still occupies what was the area of the excursion; and the right understanding of a people includes the right understanding of their religion.

Instead of a sketch-map of the ground passed over this year, which, indeed, would be of little or no value, I prefix to this volume a really good map of the whole country. For this I am indebted to Messrs. Keith Johnston of Edinburgh, and of 18 Paternoster Row, London. It will be found useful not only for the 'Month' of this year, but equally for that of last year, and even for ordinary travelling purposes, for it gives the roads, railways, mountains, and glaciers both of Switzerland, and of the contiguous region of France and Italy.

F. B. Z.

WHERSTEAD VICARAGE: *Nov.* 24, 1873.

CONTENTS.

CHAPTER I.

Bretzwyl—Berne—Zurich—Interlaken—The Allmends of the Delta of the Lütschine 1

CHAPTER II.

A cultivated Italian 16

CHAPTER III.

The Brünig—Lungern—Sacheln—Sarnen—Alpnach—Stanz—Ennetburgen 22

CHAPTER IV.

Buochs—Gersau—The Bay of Uri—Altorf—Am Stag—Wasen—Göschenen-Schöllinen—The Devil's Bridge—The Urseren Thal—St. Gothard 39

CHAPTER V.

Val Tremqla—Airolo—Dazio Grande—Faido—Bodio—Bellinzona—Locarno—Lugano—Bellaggio—Como 62

CHAPTER VI.

Bellinzona — Airolo — St. Gothard — Andermatt — The Oberalp Alpe 85

CHAPTER VII.

Am Stag—Klus—The Surenen—Engelberg 101

CHAPTER VIII.

Stanz—Beckenried—Schwyz—The Hacken Pass—Einsiedln . 120

CHAPTER IX.

Einsiedln 136

CHAPTER X.

The Lake of Zurich—Rapperswyl—Glarus—The Linththal—The Pantenbrücke 161

CHAPTER XI.

The Klönthal — Vorauen — Richisau — The Pragel — Muotta—Brunnen—The Rigi Kulm 183

CHAPTER XII.

Lucerne — Alpnach — Through Unterwalden — Meiringen — The Kirchet 202

CHAPTER XIII.

The Grimsel—Obergesteln—Munster—Viesch—The Eggischhorn . 225

CHAPTER XIV.

The Rieder Alp—The Bell Alp 247

CHAPTER XV.

Brieg—The Valais—Lausanne and Gibbon—Details and Plan of the Excursion—Conclusion 272

CHAPTER XVI.

The Swiss Allmends 297

INDEX 363

A SECOND MONTH
IN
SWITZERLAND.

CHAPTER I.

BRETZWYL—BERNE—ZURICH—INTERLAKEN—THE ALMENDS OF THE DELTA OF THE LÜTSCHINE.

Stand, and unfold yourself.—SHAKESPEARE.

ON the afternoon of July 30 I found myself at Bretzwyl, a village some twenty miles to the south of Bâle, far from any tourist-beaten track. I had gone there to see M. Heusler, *Professeur de Droit* in the University of Bâle, and author of a valuable work on the commonable lands of the Canton of Unterwalden. He was then taking his *villegiatura* at this pleasant and primitive retreat in, as it would appear to English eyes, a farm-house of the ruder sort, though it was in reality the mansion of one of the chief proprietors of the neighbourhood. It was distant about a mile from the village, and known by the name of Sonnen

Halle. It was a large, long, rectangular structure. At the end of the ground-plan, furthest from the approach, was the stabling for the cattle; at the other end, that nearest the approach, were the kitchen and store-rooms. Above these departments was the dwelling-house: the best apartments being over the kitchen and store-rooms. It stood on ground that rose all the way from the village, with ground that was much higher behind it. All the land in front of it was in grass, studded thickly with fruit-trees; on that behind it, which was higher, and not so well adapted for making hay, were, here and there, small patches of grain, and of potatoes and other culinary vegetables. These patches were unfenced, and seemed taken only for a time out of the grass-land.

The Professor and Mme. Heusler were so complaisant as to insist on my spending the evening with them. I showed the Professor a paper of questions on the subject of the *Almends*, or Swiss commonable land, I had had drawn up in German, and had got put into print, before leaving England. This speedily and completely explained the object I had in view in wishing to see him. He readily gave me all the information, advice, and assistance in his power; including in the latter letters of introduction to several of the leading people in the Cantons of Unterwalden, Uri, Schwyz, and Glarus, who from their position, and knowledge of the subject, might be of use to me in my inquiries. I cannot recall the pleasant evening I spent at Sonnen Halle with the genial Professor and his accomplished wife, without, at the same time, acknowledging the very grateful sense I have of their kindness.

As we returned to the village—for the Professor insisted on accompanying me back to the little Inn at which I had ordered a bed—there was wafted up to us, on the night air, across the meadows, the sound of music. On entering the village I found that the villagers were concluding the day with a dance and concert; songs, in which many voices joined, alternating with dances. This entertainment was being held in a large upper room, which externally bore the appearance of doing duty as the *Hotel de Ville* of the humble Commune. Those who had not the right of *entrée*, or who preferred the cooler air outside, were standing in groups in the street. While driving through the village, early in the afternoon, I had found the roadway blocked by a crowd that was collected round the stage of a cheap jack, who was putting up to auction lots of gaudily printed cotton handkerchiefs. I afterwards found that these were not the whole of his stock in trade. The stir was great. I had heard the sound of loud merriment before I reached the crowd; and, when I was passing through it, had observed in the faces of most of those who composed it, much eagerness and animation. Such an advent from the outer world was an event of some magnitude in such a village, which its miniature proprietors can seldom leave. With many it was their only chance, for the twelve months, of investing a little of their precious hoard in a little long-wished-for finery. It was an event that moved every mind—minds masculine as well as feminine; that brought everybody into the street; and that was worthy of being commemorated in the evening with a dance and concert; which, too, would act, in so Arcadian a community, as a safety-valve for carrying off the highly wrought excitement of the day.

On being shown to my bed-room, I found that it was a long corridor with beds set head to foot, reaching from the door to the further end. On each was a loftily puffed out eider-down quilt. The day had been unusually hot, and the night was correspondingly warm. I, therefore, lifted the downy mountain from the bed nearest the door, which I had selected for myself, and deposited it on the next, the second bed. As I did this I looked beyond the mountain of eider-down on the third bed. This led to the discovery, on the pillow beyond the eider-down, of a shock of black hair. I was to be, then, not the sole occupant of the many-bedded corridor. By this time I had made also another discovery: there was in the room an overpowering odour of cows and horses. The corridor, therefore, was only the upper storey, with us it would have been the hay-loft, of a long line of stalls for cattle below. As every bed had a window opposite to it, not a yard distant—the shock of black hair had intended to spend the sultry night, under his eider-down, with every window closed—I set the one over against my bed wide open. This, by allowing the exit of the warm air from the room, and the entrance of fresh air from outside, speedily removed the accumulation of stored up effluvium. The room itself, and everything in it, walls, ceiling, furniture, bedding, &c., were of snowy whiteness, and faultlessly clean.

I was up early next morning : but not so early as the good women of the village, for as I was dressing I heard from many houses the clatter of the shuttle. Bretzwyl, then, is still so primitive as not yet to have abandoned hand-weaving ; though even there it must be confined to fabrics of silk, or of wool. Money must be very hard to come at, and a little of it must go a long way, in a place where the human hand can compete with the power-loom. Being a guest of a rather unusual calibre for Bretzwyl—I had even engaged a private carriage to take me some dozen miles to the railway station at Liesthal—my breakfast was served not in the bar room of the little Inn, but in the parlour. The chair was so placed for me at the table as that I should look on the back of the door of the room. On that door was suspended, as a trophy, a work of art, a precious possession, the object which, in the general excitement of yesterday, the mistress of the house had conceived the desire of acquiring, and had bid for in the presence of the village, and paid her money for, and carried home with no ill-founded pride. And now it was displayed on that door for all to contemplate. All would be glad at least to look at it. Perhaps some favoured few might be allowed to take it in their hands, and examine its materials, and structure. It would have shown an unnatural state of mind, and an inability to enter into other people's feelings, if such an object had forthwith been put away in a box, or drawer. It was done more considerately, and with a truer sense of the conditions of the matter, to place it where al' might come, and take their fill of looking at it, anc might admire it, and might understand how happy its possessor must be ; for was it not—to the possession of which the aspirations of no Bretzwyl dame, or maiden, had previously risen—an embroidered, fringed, riband-trimmed *panier* ?

July 31.—Went to Zurich to see another learned Professor, to whom I had a letter of introduction. I found that he had gone, for his vacation, to the Simmenthal. But I had also a secondary object in going to Zurich, for I wished to take another look at the collection of objects from the sites of the old lake-villages, of which I gave some account in the 'Month in Switzerland' I published last year. Again I regarded them with undiminished interest, as everyone would, who has any tincture of history in his composition : for they are an historical record, in which there can be no misrepresentations, or deceptions, of the resources, manners, customs, and life of a branch of our remote progenitors, unconsciously bequeathed to us by themselves, and upon the possession of which we have only lately entered. I missed, however, the custodian of last year, who had spoken of the interest of the objects in the collection, to which he was in succession directing the attention of his visitors, with the bated breath of heartfelt reverence.

August 1.—To Berne, by the first morning train, for a letter from M. Ceresole, the President of the Swiss Confederation—I knew it was awaiting my arrival—in which he would request all Landammans, and other official people, wherever in the country I might go, to give me what aid might be in their power, in furtherance of the inquiries I was desirous of making.

Having reached Berne, and received the President's letter, which, as I had expected, was ready for me, I ordered an early dinner at the Schweizer Hof, a large new Hotel, the back balcony of which commands an admirable view of the mountains of the Bernese Oberland. I occupied the interval with a walk down the main street to the bridge over the Aare, returning by the parallel street that takes you by the Cathedral. During dinner I looked at the distant snow-capped peaks with some thought of the thousands from many lands, who were at that moment around, and among, and upon them. I reached Interlaken as the evening was closing in, having witnessed some of the effects of a fine sunset from the lake of Thun.

At Interlaken took up my quarters at the Jungfrau, in the *dépendance* behind the Hotel. My room commanded, even as I lay in bed, a view of the Jungfrau itself. This being the height of the season the place was full with the part then *in transitu* of the 150,000 travellers who are said to visit it, now, yearly. Sixty years since a carriage could not be found in the place, nor a building that was not of wood. A comparison of these two statements, I do not call them facts, for I have no means of verifying either, will help us in an attempt to measure the progress both the Swiss world, and that beyond, have, in the interval, made in wealth, and in the means of locomotion.

During the night two violent thunderstorms burst on this neighbourhood, separated by a lull of about an hour. They were accompanied by an amount of rain greater, I was told, than any that had fallen, at one time, in living memory. I afterwards saw much of the devastating effects of these storms. I had passed through a very similar one, on the night of the previous Tuesday, between Paris and Bâle. The rain had then come down not so much in drops as in descending jets, and the lightning had appeared to accompany, and invest the train, being before and behind it, to the right and the left of it—everywhere, equally

—at the same time. At the end of the following week, I fell in with a third storm of the same kind, to the south of the Alps, again at night. As far, therefore, as travellers, and particularly pedestrians, were concerned, their effects were only advantageous, for they lowered the temperature for a time, and washed away the dust. All this time the weather was unusually warm.

August 2.—Asked the master of the Hotel to see whether he could procure for me a guide, who understood the *patois* of the Forest Cantons, and could also speak English and French ; and then, as the storm of last night had brought a pleasant morning, went out to take a look at what we here at home would call the allotments of the peasants, but which, in those Swiss Cantons, where they are found, are their own immemorial common property. Though, indeed, in the word allotment is embedded the historical fact that such land was, in this country, once common ; and that it was from time to time reportioned, and reassigned to the common holders by lot. For the purpose I now had in view I had to walk over the eastern part of the level tract of ground on which Interlaken stands.

But first a few words about this level tract itself. The whole of it was evidently formed by the Lombach and the Lütschine. Originally the two lakes of Brienz and Thun were one continuous sheet of water.

At this middle point of the old continuous lake, it happened that, by a convex bend to the south in the mountains that formed its northern boundary, and by a projecting spur, to the north, of the mountains that formed its southern boundary, the width of the old lake had been narrowed from its average of two miles to about three-fourths of a mile. It also happened, by a fortunate coincidence, that, just at this narrowed part, the torrent of the Lombach entered the lake from the north, and that of the Lütschine from the south. Each was impetuous, and often swollen, and so brought down a very large amount of detrital matter. The result was inevitable: the three quarters of a mile of lake must be displaced by transported fragments of rock, sand, and soil. As the two streams worked against one another just where Interlaken and Unterseen stand, this became dry land first; and for the same reason the deposit was here heaped up somewhat higher than it is now, when each is working out only into the still lake. Having jointly in this way put a bar across the lake, they turned their backs upon each other, and the Lombach began to deposit to the west of the bar, and the Lütschine to the east of it; and then they continued their work in these opposite directions, till the Lombach had filled up all the space to the foot of the mountain to the west, and the Lütschine all the space to the foot of the mountain to the east. The alluvial tract thus formed may be spoken of, roughly, as about four miles long, and two miles wide; with the spur, on which stands the Jungfrau Blick Hotel, protruding into it from the south. Of course the Aare kept open for itself a channel through the alluvium. It is obvious that the Lombach, coming from the north, would force down the channel of the Aare as far as possible to the south, and that the Lütschine, coming from the south, would force up the channel of the Aare as far as possible to the north: and this is precisely what each has done. The Lütschine, being by far the larger stream of the two, has done far the greater part of the work. Every particular, as it presents itself to us, is perfectly intelligible. We see what had to be done; and under what conditions, with what means, and in what manner it was done.

What, then, I had gone out to look at was the allotments of the peasants in the eastern side of the Delta of the Lütschine. This eastern side, from Interlaken to Böningen, is about two miles at the base, and about the same length from the base to the apex. Of course the land is highest, driest, and best at the apex, and gradually deteriorates as you approach the base. As you go along the road, which is a straight line not far from the base, on your right hand spade-husbandry preponderates; on your left is grass, worsening into marsh, and ending in swamp. The cultivated part belongs to the villages that surround it. The lower part belongs chiefly to Interlaken. I walked to about the middle of the road; and then turning to the right among the allotments, walked to the apex, that I might see in what way, to what purpose, and with what ideas and feelings, it was cultivated. The wheat, which was not in a large proportion, was of a coarse and unproductive kind, though doubtless it was suited to the rather wet soil. It was nowhere a heavy crop. The ears were small, being only two-set, and with only six lifts. Compared with our English wheats, it would give the miller much offal, and not much flour. The barley varied much in yield. It was a good ear that had twenty-six grains. Maize was a favourite crop. This also varied much: some was very good, and some very indifferent. Potatoes were still more largely cultivated than maize, and formed the chief crop of all. In Switzerland they are generally of a small sort, small both in the haulm and in the tuber. The latter is unusually hard; and, therefore, probably hardy also, which may be its merit, in the eyes of the utilitarian Switzer. There were several patches of haricots, some of cabbages, and a few of hemp. The land was, for the most part, insufficiently manured. In some places it was clean enough, but in quite as many very foul with weeds.

There were here no indications of that love for the land, which, in Switzerland, is so pleasing a sight, wherever it is the absolute property of the man who cultivates it. Nowhere did I see anyone on these allotments, either pulling up weeds, or come to note what damage the heavy storm of last night had done.

It was evident that the heart of the cultivator was not in his land. It was regarded not at all as the beloved associate of a life, as a sympathizing helper, as a kindly nursing mother, but was treated, as a slave, with grudging niggardliness, only with the thought of extorting all that it could be compelled to yield to such treatment. It was manifest, at a glance, that the property in this land was common, and that it was reportioned, and reallotted from time to time.

I walked upon, and by the side of the embankment of the Lütschine from the head of the Delta down to the lake. The rapid, turbid stream, five-and-twenty yards wide, was flowing at a height of two, or three feet above the level of the Delta, heavily charged with ash-coloured mud. As much of this as might be required might easily be warped on to the land in the fashion so successfully practised in some parts of England. It might be brought on to the low, marshy, swampy land to the left of the road, so that, when the mud had been deposited, the clear water might ~~then~~ pass off into the lake. This would rapidly raise the low swamps, now producing only reeds and aquatic plants, to such a level as would enable them to produce excellent grass. This is undeniable, for the deposit would be of precisely the same soil, chemically and mechanically, as that of the most productive part of the apex. As the low swamps along the base belong to the municipality of Interlaken, this will probably some day be done. I suggested the scheme to one of the chief people in the town, and found that, as far as he knew, the possibility of turning to such account the mud of the Lütschine had not yet been debated.

Having finished my inspection of this part of the Delta, all, that is to say, that lies on the left-hand bank of the Lütschine, I crossed the bridge to look at the commonable land on the right-hand bank. This belongs to the Commune of Böningen. The only difference I saw here was that the land was somewhat drier and better; and that it had upon it a few fruit trees. This was a pleasing feature, and results from the enforcement of a regulation in this Commune that a certain number of such trees shall be maintained upon the allotments by their shifting and temporary occupants.

On returning to the Jungfrau, was told by the proprietor that the kind of guide I wanted was nowhere to be found in Interlaken. I, therefore, applied to the proprietor of the neighbouring Victoria, the largest Hotel in the place. He advised me to take Heinrich Ammer. As Ammer had been recommended to me at Berne also, and as I could hear of no one else, after some little conversation with him, I engaged him for three weeks, at eight francs a day, *tout compris*. I had more than misgivings as to Heinrich's sufficiency for my purpose; but, as will sometimes happen under such circumstances, I was impatient; and so I persuaded myself that I had no time for making further inquiries; and then I went a step further, and said to myself that if he were to prove insufficient, it would be a matter of no great consequence.

Reader, in the foregoing pages we have been whisked along the rail to, and through, some places we visited together last year. What has been said by the way will have given you to understand, that I had in view a special object. You will now also know what that object was, and will see that it was one, which might be sufficiently attended to without much interference with the ordinary objects of a Swiss excursion; if they are, as I take them to be, for the mind the enjoyment of mountain scenery, and for the body more or less vigorous exertion. For an excursion of this mixed kind, carried out in a leisurely fashion, and with some contentment, in the narrative of which the special object will take the position, as it did in fact, of so much collateral by-work, I would now bespeak your friendly company.

CHAPTER II.

A CULTIVATED ITALIAN.

*He cannot be a perfect man,
Not being tried and tutored in the world.*—SHAKESPEARE.

BUT before we enter on the narrative of the excursion itself, which will afterwards be uninterrupted throughout, I would ask leave to give a short account of a meeting I had with a fellow wanderer at its first step—while I was crossing the threshold to enter upon it. It was one of those little incidents that are ever occurring in travel, and contribute in no small degree to its pleasure.

August 3.—At a little before 9 A.M. I was on board the boat for Brienz. The morning was fresh and bright. Only here and there a streak of thin white fleece flecked the clear, smooth, unfathomable blue. The late storm had given to the atmosphere a transparency that to the eye brought the mountains very near. I placed myself on a bench athwart the vessel, that I might have the lake before me, and be able to look on the mountains on each side. I had just taken this seat, when a gentleman walked up to me, and asked, if I knew at what hour in the evening the last train left Interlaken for Berne. My interrogator —for we get into a habit of taking an inventory of people, under such circumstances, at a glance—was not stout, but inclined to become so ; well-dressed, carefully, but quietly ; middle-aged, but looking young for his years ; with light hair slightly silvered, the gray just beginning to be perceptible; and of a fresh complexion. He had the assured manner of one, who, from having mixed much in the world, has acquired a facility in making his way, with, under the conditions of the moment, the least amount of friction. I was able to give him the information he wanted.

'Excuse me,' he replied, 'but are you sure that that is the time?'

My authority, I said, was Bradshaw. It happened that I had been asked the same question yesterday.

'Again excuse me,' he rejoined, 'but is your Bradshaw that for this month?'

Somewhat amused, I answered that it was not; and added that, if he would allow me to say so, he was as exacting in his reception of evidence as a lawyer.

'But,' said he, 'I am not a lawyer.'

'Perhaps then,' I ventured with a smile, 'a philosopher, who ought to be not less exacting.'

'Of that, perhaps, a little,' was his answer, returning the smile, and taking his seat beside me.

We remained in pleasant conversation, without leaving our seats, for the hour that elapsed from the time we came on board till we reached Giesbach, which was his destination. At first I had supposed from his appearance and language that he was an Englishman. I soon, however, found that he spoke French and German with equal ease; and that he was an Italian.

When he had left the boat I tried to recall what we had been talking about. As the subjects came back to mind, I was somewhat surprised at their range and variety; not, too, without some sense of humiliation on thinking how few Englishmen, notwithstanding our vaunted public schools and universities, and the large proportion of us who are able to devote their lives to culture, have the breadth of culture of this Italian; and the power of so using their acquisitions as to make them contribute, as he made his, to their own enjoyment, and that of others.

He appeared at home, as much so as if he had made a special study of it, on every subject on which we conversed. He quoted readily, and accurately, from the Greek and Latin Classics. For instance, on my telling him, in reply to the question whether I had any particular object in visiting Switzerland, that I was desirous of looking into the history and existing state of the commonable land in some of the Swiss Cantons, I found him well up on this subject. He repeated, *verbatim*, what Tacitus says of the land customs of the ancient Germans, giving his interpretation of the passage, and his reasons for so interpreting it. He was familiar with the land system of England; and thought it impossible that what had results so much at variance with the wants and spirit of the age, could be maintained much longer. He approved of the French system to the extent implied in the remark, that the State, presumably, had a right to take care that parents, who can provide for their children, should not leave any of them destitute, or in a condition in which they are likely to become bad citizens, or in any way a burden to the State. He knew how loudly the doctrine of *laissez faire* was proclaimed in England: but this was only what might be expected from those, whom our system placed, and maintained, in exceptionally favourable conditions.

Something having been said that led me to remark that, for many centuries, in the pre-Homeric, almost prehistoric, period, Phœnicia had been an autonomous dependency of Egypt, he was ready with the parallel of the partial dependence of Genoa upon Spain: a position that was not altogether disadvantageous for a commercial community that needed protection against powerful and jealous neighbours.

We talked of the effects modern knowledge, and love of nature, are producing in men's ideas and opinions; of the causes, in literature and art, of periods of brilliancy, and then of obscuration; of the present state, and future of Europe; of the attitude and policy of the Papacy; and of the prospects of religion.

The bearing and appearance of the representatives,

on board the steamer, of the fairer half of creation led us to notice the rapid decay, in our time, of female grace. Women seem now hardly to aim at it, men hardly to look for it. This indicates a great revolution in ideas and sentiments. The loss may be accompanied with counter-balancing advantages, still it is a loss very much to be regretted ; and, I think, we were quite in agreement both as to the fact, and in a preference for what was being lost to what might be gained.

He had reasons to give for the opinion he had formed upon the relation of the Latin of Cicero, and of the Augustan, or rather, for that would be too short, of the golden period of the language, to that of the rest of Italy ; and of that again to modern Italian ; and upon the character of the civilization of ancient Etruria ; and upon the probability that its upper governing class was not of the same race as the subject population.

I do not know whether he was a scholar in our narrow sense of the word scholarship, but he had made a higher and better use of the Classics, for he had studied them as an indispensable introduction to the right understanding of the modern world. Though very largely familiar with books, there was nothing bookish about him. He spoke of books as a man of affairs, and of the world, speaks of his experience and observation of the world. He was clear and logical in thought. His knowledge was full, and at the same time accurate. His judgments were balanced. He looked at subjects from all sides. He took into consideration what others thought and felt; and the way in which circumstances affect opinion and conduct. His statements and conclusions gained much in persuasiveness from the pleasing manner in which they were put. In him everything appeared to have been cultivated — the tongue as well as the mind and the tones of the voice as well as the ability to use the right word in the right place.

CHAPTER III.

THE BRÜNIG—LUNGERN—SACHELN—SARNEN—ALPNACH—
STANZ—ENNETBURGEN.

    Liberty,
    Whose touch gives double life—THOMSON.

AT 10.45, got on our legs at Brienz. The sun had now become warm, but there was a fresh air. Two four-horse diligences were waiting for the arrival of the boat. I placed my *malle* weighing 30 lbs., and my *sac* 12 lbs., on the roof of one of them, with orders that they should be left for me at Lungern ; and we were off.

One begins a walking expedition jauntily. You are going to do the work yourself ; and you feel equal to it. You are breaking away from the conventions and bondage of society. The cords snap as you step out. You will be emancipated from the clock. You are shaking off the incubus of duty. Responsibility, duty's daughter, goes with her. You shrug your shoulders to make sure that they are going. Conscience means now to go where you please ; and to stop when, and where, you please. You are strong and free; and the sense of strength and freedom is intoxicating. Liberty, thy law is good, and shall be mine! Your heart beats gaily. You have simplified the grammar by abolishing the conditional mood: henceforth you will deal only in the indicative and the imperative.

For the first two miles, or so, the road continues in the valley with the newly embanked channel of the Aare on the right, and some high cliffs on the left. It then begins to ascend the Brünig. We reached Lungern—the books say the distance is $10\frac{1}{2}$ miles —in $2\frac{1}{2}$ hours. The two diligences drew up at the door of the hotel as we were entering it. They had, therefore, taken just the same time as we had to come from Brienz. We, however, had for some part of the way come by the more direct line of the old horse road; and when using the carriage road had cut off the zig zags. There are some good views on the Brünig in both directions. To the south, there are spots from which it commands parts of the Vale of Hasli, with many snowy summits beyond. To the north, the eye ranges over the top of the forest, along the whole valley of Unterwalden, between its two bounding ranges, with very varying outlines, over the lakes of Lungern and Sarnen, to the distant Pilatus.

The interest of a walk among the mountains never flags, whether they are naked, or clothed with forest; and still more, if the ground you are passing over is diversified with forests, prairies, rocks, upland pastures, and streams. On the north side of the Brünig are some charming bits, where lofty trees, beech and fir, with straight stems, reach up to you from below, on your right as you descend to Lungern; and others on your left, with straight stems also, springing from above the road, here cut in a groove, tower above you. And, then, if you lift your eyes from the immediate *entourage*, you have, in the distance, Alps and valley combined; and below you spots of greenest turf with detached trees and *châlets*. In the short cuts through the forest you have the chequered light and shade, luxuriant ferns, and the odour of the pines. On this day it was cool under foot from the soaking the hills had got two nights back, and which had also so thoroughly washed the road that no dust was anywhere to be seen.

I remained at Lungern for the rest of the day, that I might look at the allotments of the peasants. These were chiefly in the 500 acres of bottom land, which had been gained by lowering the lake. This work was accomplished by the peasants themselves, by cutting a tunnel through the rocky ridge that forms the foot, here the northern boundary, of the lake. You everywhere see the old margin of the lake, about 120 feet in vertical height, above the present level of the water. The diminished lake, like its neighbour of Sarnen, abounds in fish, which this day contributed to both my dinner and supper. While I was taking the latter, with no companion but my own thoughts, a young woman, connected with the Inn, approached, and leaning against the sill of the window opposite to my chair, entered into conversation with me. At first I supposed that she was prompted merely by the good-natured desire that a solitary stranger should have some one to talk with. But she soon told me that her object was to find whether I could assist her in carrying out a wish she had to get to England, to learn English. She was willing to give her services, *sans gages*, to a family that would board and lodge her, and give her a lesson daily in English. Of course, this little scheme was not motived by a disinterested thirst for knowledge, but by a praiseworthy desire to get on in the world. For an acquaintance with English is an accomplishment which at present secures for those, who have attained to it, well-paid places in Swiss hotels.

Aug. 4.—Had breakfasted, and left Lungern at 6 A.M. Sent on my *malle* and *sac* by a porter, who started 15 minutes before me. Reached Sacheln at 8.30, and found that the porter had already arrived. The road passes along what remains of the lake of Lungern, next along a gentle descent of two or three miles, and then along the lake of Sarnen. At Lungern I found that the carriage traffic had been interrupted for a time by the storm of Friday night. It took all the labour, that could be brought upon the road, during the two following days, to render it passable.

As I walked along, I counted twelve places where torrents had, on that night, in their descent from the mountains, cut through the road, or deposited barriers of mountain *débris* upon it. In two instances culverts, for carrying torrents beneath the road, had been swept away. As such a storm had occurred, I was glad to have an opportunity for seeing its effects. In some places, where the storm-torrents had cut for themselves channels on the mountain side, only soil had been brought down, and in some only small stones. These were places in which the incline was not great. In other places, where the mountain side was precipitous, large rocks had been undermined, and dislodged, and swept down by the rush of water. The largest rock I saw on the road—I did not go off the road to look for effects—was in a place where it passed through a wood, and a bridge had been carried away. Here the prisoners from the jail of Sarnen, with shackled feet, were at work under the inspection of a *gendarme*. This rock was a cube of somewhat more than 3 feet. There were tens of thousands of tons of rocks of less size above, and below, and around. One can imagine with what crashing, and thundering, they must have come down through this wood—a torrent, a continuous avalanche, of rocks.

I observed in one place, where a torrent had at last reached a gently sloping meadow, that it had formed for itself a levée on each side, and had rigidly confined itself to the space between the two levées.

The pieces of wood and stone, and the earth it had carried along with it, when running down a greater incline, it had, when it reached the meadow, where, from flowing with less rapidity, it was no longer able to carry them along, dropped, and piled up on the right and left. And, then, these torrent-constructed barriers had confined the torrent, that had constructed them, to the intermediate space. The grass, just fit to be cut for the second hay crop, was standing outside the levées, as erect as if there had been no storm at all; but between the levées it was either completely washed up by the roots, and carried away, or flattened down to the ground. It was interesting, and instructive, to have presented for leisurely examination this instance of the way in which rivers often embank themselves. The immediate bank of the Nile is generally raised considerably above the level of the country it is passing through; and so it must be with all rivers whose waters are at times much charged with solid matter, readily deposited. If during the coal epoch the amount of rain-fall in this part of the world, or generally throughout the world, was greatly in excess of what it is now, the kind of work exhibited in my walk of this morning, that is to say the transportation of soil and broken rock from higher to lower levels, must then have been going on upon a grand scale. There are, I suppose, reasons for believing in a wet epoch at that time, just as there are for believing that there was once a glacial epoch.

On the gently rising mountain, on the side of the lake of Sarnen opposite to the road, there is a great deal of land in small prairies. It may be inferred that almost all these prairies are private property from the way in which they are interspersed with *châlets*, and planted with trees. Here and there are patches of grain, the golden colour of which, at this season, contrasts well with the bright green of the prairies, and the dark green of the trees, and patches of wood. Above, are more extended forests, and mountain pastures. Many of both of these latter belong to the Commune. In the foreground is the blue lake. The whole is a varied, quiet, charming scene.

I called a halt at Sacheln, as I had a letter to one of the magnates of the place—in the address he was styled as Bundesrichter—who had paid some attention to the history, and present working, in Unterwalden, of the Swiss system of commonable land. I intended in the afternoon to go on to Sarnen. I put up at the Rössli Inn, between the road and the church, kept by Von Ah. He is a rough-looking fellow, but I found him good-natured, talkative, and intelligent. He had much to say about the past history of the Canton, and the present condition of the people. He was proud, and with good reason, of the *gaststube* of his wooden house. Its walls were covered with carved panelling. The *buffet* was very rich in carving, into which was introduced the date of

1619. The clock, by the same token, had been ticking for a hundred and one years.

For dinner he gave me two kinds of fish from the lake—alet and boriksen, as the rosy, black-eyed damsel in attendance told me, with pleasure at finding that she could answer the stranger's questions. Then came, in succession, a veal steak, a mutton stew, stewed prunes, cheese, dessert, and a bottle of eau de Seltz. As the good man's charge for all this was but two francs, and, to be precise, ten centimes, he must have taken the satisfaction he had felt at showing his *gaststube* in part payment.

I found the Bundesrichter ready to give me the information I required, and to aid me in any way he could. He procured for me a printed copy of all the regulations relating to the public property of the Commune; and offered to answer by post whatever questions might subsequently occur to me.

At Sacheln, of course, one goes to the church to stand before the bones, and the old coat, of St. Nicholas Von der Flüe, for the sake of the thoughts the sight may give rise to in the mind, on the spot. He a saint! Heaven save the mark; and some day send the simple folk of Unterwalden better ideas on what goes to make a saint. This saint was one only because to indulge a morbid crotchet, at all events a mistaken and mischievous idea, he deserted his family, and the duties he owed to them, to his neighbours, and to himself, to live in solitude, and mortification, in a cave ; and who gave out, as vouching for his sanctity, that for eighteen years heaven had supported his body with no other food than the sacramental wafer, received once a month. This was what made him a saint. Why, there is not a rural parish in England without its poor Hodge, who is a better man, a truer saint than he ; and who, if at last he were to break down under the strain on mind and body he is now manfully sustaining, and attempt what invested this old crazy ascetic with the halo of sainthood, would be bid by the law to maintain, and not to desert, his family. And who, if he were to defend his dereliction of natural duty by the assertion that heaven was keeping him alive without food, would be regarded as belonging to the same class of impostors as the Welsh fasting girl. And yet here, in this church, dedicated to the God of truth, and Who is to be served by truth, are exhibited the troglodyte's bones, and his old coat, by the priest who ministers at the altar, and by the ecclesiastical authorities who stand behind the priest ; and who are teaching the peasants of Unterwalden that these bones, and this old coat, work miracles. Over the old coat they have set up the text of Holy Writ, from the nineteenth chapter of the Acts of the Apostles, which tells us that 'from the body of Paul were brought unto the sick handkerchiefs and aprons, and the diseases departed from them, and the evil spirits went out of them.' And there on the walls around are the tablets which affirm the miracles this old coat has worked. It must have worked them, for the infallible authority of God's Vicar will vouch for it. Poor Hodge! let us hope that your turn will some day come; and that the miracle of patient and unnoticed self-denial, your life exhibits, will work the mighty miracle of bringing some of us to understand in what virtue and sanctity consist, and of casting out the evil spirits of discontent, selfishness, and vice.

From Sacheln to Sarnen I went by the lake. The boat was of unpainted deal, of the size, form, and colour of the boats you see on all the Swiss and Italian lakes. It was propelled by two men, standing up, and working their paddles, *vis-a-vis*. You are reminded of a gondola, though why is not obvious, for the resemblance is as lacking in body as that between Monmouth and Macedon. These lake-boats are flat-bottomed, with their bows rising out of the water in the segment of a circle. Any village carpenter might put them together. The flat bottom is connected with the perpendicular sides by wooden angle-pieces, fastened with wooden pins. Till recently iron was dear in Switzerland; and wood, and, in winter, time were cheap. The same cause led to the same practice in the construction of their *châlets*, for which wooden trenails were used. In the English church at Meiringen, hardly yet finished, I observed that the fastenings of the benches, of the church furniture, of the window mullions, &c., were of the same material, though by the aid of the railway iron fastenings must be now of much the same price in Meiringen as in Belgium and Germany. In this, as in many other things, a practice, long after what gave rise to it has been removed by a change in circumstances, is still conserved by custom.

To Sarnen the lake is about three quarters of an hour. I was satisfied at finding myself on the water; not merely because it was a pleasant change from exertion to repose, but also because it gave an opportunity for seeing both sides of the valley to advantage. But that was not all. There is in water something that is of itself pleasing. We may not be able to define precisely what it is that makes it so, but we feel that it is so. It has a kind of history; a kind of life; an intelligible purpose. It came from far, from other parts of the world, on the way it had passed through other forms. It is moving back to the great ocean from whence it came. It will, as it returns, be supporting organized life. To the eye, to the ear, to the bodily sense, it is pleasing: and so is it also to the mental apprehension.

As you enter Sarnen you pass its asylum for the destitute. Upon its front is the inscription 'Christo in pauperibus.' I suppose this is meant as a reference to His saying that whatever is done to the least of His brethren—it being implied that those who have nothing in this world are least of all—He will regard as done unto Himself. He, then, is in the pauper, looking for, and ready to acknowledge, the charity of the disciple. The expression is worthy of the idea, and of the sentiment that animates the idea.

Sarnen is a quaint, quiet place. Ammer would have me go to the *Hotel de Ville* to see a model in relief of Switzerland, and the portraits of some score, or more, of landammans, enriched and sanctified, of course, by that of Nicholas Von der Flüe, for he is everywhere in Unterwalden. The preternatural ugliness, the out-of-the-world expression, 'the abominable imitation of humanity' of these old local celebrities seemed, somehow or other, in keeping with the place. The expression of the features is the expression of the mind: that, sometimes perhaps its absence, is what they express. But the generations of worthies, who had successively vegetated in this then both unvisited, and imprisoning, valley, which had neither ingress nor egress, could have had but little mind to express in their features. Some of them, methought, looked, what at the best they could have been only a remove or two from, like cowherds who had prospered in their world, and after a life spent on the mountains in summer, and in the stables in winter, waiting on their cows, had arrived at last at the happiness of being able to eat as much cheese as they pleased, without the trouble of making it: and so had grown fat. But this only puffed out, and so made more obtrusive, the indelible cowherd expression. Perhaps, too, their portraits would have been more pleasing, and more indicative of mind, if the worthies, and their fathers before them, had not been taught to believe in their troglodyte saint; and, as another perhaps, we will hope that the railway, by bringing the world to the rising generation, and taking them into the world, may do something to make their features and expression an improvement on those of their ancestors. At all events it will, I think, have the effect of lowering the place of the saint's coat in the therapeutics of the valley.

August 5.—Left Sarnen at 6 A.M., and in little more than an hour reached Alpnach, where I breakfasted while waiting for the steamer, that was to take me to Stanzstad. Alpnach is a populous village at the head of the Alpnach See, a branch of the lake of the four Cantons, which from this point stretches away to the north-east. It stands at the bottom of the south-east slope of Pilatus, the well wooded flank of which here comes down to the lake. The walk had been through a broad grassy valley, thickly planted, in some parts, with fruit trees. Perhaps the walk on the eastern side of the valley, through Kerns, to Stanz, my immediate destination, would have been over more diversified, as it would have been over higher, ground. And this, I believe, would have brought me to Stanz sooner than the route I took, for I lost at Alpnach an hour in waiting for the steamer. The water was the attraction, and the view, I should have from the water, of Pilatus. But I was satisfied with the way I went, and that was enough.

The steamer was not long in reaching Stanzstad, where we again got on our legs, and in a little more than half an hour were in the Angel of Stanz—a quiet inn, about the centre of the place, facing the church. As the Commune of Stanz possesses an unusual amount of cultivable land, so much as to enable it to give to each of its numerous burgers an unusual amount of garden ground, I spent the rest of the day here in looking into the working of the system. And again the next morning on the way to Buochs, where I was to take the steamer for the Canton of Uri, I inspected a large part of the Almend ground of Stanz. Each burger peasant is allowed 1,400 klafters, which is about equal to an English acre. Of this amount I found 800 in garden ground, and the rest in marshy grass. Switzerland, speaking generally, has very little straw for foddering cattle, but a great many cattle to fodder. The rushes, sedges, and young reeds cut from such land, and dried, go some way towards supplying this want. This difficulty is so great that I have seen horse-keepers resort for bedding to a mixture of sawdust, and of leaves and weeds that had been collected in the woods, and then dried and stored away.

August 6.—While waiting for the steamer at Buochs, there was time to contemplate a charming piece of Swiss life, which is held up for you, to take your fill of looking at it, on the long slant of the opposite mountain, beyond the blue lake. It is on the broad south-eastern slope of the mountainous promontory called Obburgen, that runs out into the lake, midway between the Rigiberg and Pilatus, and would, but for two narrow straits, join on to the former on the right, and to the latter on the left. I see in Dufour's map the place is called Ennetburgen. I did not set foot in it myself, nor am I acquainted with any one who has, but if the working of inner causes may, sometimes, be read on the outside of things, then, industrious, frugal, contented, happy Ennetburgen! that has neither riches, nor poverty; that knows neither waste nor want; and where every man feels that he is a man, because a portion of the earth, the common and ennobling inheritance of all, is his! For two thirds, or so, up the mountain, its gentle ascent is almost all in small prairies, very green, and thickly planted with fruit trees, with just here and there, as at Sacheln, small patches of, at this season, golden grain, to enrich the tender green of the grass, and the darker green of the fruit trees. The upper third of the mountain is in forests for fuel, and in summer grazing ground for cows. But the characteristic feature is the houses. There is no town. That has, as it were, been taken to pieces, and evenly dispersed, house by house, over the whole space of some thousands of acres. Each house is a modest carefully kept home.

This is a scene that tells its own tale. The properties must be small, because the owners of these dispersed houses must possess, each, the land immediately around his house; for, of course, in such a place there can hardly be any other means of living than that derived from the land. And nothing, but the fact that, here, each man cultivates with his own hands his own land, can account for the completeness with which the rocks have been quarried, and removed; and for the loving care with which the grass, and fruit trees, are tended. How unlike was this to the aspect of the Almend lands of Stanz I had just been looking at. There the plan is to do as little as possible for the land, and to get as much as possible out of it this current year. Next year, or at all events in a year or two, some other transitory occupant will be treating it with the same thoughts, and in the same fashion. Here the heart of the owner is in his land, as, for many generations, the hearts of his forefathers have been. We can show nothing of this kind in England. With us there is not the relation of man to the land which can alone produce such a scene. But I believe that in old, almost prehistoric Italy, before it was devastated, and ruined, by the greed, and brutality, of Rome, many such scenes might have been looked upon. The same careful culture of small properties was, probably, in very many places there the rule then; with the addition, in harmony with the circumstances of those times, of some loftily walled place of refuge, seen from far, on its coign of vantage : as Virgil describes them, 'Towns perched on precipices of rock, with rivers gliding by beneath their antique walls.'

CHAPTER IV.

BUOCHS—GERSAU—THE BAY OF URI—ALTORF—AM STAG — WASEN — GÖSCHENEN — SCHÖLLINEN — THE DEVIL'S BRIDGE—THE URSEREN THAL—ST. GOTHARD.

> Oh! how I love with thee to walk,
> And listen to thy whispered talk !—THOMSON.

As you leave the bay of Buochs you find that the mountains on all sides show well from the lake. Behind is Obburgen, at which we have just now been looking. On your immediate right is Buochserhorn. Beyond it is Seelisberg, though not yet itself visible, but only the way to it by Beckenried, on the east face of which is the Sonnenberg Hotel, a headquarters for much that is good and interesting. On your left is the Rigiberg. Before you, in sight of which you soon come, is Brunnen, the port of Schwyz, which is seen three miles back, at the foot of the rocky and precipitous Mythen. A fair expanse, how fair! of bluest crystal, set in a glorious frame of multiform mountains, superficially more or less subdued by long ages of human industry : this, however, being possible only to such a degree as to diversify, and enrich the interest of the scene. In itself a glorious scene! but there is, besides, all about it the glamour of the memory that it was the cradle of Swiss liberty.

Along the beach at Buochs I had seen several peasant women, turning over in the bright sun to dry, as if it were so much wet hay, the roots and fragments of wood they had collected from what the storm of Friday night last had swept from the mountains into the Engelberg Aa, which had brought them down to the lake. This was to be added to their store of winter fuel. Fuel has now become very dear in Switzerland, not only from its participation in the general rise of prices—that affects everything—but also from an exceptional cause. The recent increase of population has led to a corresponding increase of cultivation; and this has been effected chiefly at the expense of the forests, which are here the only source of fuel. While, therefore, the number of consumers has increased the supply of fuel has diminished. On reaching Gersau I came on further evidence of the violence of that great storm.

But first a word about Gersau itself. Its history is interesting. Its territory is a little valley in the Rigiberg, every rood, tree, and house of which is taken in at a glance from the deck of the steamer. Its population may now number about 2,000 souls. The increase this implies is due to the advantages of its situation, and to the industry of its inhabitants, having enabled it to keep abreast of the general advance of the whole of this much-frequented region.

GERSAU.

To it belonged, for many centuries, during which its population was much less than at present, the distinction of being the smallest independent sovereign state in Europe. San Marino was four times as populous, and had a proportionately larger area. Its valley, which looks to the south, is about three miles in length. It rapidly descends from the top of the *col* to the lake. Its sides, east and west, with far more rapid descents, are about a mile, each, in width. The whole of this area is covered with little green prairies, studded thickly with fruit-trees, and with dispersed houses. The toy capital is at the bottom of the valley, on the margin of the lake. All the water that flows from natural springs, or that, in heavy rains, runs off its surface, will evidently reach the lake by the central trunk-channel that passes through the little town. This flow of water is sufficient in ordinary times for the machinery of a silk-mill, which has been placed at its mouth.

Against such a storm as that of Friday no adequate precautions had, or probably could have, been taken. As the steamer approached the pier, we saw heaps of fresh rocky *débris* piled up on the beach, and observed that the main street had been cut up, and the materials of the road partly carried away, by the torrent that had swept over it. The silk-mill had been pretty well wrecked, and a great many houses, and much land injured. Some of the rocks brought down into the town were so large that they had to be broken up by blasting, before they could be removed. I, afterwards, saw in the Swiss papers that a collection was being made to assist those of the humbler classes here, who had suffered by the storm. I heard also that the new road that passes along the margin of the lake, from Brunnen to Flüelen, had, like that through the valley of Unterwalden, in some places been blocked with *débris*, and in some cut through. As to the poorer sufferers at Gersau, we may be sure that, whether aided from without, or not, by the proposed subscription, the long tradition of self-help is not yet forgotten in this little community; and that it will soon repair the damages it has sustained, as effectually as a hive of bees would an injury done to their comb.

As far as Brunnen, which is about four miles beyond Gersau, our steamer's course had been due east. Her head was now put due south, down the bay of Uri, which is the southern branch of this tortuous lake. The character of the scene changed as rapidly and completely as the direction of our course. The mountains no longer, as at Buochs, Ennetburgen, Beckenried, Gersau, and Brunnen, gradually shelve down to the water, offering space for little communities, whose successful industry, and careful thrift, it is so pleasing to contemplate. Their sides are now mostly naked precipitous rock; in some places rising a thousand feet, sheer above the glassy water, which, in its turn, is another thousand feet deep.

But even on these mountains, which like some old-fashioned fish, wear bones on the outside, and, going further, are bone to the heart, the industry of the people, which will take no denial, has set its mark. Wherever a little space could be found for grass, there its emerald green gems the rocks, just as some bright parasite might the ganoid fish. So, too, wherever a little wood, or even a tree, or two, could be made to grow, there it springs from the mountain side. On the left you face the line of the new road to Flüelen, with the Axenstein Hotel above it; on the right, two or three thousand feet above the water, you look up to the Sonnenberg Hotel. Above and beyond the latter, reaching on for some distance in front, a combination of snow-fields, and of naked peaks, appropriately completes a scene, which once beheld is for ever remembered.

In some places you see sections of rock, exposing strata that have been contorted into zigzags. This convolution of the rock, the mountain high precipices, and the depth of the water, indicate how great were the forces that have been at work here, and with what mighty throes they worked, or through how long a range of ages.

I reached Altorf, in time for the 12 o'clock dinner, at the Golden Key. There were twenty-five people at table, among whom I was, I believe, the only Englishman; the rest being Germans, or Swiss.

English people, however, do not like these hours; but I had breakfasted early. Altorf, though the capital, is not itself a Commune, but belongs to the quasi-Commune of Attinghausen, as Am Stag does to that of Silenen. I use the word quasi-Commune, because politically all the Communes of northern Uri, speaking roundly, and subject to some qualifications and explanations, form one body; each being a distinct body, again with qualifications and exceptions, only for economical purposes. This is the case also with the Communes of Southern Uri, or the Urseren Thal.

After dinner I walked over the whole capital in a vain search for a shop, in which I might get some statistical account of the Canton. Not one was to be found in which printed matter of any, even the humblest, kind was sold. Ammer laughed at my simplicity. 'In Uri people do not spend money on books. But if I were to go to the *Hotel de Ville*, where the authorities were then holding a sitting, I might find the Archivar, or some such officer, who possibly might be of use to me.' I acted on the suggestion; and brought away with me an abstract of the last census of Uri. But I found that in the capital of Uri printed matter, in accordance with the general rule in all matters, was dear in proportion to its scarcity. For a few figures—for the population of the Canton is only 16,095—printed on a small square of coarse spungy paper, not good enough to wrap up grocery in, I had to pay a franc. But I hold that the franc was not ill spent, as I found that, under the head of 'Confession,' of the above given number 16,025 were 'Catholics;' 60 'Protestants,' 1 (with commendable precision) of 'other Christian professions,' and 3 'Israelites, and of other non-Christian professions.' Considering the relation of Israelitism to Christianity it is not quite right to class it with all kinds of heathenism; though perhaps this heading may be defended by our own 'Jews, Turks, Infidels, and Heretics.' But what a Priest's Paradise must Uri be! Only 4 per thousand, not nearly a half per cent., of heretics and misbelievers of all kinds; and then not a book to be bought! How long will it be before these one-minded and unreading folk reach the debate of the old question What is truth; and come to understand that demonstrable fact is an alternative answer to the thimblerig of authority?

In the afternoon, having left my *malle* in charge of the landlord of the Golden Key, I went on to Am Stag. So far there is bottom land in the valley; broad at Altorf, and narrowing all the way to Am Stag, where it ends. The bounding ranges are always interesting, as seen from the road, which runs pretty straight, and pretty much on a level, for the intervening nine miles, among meadows, in which numerous fruit-trees, as elsewhere in Switzerland, appear to be of little, or no, detriment to the grass.

Am Stag was reached at 6 o'clock. This gave time enough to look at the village, and its *entourage*. It is a small place created by the traffic through the valley, to which it is a kind of half-way house, where *voituriers* bait their horses, and the diligences take fresh teams. The mountains close in above and below it, forming a deep hollow of about a third of a mile in diameter. The environing mountains look unusually hard and pitiless; in part of naked rock, in part clothed with stunted woods. On the west side of the village the Reuss races by, being joined in the village by the stream of the Maderaner Thal, of about the same volume, and quite as noisy. These, with the breadth of sky above, are all the objects in nature the peasants of Am Stag have to contemplate. And in winter everything is buried in snow. And, then, the capital, for the dissemination of ideas, is Altorf. The time must be still distant when the coming bookseller of Altorf will have a customer from Am Stag.

From several conversations I had, during this excursion, with young women in these Catholic cantons, I came to think that they are not so keen and hard as, more gentle, artless, and pleasant to talk with than—to make the comparison as personal as possible—they would have been, had they been brought up under a different system. They seemed to wish to be friendly, and not to be afraid of being so; and not to have *des arrière-pensées*, nor to suspect other people of having them ; and to be taking life as it came, as if it were not they who were responsible for what it brought. This may be a mere fancy of my own ; but, because I think it something more, I set it down here.

What is the intellectual life of the peasants of Am Stag ? If even in a broad country-side, where a bookseller can live, and the world is not quite unknown, the one subject of conversation that interests all, and alone never flags, is one's neighbours, and their affairs ; and if, even in its larger atmosphere, petty jealousies and heart-burnings abound ; and often grow, for the soil and atmosphere have some qualities that stimulate such growths, to not insignificant dimensions, from beginnings no bigger than, and as unsubstantial as, the midge's wing ; what, in these matters, must be the state of this little community, when imprisoned for the winter in its mountain cage? How A. manages, now that he no longer has a cow ; or how B. managed to get one, are fruitful topics, that will not be dropped till next summer. That C. has, or is supposed to have, beaten her cat, that D.'s hen is reported to have laid an egg, will not be without interest, though the former particular, however long and sedulously nursed, may never get beyond the stage of inference. This, however, will not unfit it for many improvements; which, perhaps, the intervention of the Priest, in his capacity of moral policeman, may sometimes prevent being carried too far. For, though his authority may not now be always quite unquestioned, he still wields a machinery which, under the circumstances of the valley, leaves him master of the situation.

As to A.'s not having any longer a cow to send up to the common pasture—poor fellow! he does not see exactly how this came about. But it is not inexplicable. He is a peasant burger, with a pedigree as old as that of the Hapsburgs. His ancestors, each in his day, to a time back beyond history, had a cow or two to send in the summer. He does what he can; and yet, though still a co-proprietor of the old pastures, just as his ancestors were, he has no cow to send. That is the puzzle. His voice is as potent as that of any of his fellow-burgers in the management of those pastures. He is as much co-owner of them as they. Nothing can divest him of his right in their common use. It is a personal right inherent in his blood. But now he can turn it to no account. He looks on as the rich Innkeeper sends up his dozen, or score of cows, while he has himself none to send. As the herd is driven by, through the village, with bells tinkling, and joyous at the prospect of returning at last to the fresh, thymy, mountain herbage, he looks on in silence, with his mouth open, as if his hopes, and his wits, too, were departing from him, through the passage he is providing for their exit.

He cannot understand how things have come to be as they are. He worked hard all the summer. But, then, he worked for wages: and that is the key to the puzzle. The valley is now advancing into the condition in which, on account of the traffic and business it supports, there will be some who will have to employ others; and many, as population is increasing, who will have no means of living except that of being employed by others. Those who employ others will have cows, some of them many, to send up to the common pastures; some very many more than any had in old times. Of those who are employed by others, many, having necessarily been otherwise occupied, were not able in the foregoing summer to collect food for keeping a cow through last winter, and so this summer, and among these is our poor friend, have not one cow to add to the herd, that is now being collected from the village for their three months' sojourn on the mountain pastures. These he can no longer turn to account. And he will not emigrate to a new world, where there are openings for his industry and thrift to make him a richer man than anyone in his Canton will ever be; nor will he even leave his Canton for another. And all this for the sake of his long line of burger ancestors, and for the sake of his common rights in the land, which—as far as pasturage go—are of no manner of use to him. It is the sentiments, so lovely and so human, of home, of kindred, of the accustomed locality, of country, that have fastened themselves to, and fed on, the now valueless corporeal hereditament, that bind him to the spot with a chain he has no power to break. The hopes and chances of the distant world do not allure him. For them he will not sell the inheritance, nor leave the graves, of his Fathers.

And as it is, here, with the common pasturage, so is it in some degree with the produce of the common forests. In conformity with immemorial usage, the fuel, and timber for repair of houses, are distributed in proportion to the size of the house. A large house, in which many fires are needed, and which will require more timber for repairs, will receive its proportion. So will also the poor man's humble tenement. To him this will perhaps give for fuel one klafter, which will not be enough for his wants. But to his rich neighbour, who could well afford to pay for his fuel, it will give four or five klafters. A klafter of wood is a solid measure, six feet long, wide, and high, and three feet deep. This method of distribution, which worked fairly enough under the old condition of things, when none were rich, and none were poor, works unfairly now, when there are opportunities, of which some will be able to avail themselves, for getting rich. A man may now prosper at home in ways unknown formerly; or he may go out into the world, and make several thousand francs, as my Am Stag informant had done, and then come back, and resume his rights, none of which absence forfeits; and he will be rich, and will, therefore, build, and live in, a large house; and this will entitle him to a large proportion of the common fuel and timber. There will, therefore, be so much the less to divide among his poorer fellow-burgers.

August 7.—Had breakfasted at the Croix Blanche, and cleared out of Am Stag, by 6 A.M. I was never in bed after 5. The bottom land having now completely thinned out, you here enter on the ascent of the St. Gothard Pass. Henceforth the road is cut in, or built upon, the mountain side, and frequently changes from side to side of the Reuss.

At the last bridge before you enter Wasen, the Reuss flows below in a channel it has excavated for itself, so deep, dark, and narrow, that you cannot make out where the water is, till you have looked for it. On the left of the bridge, the eastern bank of the torrent is much higher than the opposite side. The place is called the Priest's Leap — Pfaffensprung. Here Ammer repeated the legend, you will find in the books, of the enamoured Priest, who baffled his pursuers, in the days before the bridge, which were also the days of faith, by leaping across the stream, with the cause of his lapse in his arms. He concluded the story with the comment, that, 'if the Priest did it, the devil must have helped him;' then adding, as a comment on his comment, that 'in these days the Devil has become inattentive to his friends, and does not aid them as he did of yore.' This legend will help us to understand how it came about, that, in order to promote morality, the people of these Cantons persuaded their priests to keep concubines.

I was at Wasen, seven and a half miles, by 8 o'clock. The road, all the way, was at this time of the morning, in the shadow of the eastern mountains. Yesterday evening at Am Stag, I had debated with myself the question, whether it was better to have, or not to have, an object. I had walked a little way up the Maderaner Thal, under the influence of a growing desire to give up my pre-arranged route—arranged because I had an object—and to take to the mountains. There was before me an inviting opportunity, the charming Maderaner Thal, by which I might find a way to Dissentis. But virtue triumphed. And now that I was at Wasen, and saw a party starting for the Meien Thal, the same question recurred. I had had enough of carriage-road valley-work for the present, and wished for something rougher and harder. Having, however, once entered on the path of virtue, you keep it, if only for the sake of consistency. This was the first time I had ever travelled, when on my own hook, along a prescribed route. In former excursions, I had always left the route throughout, from day to day, an open question. It is very pleasant, so unlike staying quietly at home, to be going you do not at any time know exactly where, and you do not at all care where. An object, which requires a plan, makes this impossible, and substitutes bondage for what the recollection of former excursions tells you would be freedom. An object is not bad, still no object may be better. But I had also another reason for adhering to my pre-arranged plan, which was, that it would bring me to Andermatt, where I was to meet my wife, and the blue boy of last year's excursion; and some mountain work with them was part of this pre-arranged plan. But still I said to myself this morning, It is all pre-arranged, and that excludes liberty.

Above Wasen the road, having crossed to the eastern side of the valley, passes through a pine forest. The trees are well grown, and the roadside is full of ferns. The Reuss below is unusually noisy. In places the lofty mountains ahead are in sight, and through openings in the forest, occasionally, the mountains on the opposite side of the valley, with here and there on their flanks a little prairie; on some of these a small summer *châlet*, or hay-grange. As I walked on alone, a little ahead of Ammer, the feeling came over me that I was advancing into one of Nature's sanctuaries, one of her great laboratories. It was as if I was being admitted to see the anatomy and mechanism of nature, the rocky skeleton, the mountain-ribs of the solid earth. 'And here too,' I said to myself, 'she is busy making the rivers, and' (as the dinning noise of the Reuss reminded me of the hundreds of glacier-fed rills out of which it was formed) 'she is making them out of the glaciers; and the glaciers she had made by lifting up the mountains to attract the clouds, the vapour of distant oceans; and then causing its precipitation from their cold and rarefied atmosphere. So is she forming rivers. And these mountain Reusses are grinding down rocks and pebbles, and floating off the vegetable mould, to become the particles of the soil, that is, down below, to form broad green meadows and fruitful golden cornfields. The skittish, noisy stream is young and playful now, and leaps from rock to rock like a young lion. When it has attained to its maturity it will move majestically. Cities will then be built on its banks, and commerce will make a highway of its surface. Up here man has but very slight hold on the scene. In this workshop of Nature her work almost excludes his. He is not the master here. His business and gain here are to understand nature.' My reverie was suddenly interrupted by the apparition, at the wayside, of a woman on her knees, breaking stones for metalling the road. I could not pass her without a word: even a word would be in some sort a recognition of our common humanity. Poor soul! In a life of 57 years she had seen no more of the wide, rich, busy world than may be seen at Wasen, and a few miles above and below it. Her days were now spent in quarrying pieces of rock above the road, bringing them down to the road, and breaking them in heaps by the roadside. It was with her a good day, a very good one, when she could earn sixty cents. But she was well satisfied with a day that gave her fifty cents, just fivepence. Hard work, and exposure in all kinds of weather, hot and cold, wet and dry, early and late, had scored her face with many wrinkles, long and deep; had enlarged her mouth, and had widened her nostrils, for she had to breathe hard; and by making her eyelids swollen and pendulous, had more than half-buried her eyes. All this had given her somewhat of the features and expression of an ape. I wondered whether in her long solitary days she ever compared her life with that of the gay and prosperous thousands coming and going in carriages, in making a road for whom her life was expended. And I wondered how many of them compared their lot with hers.

On returning the following week, this way, I found her again, at the same place, in the same attitude, engaged in the same work. For a few years longer, perhaps, she will be able to continue it; and then she will have sunk, out of sight of the folk who pass in carriages, to something lower and harder, and will be looking back regretfully to the better times, when between sunrise and sunset, she could earn fivepence.

In an hour from Wasen I reached Göschenen. Here the aspect of things becomes what you might have been expecting in a great and famous pass. All the way up from Am Stag the valley of the Reuss had been narrowing and hardening: and now a break in its western wall forms the Göschenen Thal. You see the snowfield of the Damma, and the eastern glacier-shed of the Damma, of the Galen, and of the Rhone-Stock; on the other or western side of which is the vast Rhone glacier. Here, as in Alpine, and as indeed in all scenes, thought aids in deepening the interest of what is at the moment before your eyes. As I looked around I felt as the spider feels in the centre of its web. Along one thread, sensitive to thought, I passed by the arrowy Rhone to the sunny Middle sea, through thrifty Switzers, and light-hearted Frenchmen. Along another by the vine-clad Rhine to the stormy North Sea, through studious Germans and plodding Hollanders. Along a third attached to the next mountain a few miles further on, by the way of the Ticino, Lago Maggiore, and the Po, through many cities of the quickwitted Italian, cities of ancient renown in the wealthy field of teeming Lombardy, to the gusty Adriatic, and its lovely Queen, whose glories have not yet all departed.

No sooner have you passed through Göschenen than Schöllinen takes up, and advances, the interest of the spectacle. The gorge now becomes narrower, more precipitous, more iron-faced. Here it is that you come upon the mouth of the tunnel that is being bored beneath St. Gothard for fifteen miles, from Schöllinen to Airolo, all in granite, with Andermatt and St. Gothard above it. You are walking on the carriage road, a grand work completed thirty years back. The old horse-road it superseded is close on your right. On its margin, on your left, is the long line of iron tubing, of sufficient diameter for a man to crawl through, which brings from a higher level the water-power that is being used in the excavation of the tunnel for the modern railway, that will supersede the carriage-road, as that in its turn had superseded the horse-road. Our world is large and busy, but the world in which our children will play their part will be larger and busier.

You cut off a few zigzags. The way becomes more precipitous, narrower, more iron-faced; and you find yourself, a few minutes beyond Schöllinen, on the Devil's bridge. Black granite rises in sheer cliffs, mountain-high above you. The Reuss thunders seventy-five feet below the arch on which you are standing. You are wet with the spray. A sense of personal nothingness, of annihilation, comes over you. You feel as a shrimp might between the jaws of a whale.

The granite appears absolutely naked; but a closer inspection shows you a few humble Alpine plants in such crannies and crevices as their roots could find a hold in, together with a little mould from decayed lichens to feed upon. And, here and there, but never rising more than a few inches above the storm-swept surface, you will make out a Pinus pumilio, or two, but of so weather-worn, and weather-stained, and snow-crushed an aspect as to be thoroughly toned-down to the dark granite. How bravely and obstinately does life struggle to maintain itself amidst all this wrath and desolation! It will have the whole world. It will not submit to exclusion anywhere. Even up here, though so nipped, and starved, and frozen; so snow-smothered, and storm-torn, it will not shrink for asserting its universal right.

You pass through a tunnel, excavated in the perpendicular granite, which here overhangs the dashing, dinning Reuss on your right. As you step out of the tunnel the broad grass-clad expanse of Urseren Thal is before you: Andermatt at the near side; Hospenthal, two miles off, on the far side. All grass between. The mountain slopes, too, around are all in this livery of soft green. Where else did one ever see such a contrast, and so unexpected! Behind you the ruthless granite and eternal snow: before you the sheen of a smooth lawn, with these busy little communities nestling in its bosom. No one, who comes along this way, on foot, on a bright sunny day, as this was, will ever forget this contrast.

At the St. Gothard Hotel, at Andermatt, I came up with my *sac*, which I had sent on in the morning from Am Stag by an empty return carriage. I here also found a telegram from my wife—she was at Pontresina—which told me that she could not be at Andermatt till the evening of the twelfth. To-day was the seventh. Nothing, therefore, could be clearer—it was obvious in a moment—that the best thing for me to do was to go on at once to Como, to breathe for some hours the air of Italy, and to gladden my eyes with an Italian scene; returning early on the eleventh, so that I might devote a part of that day, and the whole of the next, to such inquiries as I might wish to make at Andermatt and Hospenthal. I had left Ammer behind at Schöllinen, where he had fallen in with an old friend. On his arrival, about half an hour after mine, I announced to him my resolve; and told him we should be off at 4 o'clock. It was now 1. This would give him time to get his dinner, visit his acquaintances in the place, and consume as many pipes, and thin, long, black, Swiss cigars as he pleased; for it appeared to be his custom when tired of the one to take to the other. Being of that conservative turn of mind which is averse to changes of plan, as well as of anything else; and, too, being now of the age, when exertion begins to be no longer pleasing for its own sake, he seemed to think that it was hardly worth while to leave Switzerland for so short a time. At the appointed hour, however, we were again under weigh; and at 6h. 40m. had reached the Hotel on the summit of the Pass. The books give 24 miles for this day's tramp: but this, from the time we took to do it, and the ease with which it was done, I think beyond the true distance.

From Andermatt you walk through the level mead of Urseren to Hospenthal, $2\frac{1}{4}$ miles. The grass of course is carefully cultivated, for the whole dependence of the people is on their cows and horses. Andermatt and Hospenthal are towns of horses rather than of men, for here the two great trunk lines of communication from east, along the Alps, to west, and from north, across the Alps, to south, bisect each other at right angles. It is a central point for much traffic, and so a great many horses are needed. It is fortunate that there is so much grass here, for one cannot tell what would be done without it. With the exception of some patches of potatoes, chiefly on the sunny foot of the mountain on the opposite side of this great Alpine prairie, everything that you see is grass. At Hospenthal you cross the Reuss, and again begin to ascend. The mountains are not precipitous and craggy, but somewhat rounded, as if their asperities had been planed off in the glacial epoch. On them are no trees; only Alpine pasture all the way, gradually deteriorating as you ascend. To one fresh from the Devil's bridge (I wish it had a better name), and the Urseren Thal, these mountains are full of contrast and interest. Three such scenes in a single walk make it a memorable one. Sometimes you are far above the Reuss, sometimes it is close alongside of you. Sometimes the cows are below you in a deep valley, sometimes above you on a mountain flank. At last, not very far from the summit, you cross the Reuss for the last time, by a bridge which is the boundary, on the road, between the Cantons of Uri and Ticino. It is, hereabouts, a small stream, not far from its source in a small mountain lake hard by; but what would not one give to have such a small stream passing one's door at home—so clear, so pebbly, so cool, so lively, so murmurous. For the latter part of the way the snow was often, in large masses, by the roadside. There was more of it still lingering on the mountains this year than usual, because there had been a late spring with heavy snow storms. The Hotel, nearly 7,000 feet above the sea, is on the summit of the *col*, in a deep depression, surrounded by blackish-gray, jagged, naked peaks, with snow in the interstices and ravines. But even here animal life is far from wanting ; for in the dark tarn, on the edge of which the Hotel stands, and which is sufficiently deep not to be frozen to the bottom, fish are to be found. There is another and shallower tarn close by without fish. In front of the Hotel is some expanse of grass, a part of the summer pasture of the summit, which maintains for two months 200 cows.

CHAPTER V.

VAL TREMOLA—AIROLO—DAZIO GRANDE—FAIDO—BODIO—
BELLINZONA—LOCARNO—LUGANO—BELLAGGIO—COMO.

O Italy, how beautiful thou art !—ROGERS.

August 8.—'Now, Ammer, for a glimpse' of Italy;' as, at 6 A.M., starting from the almost undistinguishable watershed that divides the head-stream of the Reuss from that of the Ticino—an affluent of the Rhine from an affluent of the Po—we began to cut off the many zigzags of the Vale of Trembling, at a good pace, as became the frosty morning—frosty at that altitude—and our inspiriting destination. In just half an hour the zigzags of this once alarming descent, whence its name, were all behind, or rather above us, and we turned to the straight road along the gorge. Here we passed the still very considerable remains of two avalanches, which in the spring had fallen from the heights, one from the right, and one from the left, and were, but now some way below the road, blocking the valley. One was of clean snow; the other was largely compounded of stones, and sods, and earth, which it had swept off the mountain side in its long *glissade.* This latter one was of such mass, that if it had encountered York Minster on its way, York Minster would either have been buried beneath it, or would have had to accompany it to the bottom of the valley.

A little beyond the remains of this great avalanche we left the carriage-road, and took pretty nearly a straight line all the way to Airolo; at first through alpes, that is mountain pastures, then through prairies, that is grass land for mowing: sometimes at very steep inclines. When we entered Airolo we had been out one hour and fifty minutes from St. Gothard. Here, as at Göschenen, the commencement of the great tunnel had caused a great deal of building. Beyond Airolo the valley often has a flat bottom; and the near scenery, at times, is tamer than you might have expected to find it in the immediate neighbourhood of a great and famous Pass. But whatever there may be of this kind, for some little distance below Airolo, is completely compensated for by the gorge of Dazio Grande.

Here the Ticino descends rapidly, broken and blustering, through a deep defile it has cut out for itself. In the cliffs above the present channel man, too, has cut out for himself his path. The best part of the gorge begins, and ends, with a bridge; and is about three quarters of a mile in length. The channel, worn by the stream through the tough rock, is narrow, perpendicular, rugged, and tortuous. The water, from variations in its depth, and in the speed at which it is moving, and from the varying effects of the light in which it is seen, is, when looked at from the upper bridge, of a brownish bottle green : while in the gorge itself it is of a clear whitish green. In several places the foam is so touched by the light as to present a pale tint of pink, which still more softens it. This softness of its colour you contrast with the force it is exerting to cut away the rock, and with the aspect of the hard dark rock itself, but which you see, notwithstanding its hardness, is being ground down, and excavated, often on the sides into little rounded holes, by what appears to be only soft, feathery, almost downy, white foam, touched with this faint tint of pink.

As I was loitering through the gorge, noting what nature had done, and was doing—the din of the water, and the engineering boldness of the zigzags, gouged out of the perpendicular cliffs, awakened and enforced attention—a party of travellers in a four-horse carriage passed down: two ladies, and two gentlemen. Of the latter one was asleep, and the other seemed completely absorbed in watching the familiar sight of the smoke of his cigar. The party were not conversing, and no notice was being taken, certainly by the gentlemen, of the scene they were passing through. Let us hope that they did not hail from England. One could not but speculate a little on the cause of such strange *insouciance* to striking and interesting natural objects as the occupants of this carriage exhibited. Was it a result, if they had come from beyond the Channel, of that estimate of all knowledge (of course, with the exception of what we call practical knowledge, that is to say knowledge that will enable one to make money) which a man's having been kept, grinding, through all his blessed youth, at that instrument of torture, our 'Public School Latin Grammar,' must, in most minds, give rise to? Here we have a not unlikely source. An affluent to this may, perhaps, be found in the ideas of what is desirable in life, which must to some extent be engendered by our English form of society : the most conspicuous exponents of which are our English dinner-parties. I do not mean to imply that our dinner-party-engendered ideas are like those of an old Squire I used to hear of—his day was a little before mine—who was in the habit of affirming that 'conversation spoilt society :' by society he meant the animal enjoyment of venison, and the port wine of his day. Still I think it may be held, and not without some show of reason, that there is a sense in which half of his idea is not far from the mark, for that society, as perhaps it would be better to have it, has in this country been spoilt to some extent ; and, too, at the dinner-table ; but that, as respects conversation, it is rather that society has spoilt it, than that it has spoilt society.

Beyond Airolo, the road is straight, and there can be no short cuts. We reached Faido, seventeen miles by road, at 11.30. We now encountered a great deal of dust, for the heavy storm of Friday, a week back, had been confined to the north of the St. Gothard mountains; I, therefore—and also because I had but little time for this little piece of bywork—gave up walking for the present, and engaged a four-horse return carriage for Bodio, which Ammer had heard of while I was taking an early dinner at the Prince of Wales. After an hour's halt we were again *en route*. The road was straight; and the wind, from behind, was moving at about the same rate as the carriage. This kept us for the ten miles to Bodio in the centre of the cloud of dust our four horses and wheels were raising. On descending from the carriage, Ammer's first thought was to get a clothes-brush. The landlord brought it himself, presenting it with the remark, that 'a dusty road with the wind behind was the devil.' 'Yes:' I replied, 'it is often so on the road. But within the Hotels he not unfrequently assumes the form of flies, accompanied with a bad smell.' I had been tormented with flies at Faido, while at dinner, and had unpleasant recollections of the stenches I had met with in many Swiss Hotels. This little sally at once placed us on an easy conversational footing. He told me that he was the physician of the place; that land in his Canton was too much divided to be of much use to anybody; that this kept everybody poor; that all their best young men were emigrating to the United States, chiefly to California; and that emigration was winnowing the population, sending away all the good grain, and leaving at home only the dross. This was during the half-hour while the carriage for Bellinzona, which he had ordered for me, was being got ready. At parting he expressed a hope that I might return the same way, in order that we might continue our conversation on the condition of the people, &c.

The merits of this valley are underrated: there is much in it worthy of notice. Its character is manifestly Italian, as is that of the people, who in all probability would feel irresistibly attracted towards the Kingdom of Italy, if only (but this is an if of the kind that interposes, in the case of such lovers of money, an impassable gulf) the taxation of the Kingdom were as light as that of the Republic. The regular increase in the variety and richness of the vegetation must strike even a somewhat unobservant traveller, as he rapidly makes the descent. The contour, too, and colouring of the mountains are somewhat distinctive. Those just below Faido had, this year, their barren tops in August flecked with snow. This attracts your eye as you are passing through fields of luxuriant maize, and trellised vineyards at their feet. You see how vegetation has struggled to ascend them. It begins by having it all its own way. Down below it covers all the ground. After a time it finds the struggle harder, and fails in places. Then comes a zone in which bare rock predominates. One step more, and to the eye vegetation dies out altogether; and cold and nakedness are supreme. All this you here take in at a glance.

Further on you pass along the foot of a long mountain range, in which the rock, wherever it is exposed, as high up as you can make it out, has evidently been smoothed, and rounded off by glacier action, or that of running water, for either could have set that kind of face upon it. I am, however, disposed to think that some, at all events, of the effects you may here observe, are due to the action of the stream of the Ticino in some remote past; for I saw little polished excavations in the otherwise smooth and even face of the rock, of precisely the same kind as those I had seen in the gorge of Dazio Grande, where there could never have been moving ice. These excavations exactly resembled the half of a reversed basin, and could have been formed by running water only. Of course they were produced by pebbles and grit being thrown by the stream against, and gradually working into, accidentally soft spots.

Was jolting over the pavement of Bellinzona a little after 4 P.M. Ordered supper at 8. Engaged the carriage and pair of my talkative acquaintance, the landlord of the Hotel de la Poste at Bodio, that had brought me to Bellinzona, to take me on to Lugano early the next morning; and there to wait for my return from Como. By the way, I observed here as in the other towns of this valley—it is the same at

Andermatt—that the main streets have granite tramways, which wear the appearance of being old institutions. I suppose their object is to lessen not so much friction, which is our object, as noise; and to keep carriages in the middle of the roadway: both desirable objects where the streets are very narrow.

I had some hours to walk about the place, and note the aspect of things. Judging from the size of the old houses with their colonnades, and the number of churches, Bellinzona must have been formerly a place of more importance than it is at present; or perhaps, which may be the true explanation, wealth, may have been more unequally distributed then than it is now. For it is impossible to suppose but that the produce of the district is worth, at the present day, a great deal more than it was in the church-building age here; and that it can support now a great many more mouths than it could when those old mansions were built. More land has been reclaimed; the culture of the vine—which pays the best of all the plants cultivated here—has been much extended; potatoes and maize have been introduced, which, by reason of their greater productiveness, have almost superseded the old cereals; silk-culture has been superadded without displacing anything else; and then the great modern stream of travellers brings, every year, into the valley, and leaves in it, a great many nuggets of refined gold. There can, therefore, be no question about there being in these days, a great deal more wealth. The only questions are what becomes of it? By whom, and how, is it held? And how is it used?

I will suggest two answers. Suppose there are a score, or so, of proprietors, who have, each of them, five or six hundred acres of land. They will be able to live in such houses as surround the old *Place* of Bellinzona. But divide these estates among five score proprietors, and not one will be able to live in such houses. And this process you may carry on, till they have all become peasant proprietors. And, then, one step more, and these landed proprietors will all be landed in semi-starvation. This I take to be an answer that accounts for a great part of the change. The other answer is, that formerly people lived in towns, because it was not safe to live in the country; but that, in these quiet and peaceable days, people live just where they find it pleasantest to live. What well-to-do people, therefore, there may still be in the neighbourhood of Bellinzona now probably live on their properties. So far Bellinzona has gone out of town.

My Hotel, judging from the position of the town as respects the river, was on the north side of the modern *Place*. There was, as far as I observed, no one staying in it but myself. At all events I was shown to what I took to be the best room in the house; it was large and lofty, and led me to suppose, that the house, which had an old fashioned air about it, dated from the time of the old mansions just referred to, and might be numbered among them. On the opposite side of the *Place* was a new-looking Hotel, which I did not see anyone enter, or leave. On the east side was a chapel—though that may not be the correct word—over the door of which was the inscription 'Divo Rocho.' I saw the congregation, that had attended Vespers, leaving it. They were all women. In the *Place* itself there were never wanting several little groups of people—these were all men—*flâneurs*—standing about, apparently for the accustomed purpose of seeing, and commenting on, perhaps of getting a little something out of, the arrivals and departures of travellers. But, this afternoon, there was not much of this kind to suggest either hope, or conversation ; and so there was nothing to interrupt their combustion of the leaf that should be fragrant. In the centre of the older part of the town, in the small old *Place*, surrounded by the above-mentioned goodly old houses, fronted with colonnades, I found a tree of Liberty surmounted by the cap of Liberty. This took me rather by surprise. What can stir the mind of Bellinzona so deeply as to prompt such an erection ? And why should these republicans be fussy about what they have, and with which there is no one to interfere ? Or was it a demonstration of that portion of the townsfolk, who are for the regeneration of society, against the richer sort, who live in country houses ? I cannot answer these questions

I can only say that the tree had the appearance of age; and so possibly may have been set up during the excitement of '48, a wave of which may have reached, and transiently stirred, the stagnancy of Bellinzona.

August 9.—As I had much before me I was up at 4.30 A.M. On looking out of the window, to ascertain what kind of morning I had for the day that was to take me to Como, I saw a woman, on the opposite side of the street, seated in front of her house, busily plying her needle. It will be some time yet I thought before her little ones begin their day. When, an hour later, I left the Hotel, she was still there at work. I was reminded of Virgil's touching picture of what I was looking on. I was sure that he had often looked upon, and read aright, such sights in the northern Italy of his day. He describes the picture as it might have been seen not at midsummer, but in winter, and, therefore, as within the house.

> The middle course of night was run, when men
> Wake from their first sleep; and the good housewife,
> Whose distaff is her slender livelihood,
> Gets her from bed, and stirs th' ash-buried fire,
> Robbing sweet rest for work; and at first dawn
> Rouses her women to their long-tasked day:
> For 'twere not life to her to live, if drawn
> To shame her husband's bed, or should in vain
> Her little darlings crave their daily bread.*

---

* Inde, ubi prima quies, medio jam noctis abactæ
Curriculo, expulerat somnum, quum femina primum,

Morality is the soul of poetry, because we are still conscious—though theology and the pulpit have done much to deaden our consciousness of this—that it is the life of life. It inspires the poet, and hallows his pictures. This was of old 'the piety of the poets, who spoke words worthy of Phœbus.' At all events there were in that old world good wives, the charm of whose goodness was felt; and so there must have

> Cui tolerare colo vitam tenuique Minervâ,
> Impositum cinerem et sopitos suscitat ignes,
> Noctem addens operi; famulasque ad lumina longo
> Exercet penso; castum ut servare cubile
> Conjugis, et possit parvos educere natos—*Æn.* viii. 407-413.

I take the liberty of rejecting the ruling of Heyne, and of the late Professor Conington, that 'impositum' is the regimen of 'tolerare.' (1) It is not necessary. (2) 'Impositum' gives importance and meaning to 'cinerem,' which would be too meagre without it. It does also, as it were, balance 'sopitos.' (3) It brings before the eye the pictures of the way in which the fire had been made up over night, to keep it alive till the morning, and of the way in which in the morning it is resuscitated. Where wood is the fuel, the ashes are heaped up, for the night, over the live coals. This excludes the air. In the morning, the heaped up ashes are removed, and the fire fed. Everyone has seen this done in Italy, and elsewhere. Virgil had seen it done; and this is what he describes.

I also suppose that 'ad lumina' means at the first dawn. The good woman herself rises before dawn, 'noctem addens operi.' But it would be hard, and unnatural, to set her women to work before dawn. That they should work through the whole day, beginning at dawn, is a sufficiently long task for them. I even doubt whether spinning and weaving could have been carried on with the feeble light of the lamps of those days; and, too, whether, if possible, it would have paid to do it for the short time before dawn. At all events by my interpretation of 'ad lumina' the good woman's motives and early rising are thrown into strong relief; and this is done without making her treat her women harshly.

been good husbands, too," whose goodness was honoured. I believe then, as the Mantuan would have believed, that my opposite neighbour of this morning was good in heart as well as in deed; and, for her sake, I hope her husband was good. If not, she was by so much the better in heart and in deed.

The road to Lugano begins on a rich and well-cultivated level. The broad, highly varnished leaf of the maize, and the more sober green of the vine, are side by side everywhere. Some country houses are passed. After five miles of this rich cultivation, grass becoming more common, and country houses less so, at Cadenazzo, you leave the valley, and begin the ascent of the Monte Cenere, by which you cross the range that separates the valley of the Ticino from the basin of Lugano. We had been for some little time slowly toiling up the zigzags; and I was at the moment noting the heath in flower, and the stunted russet brake (for there had been a long spell of dry weather) with rock everywhere protruding; and all beneath the old gnarled chesnuts; when, on coming to a masonry-supported angle of the road, projected on the mountain side, almost as if for a look out, there burst on my sight, beyond and below, at perhaps a distance of two miles, the head of Lago Maggiore, and the town, on its margin, of Locarno. I was not expecting anything of the kind; and was indeed, at the moment, intent on the heath and brake, when they abruptly vanished, and this glorious prospect took their place.

At my feet, for the foreground, was the broad, richly cultivated valley, partitioned into innumerable bright green prairies, and grain fields yellow for harvest; all full of fruit trees. Beyond were mountains of very varied outline and colour, scarred with rocky ravines of varying size, which the melting snow, and the storm torrents of ages, had cut from their naked summits down along their forest-clad sides. Snow still, here and there, spotted their summits, in consequence of the cold late spring of this year. Along the margin of the glass-smooth, green-blue lake were the white houses of the long straggling town. Above the town, scattered in woods, at wider intervals up the mountain, and for some distance from the town along the margin of the lake, were innumerable white villas. It being early morning the bright sun was full on the town, and mountains, bringing out clearly every white wall, every dark roof, every green field, every patch of wood, almost every individual tree, and every dark gray rock. It was a scene of surprising variety, interest, and beauty, that had come suddenly before me without any preparation. I was reminded that I had felt, when staying at Jerusalem, some years back, just the same kind of surprise. I had been riding up Mount Scopas, and had been occupied, as I ascended the crest, in looking at the broken pieces of red pottery which strewed the ground, and thinking that they might have been left there by the army of Titus, who, during the siege of Jerusalem, had held this summit, for it commanded a complete view of every house in the Holy City; when, on lifting my eyes from the ground, they were filled with the sight of the twenty miles of white sandy desert, in which had once been Jericho, and on the further side of this white desert was the black line of the Jordan, leading straight to the light blue of the Dead Sea; and beyond all this, the long, wall-like line, ablaze with purple, for it was verging towards evening, of the mountains of Moab, closing the scene, like a barrier of ruby and amethyst, to give promise of some brighter world beyond. The suddenness of the change, and the gloriousness of the new scene, in both cases affected the nerves of the mind with a sensation which can never be forgotten. But, however, in one case it was absolute desolation; not a tree, not a human dwelling-place in sight; all rock and sand; and the complete absence of man from a scene where of old he had often been busy: in the other case it was the complete present subjection and subserviency of the scene to man, and his busy presence everywhere, which were, respectively, the predominant elements of interest. In both scenes nature was grand; but in one grand in desolation, and in the other grand in combination with widely expanded and well-requited human effort.

As you pass on to Lugano, though you are still on high ground, there is something that tells you that you are on the south side of the mountains. It may be hard to say precisely what this something is, but it is in the vegetation, in the people, in the air. There is more of the chesnut, and less of the fir tribe. The oak is more spreading. The undergrowth in the copses, and the plants by the roadside, are more varied. The people are gayer, and more light-hearted. The air is more stimulative of life. At Lugano, as might be expected from its contiguity to the lake, the aspect of things is very different from what it is at Bellinzona. Many appear to be in easy circumstances, and at ease in their minds. This they show by the care they bestow on the exterior of their houses, and on the ground around them.

As to the lake. As far as I saw of it, its distinguishing feature appears to be the abruptness with which the environing mountains descend into the water. In many places they dip into it without any preparation at all, with no final *talus*. The deep water breaks on the clean upright rock. Still the mountains are pretty well clothed with wood. The trees, however, are much detached, and very scrubby, as if on these dry, sunburnt, rocky mountain sides, they needed a century, as probably they do, to grow into scrub. Still wherever on the margin of the lake, and a little higher up, soil could be collected for a few vines, or for a little garden, there you will see the few vines, or the little garden. One is astonished at the number of small towns on the margin. They are very conspicuous from the walls of all the houses being white. I suppose they are built of rough stone, which is then plastered, and lime-washed. An American on board the steamer, and who was acquainted only with the large way in which things are done in his own country, and with the large rewards of industry there, told me he had been fairly beaten by the puzzle, how the people in these towns could live. There was no land to cultivate. There were no factories to work in. No business. Nothing to trade with. Nothing to get a living out of.

Somewhere between Lugano and the eastern extremity of the lake, we were boarded by a custom house officer, and entered the kingdom of Italy. At the eastern extremity—the place is called Porlezza—we took the diligence for Menaggio, on the lake of Como. The road lies along a depression in the ridge that separates the two lakes. From its being much lower than the ground which separates the head of Lago Maggiore from Lugano, it presents a much more advanced stage of the idea of Italy, and of the sense of being in Italy. There is cultivation all the way. Maize, mulberries, vines everywhere. *La petite culture* only. In a little more than an hour we were going down the zigzags to Menaggio. The long expanse of Como was at our feet, backed by lofty mountains, on which snow still lingered. Everywhere on the terraced slopes, in which not a square foot of ground was anywhere lost, were not only maize, and mulberries, and vines, but also figs, almonds, and olives; and oleanders, myrtles, and magnolias. Another world with a richer life was around us; a brighter sun, and a bluer vault were above us—a glorious bit of quick-pulsed Italy! It is good for a man that his mind can be moved in response to such a scene.

At Menaggio I took a boat to cross the lake to Bellaggio—the fac-simile of the boat in which I had gone from Sacheln to Sarnen. It was propelled also in the same fashion by two men, who stood up to their work. Of course they demanded at first twice as much for their services as they were glad to accept eventually. As we got afloat the sun was shining brightly, as it had been since we left Bellinzona in the early morning; and there was just enough air to be pleasantly perceptible. At the head of the lake, however, far away to the north, we saw that a storm was raging. There all was black, and distant thunder was at times heard. When we had got about halfway across the lake, the surface being still unruffled where we were, we descried a line of broken water reaching across the lake, rapidly advancing upon us from the north. Our boatmen made all the haste they could, and succeeded not quite, but almost, in escaping the squall: for it struck us when we were but little more than 200 yards from the beach.

We had to wait at Bellaggio about an hour for

as it was to go to Como I suppose I must say, the up steamer. If I had remained at Menaggio I should have gone on by the same boat, but I was glad that I had not done so, not merely because crossing in the boat was an additional small incident in the day's work, but also because it enabled me to see the finest, I might say perhaps the grandest, display of flowers I have ever looked upon. In going down to the new pier, to the left of the road, or rather of the street, for it was still in the town, there is a long wall about 10 or 12 feet high; evidently the boundary of the grounds of a house situated somewhere behind it. I infer from the lay of the land that the grounds, immediately behind the wall, must be 6 or 7 feet higher than the roadway. Over the top of this wall, rising several feet above it, and bending down 4 or 5 feet from the top, was one thick, bushy, unbroken line of oleanders, every spray of which ended in a large truss of freshly expanded rose-red blossoms. I paced the wall, and, if I remember rightly, its length was 62 yards. The stems of the plants were invisible, being behind the wall. Crowning then this lofty gray stone wall, and hanging down over its side was a long, broad, even, unbroken line of bright blazing colour. The eye fed upon it, and was more than satisfied with the feast.

The streets of Bellaggio were sheltered from the squall. In crossing the lake to Cadenabbia it was on our starboard beam. The little wet it made on deck was sufficient to drive pretty nearly all the native below. A little further down, on rounding the point, which opens the long reach, at the bottom of which stands Como, there was no more wind: either the interposing mountain acted as a screen to keep it off; or, as is common in mountain lakes and valleys, it was a local affair along a single reach. As we neared Como, at about 6 P.M., we saw that a heavy storm was gathering at that end of the lake, and just as we were leaving the boat for the pier, the rain came down in earnest; and lasted for two hours, accompanied with much thunder and lightning.

On seeing, this evening, in the reading-room of the Volta, a file of the 'Times' down to the 6th, I was amused at recalling that for some days I had been suffering under a complete deprivation of this necessary of English life, without having once given the loss a thought.

August 10.—At 7. A.M. attended mass at the Cathedral. The service reminded me of a question, which some years ago occurred to me in the Cathedral of Montreal—What is there in this service which can lead any one to suppose that it is edifying to man, or pleasing to the Almighty? The men of Como, we may infer, are of opinion that it is not edifying, or they have some reason for refusing to be edified by it, for certainly there were not half-a-dozen of them in the Cathedral. The women, too, of whom almost exclusively the congregation was formed, were, again almost exclusively, from the lower classes. I was on this occasion horrified (for I offer to the reader everything at all worthy of notice, but this incident very unwillingly) at seeing the officiating priest, in the midst of the service, expectorate on the floor, and a few minutes afterwards repeat the offensive act. The assistant priest took the contagion, and followed his example. As, however, in matters of this kind, practice and feeling are conventional, I, probably, was the only person present whom the act shocked.

After the storm of last night the day was bright and fresh. I was due at Andermatt to-morrow; and, as we have so often heard with respect to political questions, there were three courses open to me. I might return to Bellinzona by Lago Maggiore, which would so far have been new ground. This, however, I rejected, because I wished to see Lago Maggiore in a more leisurely manner. Or I might, by way of the Splugen, reach Andermatt late on Monday night. This also I rejected, because the Splugen appeared to belong to a district I wished to reserve intact for another day. Or, finally, I might, throughout, retrace my steps: and this was what I did. Nor was I dissatisfied with my decision; for I found that a second sight of the lake of Como, and of its lovely shores, was almost as pleasing and interesting as the first had been, though the two were separated by the interval but of a single night. It is a sight of which you feel that you can hardly have enough. The surprising number of towns that embroider the margin, and which are almost everywhere, all along, connected by villas, is in itself a pleasing sight. They show how near you are to Milan, and to many other wealthy cities, the dwellers in which are glad to exchange for a time the dust and dirt, the heat, the moil and toil, of city life for some months of quiet in a scene where Nature has done all she could to make quiet soothing, and remedial for damages and overstrains of either body or mind. It is a *sanitarium*, provided by kindly and provident Nature, for the exhausted and injured powers of the mental workers of Europe. Here is space enough for all; and all the space good, for the direction of the lake is mainly from north to south; every part, therefore, of each shore gets daily enough light and warmth, and not too much; one side being cool in the morning, and the other in the evening. The lake, too, being 30 miles in length, has, with the addition of the branch to Lecco, more than a hundred miles of shore: a hundred miles of its embroidered border of towns and villas; and of gardens, terraces, and pleasure grounds. The water, also, being only between one and two miles across, your opposite neighbours are within visiting distance by row-boat. And, now, steam has brought within visiting distance the inhabitants of all the towns, and of all the villas, throughout the whole hundred miles. And, then, this blue highway, and its charming margin, are set in a frame of most varied and picturesque mountains, with the purest and freshest air for you to breathe; with the richest vegetation to delight your eyes; and all canopied by the clearest and brightest azure. And this within an hour of Milan; and no city of northern Italy, if distance be measured by time, far off; and, when the tunnel under St. Gothard shall be completed, northern Europe brought close: and the sojourner, though on the shore of Como, yet, all the while, by the aid of the telegraph, at home.

As I descended Monte Cenere I was on the look out for the glimpse I had had, yesterday morning, of the head of Maggiore. But in these matters there is often a wide difference between evening and morning. The sun was now to the west of the mountains, behind Locarno. The lake was no longer blue, but hazy. The same haze shrouded Locarno, and its environs. Everything that had given life and interest to the scene then, was veiled from sight now. Its present aspect was too dull and dead even for imagination to work upon. The disappointment was just that so common in human lives, when, where we look for a garden of roses, we find desolation.

CHAPTER VI.

BELLINZONA—AIROLO—ST. GOTHARD — ANDERMATT—THE OBERALP ALPE.

Thought is the slave of life, and life time's fool. · SHAKESPEARE.

AT Bellinzona I wished to take a carriage and pair to Airolo, but in this extortionate place I could not hear of one for less than 75 francs. Probably 50 would have been gladly taken; but I was not in the humour for higgling, and so I went by diligence for 9 francs, 50 centimes, with the same for Ammer. As I got a place in the *coupé*, the diligence was as comfortable as, perhaps more so than, a private carriage would have been at night. I was saved, too, the possible troubles of long unnecessary halts, and overcharged *bonne-main*. We left Bellinzona at 10 P.M.

August 11.—I knew nothing of what passed from that time, till I was woke in the gray dawn, some way above Faido, just below the lower bridge of Dazio Grande, by a shock, which shivered the glass before me. This was caused by our diligence having come into collision with the down one from Flüelen over the Pass. The two diligences had got locked together; and it was some time before they could be disengaged, as the wheelers were unable to back such lumbering machines. The collision had been the doing of a young gray in our team, the off-horse of our three leaders. Though the middle horse of the three was an old hand, and—like the trained elephant, harnessed with the wild one, to teach him how to be tame, and to do his work quietly—did all he could to keep our unruly youngster straight, one of his jibs, just at the moment of crossing, diverted the vehicle an inch or two from its course: hence the mishap. He was punished quite enough for this escapade; for as soon as the diligences were got clear of each other, we were put into a gallop, and the offender was flogged all the way up the gorge: he resenting the whip with kicking and jibbing, always to the near side; and his tutor and trainer always steadily pushing him back. When we had got above the ravine, on to the level ground, the flogging and galloping was kept up pretty well all the way to Airolo. This I suppose is the fashion in which refractory young blood is tamed for Alpine roads. The diligence horses are strong bony animals, and are well kept; but they must have a hard and dreary life of it. One sympathized with the objections of young blood to begin such a life: but, then, the choice is between it and, perhaps, something worse.

It was just 6 A.M. when we reached Airolo. Here we left the diligence, and were glad to get once more upon our legs. By taking a highly speculative way over the steep grassy hill above Airolo, which proved a successful speculation, and by cutting off, as we had done in the descent, all the zigzags of the Val Tremola, we reached the Hotel on the summit of the Pass at 8. Here we breakfasted. At 9 we were again on the road. At 11.30 we were again at Andermatt, in our former quarters at the St. Gothard Hotel. Here I found a letter awaiting my return, in which I was given to understand that my wife and step-son would arrive from Pontresina to-morrow evening; that the following day would be spent in rest, and in such selection and condensation of the baggage of the trio, as the light marching order of an expeditionary party would require, and which might make it, should that be possible, not too much for a single porter; and that on the next, that is to say Thursday, morning, tents would be struck, and the march commenced. This gave to Andermatt an afternoon and two days. As I replaced the letter in its envelope, I said to myself, 'If I had known this when at Como, I should not have left the Splugen for another day. Still it will stand over very well; and there is abundance here, at nearly 5,000 feet above the sea, to occupy one for twice two days and a half.'

The morning had been bright and cheery; but in

the afternoon a cold, wet, leaden mist, sometimes worsening into a shower, rolled over the mountains from the direction of the Devil's Bridge, and settled down doggedly on the broad deep depression of our valley of Urseren. There was no breeze to sweep it away, even to give it the slightest movement. On the side of the mountain to the south of the village, just about the height of the little wood, which partially shelters it from avalanches, that is to say a few hundred feet above our heads, patches of dense cloud hung for hours together in the somewhat less dense mist, without moving, without even any alteration of shape. The mist was in the Hotel. It was everywhere. It penetrated to one's bones. In the reading-room men buttoned their coats, and lighted their cigars, wishing that the stove, too, were lighted. Last week, when passing through Andermatt, on my way to St. Gothard, I had sat for half an hour in the shade of the Hotel, on the bench in front of it; and had thought that nothing in the way of climate could be more freshening and delightful than the shade, on an August day, at such an altitude, with the flood of pure sunlight poured on every object around. But, now, the difference was cruel to those whose bodies, as well as minds, respond with too sensitive a readiness to the skyey influences of such altitudes. A fine, bright day quickens them into unwonted life; they feel as if they had been bathed in, and were breathing an exhalation of, champagne. And even mortals whose fibres are of the ordinary callousness, find it hard to be jolly, when for the exhalation of champagne has been substituted a cold vapour bath.

When Andermatt is in the clouds, the only local resources are the streams of carriages, and the arrival and departure of the diligences. The rolling rattle of the carriages, the jingling of the horses' bells, and the clatter of their feet on the granite pavement, are incessant. The new monster Hotel, the Belle Vue, being a little to the north of the new road from the Rhone valley to the Grisons, sees and knows nothing of the up and down traffic on this line. The Old Hotel, however, the St. Gothard, in the main street of the village, is in the way both of this traffic, and of that which passes, to and fro, over the St. Gothard Pass, wherewith, in such weather, to divert the thoughts of its prisoners from themselves. It all passes in front of the reading-room, within arm's length of the window. This advantage was not, this afternoon, thrown away; for some found, or endeavoured to find, a grain of comfort in the remark that the occupants of the carriages, at all events the gentleman who is generally seen seated on the box, by the side of the driver, must be very wet and cold. One, however, of the party, who appeared to have a scientific turn of mind, refused to be comforted by a comparison which might soon be to our disadvantage; and therefore remarked, unfeelingly, that such weather was generally very local, and that the occupants of the carriage would, probably, soon be in sunshine, in the Rhone valley. The majority at once saw the advantage of adopting his view; as it would give an additional justification for their discontent, and so aggravate their discomfort.

The well of conversation appeared to have been pumped dry. Fortunately, however, an opposite neighbour, some few paces lower down the road, who had a little piece of grass a few square yards in extent, kept geese. And these sagacious birds, having found that the road was no longer dusty, had sallied out in quest of a puddle, in which they might wade at least foot-deep. Their advent was hailed by those at the window as an event worthy of notice. This opened a new fountain for conversation; and it turned out to be one that for a time appeared inexhaustible. The first observation made was the most obvious one, that these Andermatt specimens were not much more than half the size of our English geese. The gentleman with scientific proclivities immediately suggested the effects of a cold climate in stunting animals, with a reference to Shetland ponies, as an illustrative instance. He was met with the remark that the Arctic bear is larger than the Westphalian. The last speaker for a moment appeared to have received a check by the observation that they do not belong to the same species. From this momentary check, however, he recovered by requesting his interlocutor to define species. The interlocutor being unwilling to lose his supposed advantage, retorted by the announcement that to ask for a definition of what all the world had always understood very well, implied belief in Darwinism, which was the demonstration of the absurdity that there was no difference between a man and a monkey. This, having been delivered with a show of denunciatory earnestness, was followed, as might have been expected, by a pause. But in the now ascertained dearth of subjects for conversation, one in which many were looking forward to taking a part, was not to be put aside in this way; and so there now commenced a recital, by several of the party in turn, of what each had observed, or heard, or read of geese. One prefaced what he was about to narrate by announcing that it was extremely curious. This was injudicious, for it excited more expectation than what he had to tell could satisfy. He thought it a proof of the justice of common opinion in regarding the goose as a stolid bird, that it always, as it crosses the sill of a barn door, cranes out its neck, and lowers its head, for fear of striking the lintel, generally some 10 or 12 feet above. There was nothing curious in this but the speaker's mistake; for the goose cranes out its neck, and lowers its head, because it very sagaciously supposes that it is not improbable that the barn, it is entering, may contain some enemy; and this is its attitude of cautious observation, and of defiance. A second, who appeared to have had some experience of the fallibility of testimony, or of the incredulity of mankind, acknowledged that what he was about to narrate had in it something marvellous. It was a story of a goose having contracted so devoted a friendship for a horse, that fed in the same paddock as itself, that it was never easy except in the society of the horse. There was, however, nothing very marvellous in a highly gregarious animal attaching itself to the only other animal with which it could associate, notwithstanding that that other animal belonged to a different natural order. Talking of geese reminded a third—it must have been on the principle of the game of dominoes—that he had once bought his Michaelmas goose at a poulterer's, four of whose children, he afterwards heard, were laid up at the time with small pox. This was evidence that the subject of geese was worn out. And, as no successor for it could be found, the party dispersed; some to their rooms to attend to any small matters they were so fortunate as to think required attention, and some to the post office, to see the arrival and departure of the afternoon diligences.

The number of diligences, that pass through Andermatt, surprises one, who does not consider that they not only carry the letters between northern Germany and Italy, and between southern Germany and France, but also a large proportion of those who travel in Switzerland, and no small amount of goods; for both the latter fall within the purview of the Swiss Post Office. You may twice a day, at the hours in the forenoon and afternoon when the diligences are timed to meet here, from north, south, east, and west, see as many as half-a-dozen together in front of the post office ; which, by the way, is kept by a woman, and, in her absence, by a boy. As to the diligences, the driver is the servant of the conductor, who is the responsible official, and wears a kind of uniform. The conductors are, generally, very civil and obliging. They are well paid by ascending salaries, which at last reach 3,000 francs, besides the *bonne-main* they get from travellers.

At dinner I was placed next to a party of five young men. At a glance I inferred that they were Americans. I was sure, however, that they were not Yankees, for they had neither the features, nor the bearing of the men of the hub of the world, nor of anywhere in that neighbourhood. Judging in the same way I concluded that they were not western men. I was not, therefore, surprised—it was only what I had expected to hear—when they told me that they were from Baltimore ; the city of the United States in which I had found the American most like the European in manner, and tone of thought. They were of varying ages between the limits of twenty and thirty ; and had formed a party, as they informed me, to complete their professional education—they were all aspirants for the faculty—by visiting, and studying for two years in, and acquainting themselves with the practice of, the chief medical schools of Germany, France, and England. This reminded me of an observation I had made while travelling in the United States, that, there, in some matters, especially practical ones, larger and more complete views are taken than with us: at all events, it would be well if a like desire for study and culture were common among the medical students of the old country.

August 12.—On the following morning the fortunes of the weather-battle were evidently inclining to the side of the Sun. It had broken the ranks of the clouds, which yesterday were in complete possession of the field. They were now retreating in scattered detachments. As each trailed over the scene of their late victory, it discharged a parting volley, in the form of a smart shower. The Sun, having been forced back for a few minutes, then returned, and re-occupied the ground. By the exercise of his evaporating powers, he effaced, with marvellous rapidity, the traces of his enemy's recent work. A few moments after his rays struck the wooden roofs of the village, steam was curling up from every part of them—as much as if the interior of each house had been on fire, and the smoke was pouring up through the joints of the shingles. This was repeated several times, at lengthening intervals. At last the valley was completely cleared of the enemy, of whom nothing remained in sight, with the exception of a few small outposts high up on the mountain sides.

Ammer was now summoned, and we started for the inspection of the alpe of Oberalp. A line or two will suffice for the statistical account of this alpe, as it is given in the *Economie Alpestre de la Suisse*, which was issued in 1868 by the *Bureau de Statistique du Département fédéral de l'Intérieur*. The alpe of Oberalp is situated in the Commune of Andermatt. It is the property of the Commune. Its acreage is not ascertained. It was assessed formerly at 350 Kuh-essen (the extent of pasture required for the keep of a cow), now at 290. At present there are summered on the alpe 175 cows in milk, 140 young neat stock, 250 goats, and 40 pigs: in all equal to the keep of $328\frac{1}{3}$ cows. It is 4,400 feet above the sea. (It must be 1,000 feet higher). It is grazed for 97 days, between June 24, and September 28. For each cow 3fr. 50 cents. are paid. Each cow gives 144 livres of cheese (a Swiss livre is equal to nearly 17 oz. English), worth 50 cents. a livre; and 64 pots of whey worth 20 cents. each. The return for each cow is 85·20. The outgoings for each 5fr. The net return for each 79fr. 20 cents. The total net income from the alpe is 17,885fr. Of this 13,860fr. is from cows; 4,025 from other stock. This will give a general idea of the nature, uses, and value of Swiss mountain pastures, which are not cut for hay (if they are cut for hay they are prairies and not alpes) but depastured during the late summer and early autumn; being for the rest of the year either too cold and wet for stock, or actually buried beneath the snow.

To reach this alpe you leave the village either by the old mule-path, or by the new carriage-road, and are immediately on the skirts of the mountain, which is here quite devoid of trees, and all in grass. You do not ascend the zigzags, by which the road climbs the mountain, but cut them all off by going over the grass, straight up the mountain side. As long as you are cutting off the zigzags, and till you come out on the straight road, you will be going up, and through, about a mile and a half of prairie, where the grass is cut for hay. This is kept clean, all noxious weeds being eradicated, and, as I saw, is pretty well manured. Upon this you will see no stock in August. They will take whatever parts of it are ever fed, in their way down from the upper pastures. When you get to the road, it has become straight and level, and remains so, with only a very gradual ascent, till it gets beyond the Oberalpsee, that is to say, for something more than two miles further. It then rises, and turns to the right. But if you go straight up the mountain that is before you, facing you as you walk up to the lake, you will come, on the summit, to the end of the Oberalp alpe, and will be on the Tiarms Pass, by which you may leave Uri, and enter the Grisons.

As soon as we had reached the road, we were upon the unmown alpe, and among the stock. At its near, or lower, end were the pigs and calves. The pigs are never very far from the *châlet*, in which the cheese is made, for they get a good part of the whey. The *châlet*, of course, is placed in as low and sheltered a spot as it can be conveniently. But, wherever it is placed, you will see smoke issuing from its chimney, for at these altitudes it is too cold to make cheese without some artificial heat. We next came up with the goats. For, as they must be brought twice a day to the *châlet* to be milked, it is as well to have them pretty handy. After the goats, in the broadest grassy bottom of the alpe—for they are entitled to, and have, the best pasture—a herd of cows—I counted somewhat over 100 of them—put in their appearance. They were below the road, beside the stream which discharges the Oberalpsee, and which was, just where they were, fringed with patches of the rose of the Alps, then in flower. Last of all, on the flank of the ascent to the Tiarms Pass, at the greatest distance of all from the *châlet*, were the sheep; for they have not to be brought home to be milked. As to the pasture itself we will put it at three miles in length, and we will call the road its axis, though I do not know how far it extends laterally, beyond the two ranges of mountains that bound the view. The sward is generally clean and good. The road is on the flank of the mountain on the left to one going from Andermatt. There is a good breadth of grass above the road in most places, bounded by a ridge

H

of rocky summits. On the right there is the descent to the stream in the valley, and the rise, beyond, of the opposite mountains. The sward here, too, is good till it begins to get threadbare as it approaches, and at last becomes quite out at elbows on, the summits.

While I was counting the cows, I saw Ammer among them, picking his way across the stream from rock to rock. On his return he had in his hand a bouquet—by no means a small one—of the rose of the Alps. This he informed me was for Madame on her arrival.

Turfy mountain slopes, and cattle, are not much to go to see. You may find at home, in Wales, or Scotland, just as good combinations of these objects as at Andermatt; possibly even better, for the actually subaerial mountains here are no great height above the elevated plateau from which they spring. But, then, these turfy slopes, and these cattle, belong to the peasants of Andermatt; and that to the thought, whatever may be the case with respect to the eye, makes a world of difference. The peasants of Andermatt are a very old community. They are as little changed from what their fathers were many centuries ago, as the mountains that stand round about Andermatt. While the outside world, north, south, east, west, has been changing from century to century, they, from century to century, have continued the same. They have had neither a governing class, nor a destitute class. All the while they have, themselves, managed their own affairs. Among them there have been neither governors, nor governed; neither rich, nor poor. These alpes, as far back as their history goes, have been held in common; and by the line of ancestors of those who hold them now. They have been held, generation after generation, down to the generation whose cattle are now upon them, in precisely the same fashion. Land, elsewhere, has ever been changing hands; been held by different tenures; been turned to account in different ways; and given rise to different political constitutions. Here it has never changed hands. It has passed from the father's to the son's by an unbroken lineal succession. It has all along been held by the same tenure; been turned to account in the same way; and maintained the same political constitution. This is what gives to the sight its interest.

And now a change is coming over their little world. The great world, and its influences, are encroaching upon them. The causes, which have brought about changes elsewhere, are beginning to bring about changes among them. Some are getting rich, and some are getting poor. Some are amassing capital; some are working for wages. Oberalp alpe is already let, that is to say, its proprietors pay for sending their cows on to their own property; and the rent is wanted to defray the growing expenses of the old village, which has now become a modern town. If they did not turn it to account in this way, they would have to pay road-rates, and fountain-rates, and antiavalanche-rates. Perhaps the day is not very distant, when this alpe will be sold to a joint-stock company, who will supply with milk, butter, and cheese the two railway towns that are now springing up at Göschenen and Airolo, and the town in the high vale of Urseren, to which the pleasure-worn and business-beaten inhabitants of the cities of the plains will come to summer. And then the long communal history of the Oberalp will have ended; and those who walk through it will no longer be able to read in it the life of the past: for that will be found then only in books. This enhances the interest, with which the beholder now contemplates it. It is one of the last pictures, and a fading one, of a form of human life that will soon have completely vanished for ever. But for the present there it stands, exactly where it ought to stand. It has, as it were, taken refuge; and been able down to our own times to maintain itself, in this lofty, inaccessible, central nucleus of our Continent. But the flood of change has at last come near to it, has risen high upon its sides, is still rising rapidly, and must soon sweep over it.

CHAPTER VII

AM STAG—KLUS—THE SURENEN—ENGELBERG.

> Therefore am I still
> A lover of the meadows, and the woods,
> And mountains ; and of all that we behold
> From this green earth ; of all the mighty world
> Of eye and ear—both what they half create,
> And what perceive : well pleased to recognize
> In nature, and the language of the sense,
> The Author of my purest thoughts, the nurse,
> The guide, the guardian of my heart, and soul
> Of all my moral being.—WORDSWORTH.

August 13.—Madame and the little boy arrived, from Pontresina, yesterday evening, as expected, at five o'clock. This morning, after breakfast, he and I walked to the Devil's Bridge, and a little way below it, for I wished to see how strong he was upon his legs, and to hear his own account of what he had seen and done during the last year, which he had spent in Switzerland, at school at Aigle during the winter, and in the hot weather at Pontresina with a German tutor. In the afternoon we all went to Hospenthal. These are small matters ; but not to mention them would be to exclude the reader for a whole day from our society, which would be a violation of the understanding implied on our title-page. This is the record of a month; and an uneventful day must not be dropped out of the record, but shown to have been uneventful. What, however, was uneventful so far as matter worthy of record goes, must be taken as a part, which, though small, has its place and purpose in the sketch of the whole. The reader, too, will understand that even in a Swiss excursion an uneventful day is not necessarily an unsatisfactory one; for just as peace has its triumphs as well as war, so has repose its charms as well as exertion, and the more so if the repose comes in the midst of the exertion.

August 14.—At 6 A.M. with, figuratively, bands playing and banners waving, that is to say with a fine morning, light hearts, and the good wishes of our host and his wife, we commenced our march. Both the heavy, and the expeditionary baggage was left in charge of my wife's maid, who was now included in the former. By the diligence that left Andermatt at 10.30 A.M. she was to bring it all on to Am Stag, where she would leave what we were to take with us, take the rest on to Lausanne, and there await our arrival, whenever that might be.

Our first object was Engelberg by the Surenen Pass. With this in view we were to walk to-day to Klus, a little village about four miles beyond Am Stag. The way was all down hill, and the Devil's Bridge, Göschenen, Wasen, the Priest's Leap were in succession rapidly left behind and a few minutes after 10 A.M. we had reached Am Stag, somewhat over fourteen miles. For old acquaintance' sake I was for stopping at *La Croix Blanche*. My recollections of the good-natured, burly landlord, and his neat-handed, pleasant-mannered manageress, were obligatory. There was too—it was a warm sunny day—a most umbrageous walnut-tree alongside his house, with seats and tables beneath it, just at the foot of the eastern mountain. Only a few paces below the tree was the high road of the valley; beyond that, a few paces more, the murmurous Reuss ; and then the opposite western mountain. As it was here that our baggage was to be given up to us, we had to wait for the arrival of the diligence, which would be for two hours. We decided, however, as the day was warm, and our halting place had attractions, and also claims upon us, to stay here till late in the afternoon, and then do the remaining four miles of our day's work. Having had an early dinner, we took up a position under the umbrageous walnut-tree, and whiled away the time with coffee and ices, which we found were to be had at Am Stag, and with looking at the opposite streams of carriages, from the north, and from the south, which are incessantly passing along this arterial line of road.

As each carriage stopped before the house, down the long flight of steps would waddle the good-natured, burly landlord, to receive his visitors, in gait, bearing, and bulk not unlike a young hippopotamus going down stairs. The parties in the successive carriages had each its own idiosyncrasy, and was a distinct study. Before a word was spoken by the occupants of a carriage, the experienced landlord—for many years he had been a courier—divined at a glance whether he should welcome the new arrival in French, or German, or English. Some had a *blasé* look. They had had enough of everything, and especially of this kind of thing. They knew very well what it all meant, and just what it was all worth. Others were *riant*, and reciprocated the host's politeness. Others had a helpless expression, as if they mistrusted the French of the spokesman of the party, but brightened up when addressed in the familiar accents of the Island tongue. In one of the carriages that stopped before us was an American, as burly as the young hippopotamus, and a head taller. His carriage wheels had hardly ceased to revolve, before he was on the road; and having given an order that the fresh horses were not to be put to for a quarter of an hour, walked off, at a quick pace, to the Reuss, throwing out, as he went, the joints of a telescope fishing-rod. There was a grain of the comical in a big man, in the prime of life, who had crossed the broad Atlantic to see Switzerland, here at Am Stag, with the mountains all around him, entirely absorbed in the hope (it proved fallacious) of being able to beguile, with an artificial fly, to an untimely end, an unwary little trout.

I was reminded of an Englishman, of much the same build, I had met some years ago in Italy. He, too, was a sportsman, and had his gun with him, in expectation of falling in with some quail, or a woodcock or two. That was what, in his way of looking at the world, and all that therein is, Italy might be good for. We were at the time passing through the highly cultivated neighbourhood of Bologna, and were occupying opposite seats, next the same window, in a railway carriage. As far as the eye could reach, the rich level, we were traversing, was all in corn, planted, at regular intervals, with lines of mulberry trees, to which were trained luxuriant vines. It was thus yielding, simultaneously, the three valuable crops of maize or wheat, silk, and wine. My fellow traveller, for some time, contemplated the scene in silence; at last, when he had, with due deliberation, formed his ideas, he gave me the benefit of them. 'Did you ever see such farming as this? These people here pretend to be growing corn. Just look at their land. Every few yards they have got a hedge of miserable pollards, that will never be worth a shilling a-piece, and of old brambles.' I afterwards met the same gentleman at Venice; and asked him, if he had seen St. Mark's, and the pictures at the *Accademia?* 'Of course,' he replied, 'I have been to see them; and all that sort of thing may do very well for the sort of people you have here, but you know I am an Englishman, and can't take any interest in that sort of thing.' He had, I thought, hit the nail upon the head. It was because he was an Englishman. He was a public school and University man, and so one of the victims of our public school educational system, which, while undertaking to make classical scholars of the few, who have some taste and capacity for such studies, leaves the minds of all the rest, the great majority, who have no taste or capacity for such studies, utterly blank; and, which is still worse, engenders in most cases an insuperable life-long distaste for every other kind of study. I believe it was the attempt, at the cost of every other kind of knowledge, to force down the throat of my fellow traveller not the Classics, but a grammatical and critical knowledge of Latin and Greek, that must be held answerable for his inability to understand the agriculture of Italy, and to find anything to interest him in Venice.

As soon as Ammer had dined, I sent him on to Altorf to get my *malle* from the landlord of the Golden Key, in whose charge I had left it, and to post it for Lausanne. He was then to return in the evening to Klus. At 3 P.M. we sent on the little man, in an empty return carriage, in charge of the expeditionary baggage: he had walked 14 miles in the morning. At 4 o'clock my wife and myself followed on foot. We reached Klus a little after 5.

The Inn at Klus is quite of the village kind. The ground and first floor appear to be intended only for the accommodation of peasant visitors. The upper chambers are the guest-chambers. They consist of a small sitting-room, and three good bed-rooms. Everything in this part of the house was clean. The people, too, themselves, we found good-natured and attentive. We had intended to have had a baggage horse for the Surenen, as the distance to Engelberg is great for porters. No horse, however, of any kind, or of any degree of badness, could be had. Anticipating the possibility of this, we had tried to get one at Am Stag; but ineffectually, for every animal that could be brought into the valley, and kept on its legs, was wanted for the traffic of the road. We were, therefore, obliged to have recourse to porters; and having engaged two, ordered coffee for 4.40 A.M. next morning.

August 15.—Were under weigh at 5 A.M. A fine bright morning. At Erstfeld, half a mile from Klus, you cross the Reuss. At Rübshausen, a mile and a half further on, you begin the ascent of the mountain. All mountain ascents are pleasant in the fresh morning. You enter the forest at once, the breadth of the bottom land of the valley being hereabouts on the other bank of the Reuss. We found the forest on the mountain side frequently broken with little prairies, and enlivened here and there with *châlets*. Occasionally we got a good view down the valley, and of the opposite range.

Having climbed to the upper limits of the forest, you reach a place called Bocketobel. You have now earned something, and will be well paid. You are about to enter the upland valley of Waldnacht: but it is not yet in sight. The path is a mere groove along the top of the precipitous *talus* of the cliffs that rise on your left. You turn your back on these cliffs to make out the particulars of the scene. It is thoroughly Alpine. If you look first to your left there is before you a very fine rock-bound ravine, into which is falling, in a good cascade, the waters that drain into the Waldnacht valley from the heights around it. The opposite side of this ravine is a sheer wall of rock. This is crowned with an upsloping wood. Then a broad expanse of upsloping prairie. Then wood again to the top of the ridge. You then turn to your right. You there have a long sharply shelving *talus* from the heights above, in part forest, in part grass. Behind, and above all this, at the point at which you are standing, facing south-east, are the rugged snow-streaked tops of the Uri Rothstock. If you are fortunate, as we were, all these objects, and their minutest details, will meet your eye in full sunlight, through the diaphanous sunlit mountain atmosphere. It will, however, be very different when you look down the mountain, you have been ascending, to the deep broad valley, and to the opposite range. It is still early morning, and there is a light haze in the valley; and the sun, which is all about you, above you, and for some way below you, cannot yet reach the valley, or touch a point on the eastern side. The haze, therefore, that fills the valley below, is equally on the side of the opposite range. This haze is of a pale grey, almost white, with a suspicion of blue. It is of the tint of a glass of water into which has been stirred a drop or two of milk. This is but dimly diaphanous. The opposite mountain, therefore, and the works of man in the valley, in contrast to the clear definition of all that is immediately before you, and on either side, appear to be unsubstantial—like objects in a vision that is fading away—the mere spectres of villages and mountains. It is a scene of much variety, and of good contrasts.

Having given to it sufficient attention, and time, to allow it to form its image in your memory, you turn your back upon it, and enter the valley of Waldnacht. This, as *L'Industrie Alpestre de la Suisse* tells us, is an alpe lying within the Commune of Attinghausen, in which Altorf is situated. It now grazes 116 cows, and 16 pigs. It is nearly 6,000 feet above the sea; is available for 107 days; is worth 7,324 francs a year; and belongs to six co-proprietors. What is visible of it, as you enter it, is a long grassy oval, bounded on the south by precipitous mountains; on the north by a long grassy mountain slope, with, here and there, tufts of dwarfed alders on its side; on the east it contracts to the narrow passage by which you have just entered it, and on the west to the Surenen Pass.

What is visible may be three miles long, and in the best part one mile broad. You will understand from these particulars how completely above, and out of the world it is. The herdsmen who milk the cows, and make the cheese, even with the occasional diversion of the few travellers the Pass brings to them, must have plenty of opportunity for studying each others' character, and the characters of their 116 cows and 16 pigs.

Here we took on one of the herdsmen to assist the little man up to the top of the Pass, for in the ascent of the mountain from Klus to Waldnacht his strength, for climbing, had begun to fail. The path lies along the bottom of the grassy vale by the side of the flower-margined stream; at the western end of the grassy bottom it crosses the stream; and then the ascent begins again. In the valley you had been on level ground. This second stage of the ascent is without trees; rough and rocky, but full of flowers between the rocks. Here a part of the herd of cows was grazing. Many were on the path in preference to the rugged mountain side, though there was not much to choose between the two. The sun was hot. The way was steep. After a time we came to the end of the first stage. It was a kind of landing place in the mountain staircase we had been toiling up. On this was a field of snow about 100 yards across. The very dog, who had accompanied the herdsman, took a mouthful from it. Then climbing again. In this bit was an ice-cold spring which bursts out from beneath a rock, a yard or so from the path. I might have passed it without observing it, and so lost a rare draught, but Ammer and the porters saved me from that loss. We then came to a second ice-field about 200 yards wide. After this the ascent was sharp and toilsome for a warm day, with the sun—at that hour it is on the face of the mountain—on your back. As you near the top the path is steep, loose, and shingly.

When we had climbed to within three or four hundred feet of the top, vegetation almost entirely died out. The surface was everywhere strewn with small slaty *débris*, from which uprose, at intervals, large masses of harder rock, not yet disintegrated. Here, between these larger and harder fragments, on the scaly, leaden-coloured ground, which otherwise would have been quite naked, was a natural garden of most charming little Forget-me-nots. They stood an inch, or two, apart, as if the soil were too poor to admit of closer proximity. But, even with this amplitude of space, each plant could form no more than a single stem, without branches, perhaps two inches high, with two or three little lateral leaves. This little stem supported a single truss of pale blue flowers, with pale golden eyes. Such soft tints, and amid such hardness! Like pearls upon an Ethiop's arm. They can do little at this height, and on such a soil. Nothing else can do anything. But this frail little plant bravely holds up to the light its gem-like flowerets in the midst of cold and barrenness. The little it can do it does passing well. The slender stem is stretched up to you as far as it can reach. The little flowers, too, do not droop, but are erect also; nor are they half-closed, but each is expanded out quite level. It looks up to you with the open eye of confiding innocence, and says, 'If you are pleased with me, look at me. Take me into your eye. Forget me not.'

'No! gentle little suppliant, never! No cares, nor pleasures, of the world shall ever dim your image in the eye of memory. To recall it will be always pleasant, and at times may charm away care. May sky and sun, whose liveries you meekly wear, smile on what remains of your short day.'

As is the case with many Swiss Passes, the Surenen, looked at from below, appears to be very much less than it proves to be in the ascent. The eye takes the air line to the top, and because it sees none of the depressions, and few of the windings the path is obliged to make, naturally ignores them, till experience has taught the necessity of making due allowances. While you are in the inexperienced stage you will often mock yourself, you may do it here, with the complaint that you have got a long way from the bottom, without getting any nearer to the top. As you advance, the way only lengthens. The more you do, the more there remains to be done.

At last the summit was reached, and with something akin to disappointment, at finding that what we had been so long in toiling up to, from five in the morning till past eleven, was crossed literally in two steps, for the top is only a hog's back ridge.

Half a dozen steps beyond the summit, inclining to the left, is a little stream, with its channel cut in the short turf, which you had left behind you a long way down on the other side, but which at once reappears on the western slope. This little stream must take its rise, perhaps by some subterranean duct, from the lower stages of the Schlossberg, which is here on your left. The Blackenstock, a lower stage of the Uri Rothstock, is on your immediate right. The depression between these rugged, craggy mountains forms the Pass. Here, on the grassy marge of the little runnel on the summit, was called a halt. From this point you look down on the Surenen alpe, falling away immediately below your feet, with, on its southern side, the grand summit snow-field of the Titlis, in the distance, full before you. Between it and you are several iron-cased, iron-hearted, inaccessible-looking mountains on each side of the valley. All this will feed the eye, as you lie on the smooth short turf by the side of the glancing blithesome little runnel.

It is pleasant, very pleasant, with so much that is grand and unwonted before you—such huge masses, such dark, unpitying, unchanging hardness, pinnacles, precipices, ravines, and snow-fields—to rest on the smooth turf by the side of the cool sparkling streamlet. Your hard work is now done. The strain of the long climb—and it was sharpest at the last—has come to an end suddenly. You feel that your lungs, your heart, your muscles, are rapidly resuming their normal condition. The cigar you have earned is unusually soothing. You notice that a little puff of white vapour is incessantly curling up from the summit of the Blackenstock, hard by on your right. He, then, too, to keep you in countenance, to associate himself with you, has, by the aid of the sun, lighted his pipe. That 'chartered libertine, the air' is quiet, with only just enough movement in it to make its Alpine freshness perceptibly restorative. Your draughts of claret, mixed with the water of the lively streamlet, seem to be replacing the moisture of the bodily organism, which the effort and sun-heat of the climb had abstracted; and the sensation of the replacement is contenting. Your camp-followers, too, a few paces off, are, you notice, rejoicing in the sense of release from their burdens, which they have placed, erect in their wooden back-frames, before them, as if they wished to see, as well as feel, that they are no longer upon their backs. You pass the claret to them. They do not dilute it from the stream. To them, undiluted, it is a thin potation.

Half an hour is soon gone. Another quarter is added. And then the words *en route* are again heard, and the descent commences. You are fresher than when you rose with the sun, though a life seems to have passed since then; and you can hardly bring yourself to believe that that was the morning of to-day. *Le petit Caporal*—for the blue boy of last year now wears two stripes in the battalion of the Aigle Cantonal College—takes the lead, and keeps it all the way, till at 4.30 p.m. we enter Engelberg. But that is yet a long way off. The descent has many well-defined stages. First comes the topmost pasture—the most exposed, and with the shortest turf. Here are flocks of sheep, and the cows that are out of milk. They will not stray, for right and left they are walled in with mountainous precipices; and over the Pass they would find nothing to eat. In the next stage is a deeply sunk pasture, protected on the north by a semicircle of mighty precipices. Here are some horses and pigs, and the cows in milk, with a *châlet* for making cheese, from the chimney of which the blue smoke of the wood fire is rising vertically in the quiet air of the sheltered bottom. The third stage is composed of a long green mountain slope on the north, the successor of the semicircle of precipices, which are now transferred, mountain-high, to the opposite, the south side, but not in a semicircle. At one spot in this southern range you may count as many as six torrents, close together, streaming and tumbling down from the summits, which are needles of granite rising out of ravines of snow. In the fourth stage the valley has become narrow. The mountains on each side are naked cliffs; the only green being the narrow grass-clothed *talus* at the foot of each range. The last stage, which brings you to Engelberg, is one of woods and mown meadows. Two objects accompany you all the way, the brawling Aa at your feet, and the vast expanse of snow on the summit of the Titlis. To one descending the valley, the distinguishing feature of this grand mountain is that its upper stage rises in sheer black rock above the mountain in front of it; and then on this sheer precipice of rock is superimposed a sheer precipice of snow. It seems as if one might stand on the edge of the snow, and let down a plumb-line against the face of the snow, for some hundreds of feet, and then let it fall for some hundreds of feet more, against the face of the underlying rock. You are able, too, at the same time to see that this is not a mere ridge of snow, but that it is the edge of a vast field of snow on the flat crown of this mountain giant's head, which only gradually slopes off north, south, and west ; and which is, in the fashion just described, cut through perpendicularly on the eastern side, which is the one that faces you as you come down the Pass.

As there is no telegraph over the Surenen, we had, after our halt on the summit, sent on Ammer to engage rooms for us at Engelberg. It was fortunate that we had taken this precaution, for he was only just in time to procure them for us in the last hotel at which he applied—the large new hotel of the Titlis, on the further side of the town. The books say that the Surenen requires nine or ten hours. We were out eleven hours and a half. But then we were a family party, recruited from the drawing-room, the junior department of the schoolroom, and the study; and we did our work in family fashion, which, as far as I know, is, taken in its turn, as good a fashion as any other. At all events it is satisfactory to find that you are disposed to think so; for this will justify you in supposing that you are not one of those impetuous souls who have no idea of any pleasure in a Swiss excursion, except what they can extract from the fact that they got over a certain distance in less time than the books allow for it, or than their friends did it in: as if the merit of a book were to be measured by the rate at which it was written, or of a dinner by the rate at which it was eaten. Fair scenes and wondrous scenes are not to be scampered over, and toiled through. They have to be done with the eye and the mind as well as with the legs. What is fair and wondrous should be noted and understood. These are books which those that run cannot read. And they must be read carefully and rightly in order that they may be understood. Otherwise we cannot make them our own, so as to carry them away with us, and have them to look at (mentally) afterwards, whenever we please.

As we passed through the town we found that Engelberg was that day holding high festival. The bells were ringing; everybody was in the streets. The men were in their holiday costume, and of course the women too: each of the latter, if married, had two spatula-headed silver pins in her back hair—a local fashion, confined to the dames of Unterwalden—or, if unmarried, only one pin, the head of which was sometimes a disk, sometimes a globe about the size of an orange, formed of a kind of open filagree work. I asked one of those who was keeping the day with this festal adornment, what it was all about. The answer I received was, that it was in honour of God's Mother.

In the evening I went to the church of the Monastery for Evening Song. All the day long I had been looking on the face of nature, one of the aids allowed us for the construction of our idea of God; I would now draw near to Him, as He is presented to us in another fashion—the old accustomed human fashion. The shades of evening were beginning to come down on the valley; and the hour, now that work was over, and the day coming to its close, disposed to quiet reverence, to religious reverie. I would go for a time to the house where the sights and the thoughts of the world are excluded. But I did not find what I went for. The chanting of the monks was loud and harsh; and I could not make out a syllable of what they were chanting. And this was the more forced upon me because, they being behind a screen impervious to sight, the ear only was appealed to. The influence of the hour having been thus dispelled, I looked at the people before me. There were among them three men. All the rest were women.

Neither, then, the untutored peasants of Engelberg, nor one of the many hundreds of people from many nations, who had such culture as the world now gives, were there. How did they regard the fête and the occasion of it? Here were the old world and the world of to day face to face. I remained till the end of the service, and then, returning to the hotel, took a place on the seat in front of it.

The day was now gone by. The last traces of light were fast fading away. Darkness was deepening in the valley. In the west, in which direction I was looking, the black silhouette of the mountains was projected from the now silver-white western evening sky. One bright planet alone was seen overhead. A few remaining flecks of cloud were being fast absorbed, and were soon quite lost. The loiterers from many countries and the mediæval Engelbergers were fast disappearing from the streets. And now the last white traces of the dying day are gone from the western heavens; and unnumbered worlds, gleaming from illimitable space, are discoursing of the glory and of the mystery of the Universe. And nothing else is seen and all is still, that their discourse may be heeded.

CHAPTER VIII.

STANZ—BECKENRIED—SCHWYZ—THE HACKEN PASS—
EINSIEDLN.

> Silence is only commendable
> In a neat's tongue dried.—SHAKESPEARE.

August 16.—Stayed at Engelberg till 10 P.M. to see something more of the place. The monks declined to show us their library, or anything within their walls. To have admitted us would have been a violation of their rules. I was afterwards told that they do show their library on certain stated days: but as few people would be able, or disposed, to remain at Engelberg some days for the purpose of seeing a library, my inference was that it was not—which may be no fault of theirs—particularly worth seeing; for monks, in this respect like the rest of the world, if they have anything worth showing, are seldom indisposed to show it. In this way you may escape the unpleasant necessity of having to condemn them for churlishness.

Engelberg, as the books tell us, is 3,343 feet above the sea level: an elevation which gives it a fine, invigorating air, and a pleasant temperature in August. This, and the mountain excursions that may be made from it, among which is chief the ascent of the grand Titlis, are its attractions in these days ; and there are many who feel their force. But of all those who yesterday were coming and going, none excepting ourselves came or went by the Surenen Pass. This appears to be a district that is not greatly in favour with pedestrians ; and of those who are attracted to it, but few would wish to undertake so long a day without any snow-work, and even without any hard climbing. The Pass admits of being taken on horseback ; but on the eastern side the path would be very rough for riding, and as this would also be a very tedious way of doing it, I, for one, would very much prefer doing it on foot.

Our immediate destination was Beckenried. We went by way of Stanz. The distance is given at thirteen and a-half miles. The descent is nearly 2,000 feet, and is made in the first half of the road, much of which is through pleasant woods. The remaining part, that nearer to Stanz, is very much on a level, through meadows and orchards. The valley is not wide ; and the mountain-ranges which inclose it are at a distance which enables you to see with distinctness every object on large expanses of their slopes, from the bottom to the top.

At Stanz we stopped for an early dinner. We put up at the Angel. I had spent an afternoon, and slept there, on my outward journey ; and, as in the case of *La Croix Blanche* of Am Stag, had agreeable recollections of a pleasant-mannered and conversible manageress. At her suggestion, almost request, we visited the studio, hard by, of M. Deschwanden, the best known, at all events in his own locality, of living Swiss painters. One is glad to find an artist in Switzerland. Confining my remarks to the specimens of his work I saw in churches, and elsewhere than in his studio, I would hazard the criticism that his figures are not sufficiently suggestive of a substratum of bones and muscles, and that his colouring is too suggestive of lilies and roses. Of course the sacred subjects, in which chiefly he deals, generally require the expression of humble resignation, and of rapt devotion : still it is the resignation and the devotion of men and women, that is of organisms of bones, muscles, and nerves ; and furthermore, resignation and devotion are, after their kind, action ; and their surface, if one may so put it, presupposes the recognition, and anatomically correct disposition, of the inner mechanism. The external must be built on the internal.

In the afternoon we went on to Beckenried. Here we found that our *voiturier* and ourselves had formed very dissimilar estimates of the pecuniary value of the services he had rendered us. At Engelberg we had agreed with him for the payment of a certain fixed sum for taking us to Stanz, but had omitted this precaution for the stage from Stanz to Beckenried. For this his demand was unjustifiably extortionate. It was still early in the afternoon, and as I wished to see how matters of this kind are arranged in Switzerland, I was for laying the case before the Landamman. For this purpose I had not far to go; for this functionary was, as it happened, the landlord of the hotel at which we had just engaged apartments. The case was settled then and there, off-hand, as soon as stated, by the Landamman, standing in the middle of the road, without his hat, and with his hands in his pockets. He taxed the demand to the amount of four francs. The deduction should have been greater according to the tariff; but I was satisfied with the exposure of the man's roguery, and with the expression exhibited in his face of baffled and impotent spite.

Had this *voiturier* been a good-natured vagabond, who, in making his exorbitant demand had betrayed some consciousness of its character, I should probably have compounded his roguery—and at the same time paid the due penalty for my carelessness in taking an article without asking the price of it—by giving him half the fictitious excess he demanded. I here record his attempted imposition not at all as an instance of what people must expect in Switzerland (though, of course, there, as elsewhere, they ought to be on their guard against the possible occurrence of such cases); for this youth—small-headed, hatchet-faced, low-browed, with small cold gray eyes, meagre bony nose, and thin bloodless lips—would have been as bad anywhere else: nature had gone wrong with him in his original composition, and had denied him all human feeling except that for a franc. My mention of the matter is rather intended as a reply to the loud and frequent charges we have lately heard against the administration of justice in Switzerland. We have been told that it is so tardy as to amount to a denial of justice. This little affair, as far as it goes, points in the opposite direction.

As to the charges, about which, too, one hears much, of greed and roguery in the people one has to deal with while travelling in Switzerland, I for my part am surprised at finding so little of this kind of thing; and that what I do find of it is not carried further. In England—for of course our standard of comparison is ourselves; I say nothing of Scotland, for the Scotch are a peculiar and privileged people, to be judged only by Scotchmen—I believe that innkeepers, lodging-house keepers, horse-jobbers, and porters, are in the matters complained of, a long way ahead of the corresponding classes in Switzerland. Let us, too, make a little allowance for ordinary human nature, when tempted beyond the ordinary human capacity for resisting temptation. Here are people who have been brought up under conditions of life, confirmed by long traditions, which oblige them to believe that there is nothing in the world like francs; and who then have for three or four months in the year such temptations to act on this belief as assail no other people. During these three or four months, mobs of travellers from all parts of the world are bidding against each other for every horse, porter, and apartment in the country. Those who have what is wanted know that many of those who want these things are rich, many in a hurry, and that all must have what they want. My astonishment is that the Swiss who cater for travellers have so much forbearance, so much honesty, are so obliging, and give themselves so much trouble to please. Most people, I think, would be of opinion that in this country, under such circumstances, there would be a general break-down in these virtues. Let any one recall what he has himself experienced at home in matters of this kind. We are a very exemplary people in the knowledge of virtue. In its practice, too, we can resist everything except temptation: but here the Swiss go beyond us, for they can, to some little extent, resist even that.

Our first care on reaching Beckenried had been to telegraph to the Sonnenberg Hotel, on the Seelisberg, for rooms for Saturday. The answer had been immediately returned that we could not be accommodated till Saturday next, the 23rd. In the matter of time we could not afford a week at Beckenried; and so, with regret, we gave up the idea of staying a few days at the Sonnenberg for the purpose of visiting and investigating its interesting neighbourhood. Being, then, obliged to drop this out of our programme, we determined to go on next day to Einsiedln, which stood next after Sonnenberg in our plans.

We spent the remainder of the afternoon and the next morning at Beckenried. It is a pleasant place. There is the lake to be looked at, and to be turned to account for bathing, boating, and fishing. All the hotels have bathing-houses. There is the view across the lake; charming walks up the mountains behind and beyond it; and a great many excursions to be made by steamboat to places on the lake. As to the fishing, as you see people fishing, and as the hotels are supplied with fish, we must infer that there are fish that may be caught. But we have no reason for supposing that any in this part of the lake ever allow themselves to be caught; for all this afternoon, and the following morning, we saw, on the terrace of our hotel, patient Germans watching their floats, but did not see anything come of their patient watching; nor do I suppose that they would have got anything by watching through other afternoons and mornings. As I looked at them I was reminded of the patience with which the same good people had laboured and waited for the resurrection of the Fatherland—patience worthy of the energy and determination they exhibited when the time came for action. I fancied that I saw in the patience of these unrequited anglers some of the honest pride late events had made justifiable. One can understand their feelings. The day many generations had desired to see, but had not seen, had come at last; and when it had come they showed themselves not unequal to the supreme occasion. They had plenty to ruminate upon. At Beckenried, for them the fishing was enough without the fish.

August 17.—When, yesterday, we had telegraphed to Sonnenberg, we had supposed that it was Friday. We had therefore thought that the answer returned, that we could not be accommodated before Saturday next, the 23rd, was wrongly expressed; for was not the next day, the 16th, Saturday? It had never crossed the mind of any one of the party that yesterday was Saturday, the 16th; and so this morning no one was aware that it was Sunday, the 17th. We had lost our time-reckoning; otherwise we should have arranged for staying this day at Beckenried. The first suggestion we had of our mistake was seeing Ammer, on the steamboat pier, in his Sunday attire. We had given up our apartments at Telfer's, which, indeed, had over-night been engaged, by telegraph, over our heads; and as we had on the previous evening been rejected both at the Sun and at the Moon, the two chief hotels of the place, which were full to overflowing, there was now nothing for us to do but to remain where we were, on the pier, for the steamboat. This loss of time-reckoning is a common occurrence in travelling; at least I generally find it to be so. At home every day has its appointed work. The work, therefore, of the day of itself informs you what day of the week it is. You are kept *au courant* of the almanac by the work you have to do. In travelling you have no work at all except to go on. This is the same for every day. You cannot, therefore, remember the days of the week without a continual effort, which would be disagreeable, and of no advantage.

The steamer in somewhat less than an hour from Beckenried—we wished it had been longer about it—deposited us at Brunnen, having by the way touched at sunny Gersau, and at tiny Trieb—it is but a little *châlet*, the landing-place for the Sonnenberg, adhering to the perpendicular side of the big mountain, where it dips into the lake. In half an hour more the diligence, *en correspondance* with the steamer, took us on to Schwyz. Here we had an early dinner at the Rössli. At 12.30 my wife and the little man went on by *char* to Einsiedln. Ammer and I started at the same time, for the same destination, by way of the Hacken Pass.

As to the Hacken Pass, it is a very small affair, but a very pleasant walk. You begin the ascent as soon as you are out of the town of Schwyz. It is over the depression between the Hochstock on the north, and a spur of the Great Mythen on the south. The ascent, from the town to the top, requires two hours. It frequently brings you in sight of the lake of Lowerz, and of the two branches of the lake of the Four Cantons, which at Brunnen make an angle. Grass and woods alternate to the top; the former being in excess of the latter. As you look down, occasionally, on Schwyz, you think of the history of the men, who in old times made it a home for freedom. And, as you note the countless divisions of the plain below, you think that its existing state is not unworthy of attention; for there is evidence before you not only that the old freedom has been maintained, unimpaired, on the two bases of general possessive, and of universal political, equality, but also that unflagging industry, the associate of much manly virtue, has aided in its maintenance. You see that every little plot of prairie, or of corn land, and every fruit tree, you are looking upon, is watched, and tended, with an interest none but small proprietors can feel. You sympathize in the emotions with which the members of the little community below you regard their history, their freedom, and the modest rewards of their unflagging industry.

As you, toilsomely, climb up the mountain, in the bright sunshine, frequently shaking off, with a toss of your head, the briny drops, which are trickling down your face, and finding their way into your eyes, you will perhaps ask yourself, whether this is pleasure. Do you, honestly, like it? That you find it pleasant to be at rest in the cool shade, does not necessarily imply that you do not like exertion in the warm sun, if the exertion neither distress your lungs, nor blister your feet. There is a kind of enjoyment to the mind at all events, if not to the body also, in violent effort, when you find that you can sustain it. It is pleasant to feel that the bodily mechanism is being made to respond to the will. But be this as it may with many, there is no disputing about individual tastes. Each must be allowed his own; with respect to which he is a law to himself, without appeal to any higher tribunal.

There is something almost startling, from its instantaneousness, and completeness, in the change of view on reaching the summit of a *col*. You have been, for a long time, struggling up against the mountain: that side of it, and the mountains right and left of that side, have all the time been filling your eye. Without giving the matter a thought, you step upon the summit. Every object you have so long been looking at is out of sight; is gone; is down behind you. All that you are now looking upon is new, and generally very different—another valley; other ranges of mountains. That in the twinkling of an eye such vast objects should disappear, and such vast ones take their places, staggers you for the moment that is necessary for the comprehension of the new situation.

Having now accomplished the short, and sharp ascent of the Pass, the long and easy descent lay before me; and easy enough it is at first, being almost level, and over short springy turf. After a time you enter the pine forest, which along the path clothes an underlying ridge of the Hochstock. Here you have a made road; and before the great storm of a fortnight back

THE HACKEN PASS.

you would have had a bridge over the torrent—at this time of the year usually little more than a torrent channel—which comes down from the mountain. The storm, however, had not only carried away the bridge, but had also dug out a ravine in the loose rocky *débris* of the mountain side, to the depth, just about where the bridge had stood, of twenty feet, or more. I had, therefore, to scramble down to the bottom of the ravine, and to scramble up the other side, having in the bottom stepped over the little thread of water, to which the mighty raging torrent of a fortnight back had now shrunk. These excavations are easily formed by unusually heavy storms, because the mountain sides are generally only a *talus* of loose detrital matter that has, in the course of ages, fallen from the summits, and accumulated at the bottom, and on the flanks of the mountain, and eventually become covered with forests, and turf. This torrent, and many others on each side of the valley, had, on the occasion of the late storm, carried down hundreds of thousands of tons of stones and earth to the valley bottom, and into the Alpbach, the stream that drains the whole valley. Much of this freshly brought down stone had been spread out over the bottom of the broad channel of the Alpbach. In this way the new deposit has for a time raised its bed, that is to say till the pieces of which it is composed shall be ground down, and worn away. But while they, and the additional volume of storm-water, had to be provided with space, the Alpbach had been obliged in many places to widen its channel. This I saw it had done, sometimes on one side, sometimes on the other, by cutting away its banks. The lighter particles, those which the galloping freshet maintained in a state of suspension, had, of course, been carried down to the lake of Zurich.

Near the village of Alpthal I saw old stumps of alders and firs, that had been disinterred from grips, lately cut for the drainage of some damp prairies. These prairies, then, had been, at no very remote date, forest. In other places I have seen similar evidence of a change, which has of late been largely brought about in Switzerland in the uses to which land is put. As population increases, and, too, as more distant markets, by extended and improved means of communication, are brought within reach, more cows are kept. More milk and cheese are wanted at home; and can, profitably, be disposed of abroad. The forest, therefore, is cleared away; the rocks are quarried; and the land is laid down to grass. In this way more money is made of it. This conversion, however, by diminishing the amount of fuel brought to market, enhances its cost, which had already been enhanced by the increase of population. It is obvious that the poor, or rather those who have no land, are the chief sufferers by this change.

The scarcity, and consequent enhancement of the price of fuel, have now become in many parts of Switzerland, very considerable. In some places this has reached such a point that, as a check on its further progress, the Communes have ceased to supply their burgers with timber for new constructions, obliging them for this purpose to use stone. Great attention is now paid, pretty generally, to the maintenance of existing forests; and the profession of foresting is becoming an important one. The traveller, as he passes through the country, will, often, be struck with the care, he cannot but observe, has been bestowed on arboriculture. He sees that the rocky mountain side is supporting as many trees as could possibly be made to grow together on the space devoted to them; and that each individual tree has been carefully looked after, and scientifically pruned and trained, so that they shall not interfere with each other, but each have its fair share of space and light. In this work nature aids man's labour and thought by giving to the forests abundance of moisture; and, between the frequent storms and showers, abundant floods of sunlight and warmth. It is this, that, on the mountain sides, enables trees to take root, and grow to considerable size, on what apparently is little more than bare rock. I often observed far from insignificant conifers on the summit of detached blocks of granite—situations which, in this country, could not have kept them alive.

The same cause it is that gives to the Swiss their abundance of grass. Grass, under such conditions of moisture and warmth, will grow anywhere. You see it in Switzerland rapidly establishing itself on the tops of roadside walls. If a heap of stones has been piled up in a field, lichens and moss soon appear upon it; and, by their decay, in time, fill the interstices. Then trees spring up upon it, or a mantle of turf creeps over it. This may be the work of a century, or two. I noted multitudes of instances of every step of the process. And in excavations on hill sides I saw evidence of how the process had been repeated, again and again, as the mountain torrents had brought down successive avalanches of rocky *detritus*. Each successive layer, in turn, and in time, had become in this way consolidated with mould, and then covered with forest, or turf: only for the steps of the process to be again repeated. Indeed, the greater part of the prairies, and of the workable land in the valleys, consists of nothing but a thin film of soil, superimposed on fragments of rock. If a tree in such situations is blown over, its roots tear up this thin film of soil, and leave the substratum of fragments of rock exposed to view. The industry of petty proprietors, who both have much time at their disposal, and will, themselves, reap the whole benefit of their labour, aided by the climatic conditions of the country, has created the cultivated surface of south-eastern, and no small part of that of north-western, Switzerland.

On the way to Einsiedln I met several parties of pilgrims, almost exclusively Valaisans, it would be more correct to say Valaisannes, returning from their devotions before the shrine of the black-faced Virgin. Ammer recognized them by their costume. The day was warm, and they were going up hilL The women of between fifty and sixty years of age were, I observed, suffering less from their exertions than, and were not looking so much heated as, their younger and more vigorous companions. For the last three, or four, miles the road is very much on a level. I reached Einsiedln at 4.30 P.M.—just four hours out. As the carriage road from Schwyz makes a large loop, my wife and the little man were about the same time —only ten minutes less—on the way.

CHAPTER IX.

EINSIEDLN.

> What is't t' us'
> Whether 'twas said by Trismegistus,
> If it be nonsense, false, or mystic,
> Or not intelligible, or sophistic?
> 'Tis not antiquity, nor author,
> That makes truth truth.—HUDIBRAS.

As you enter the *Place* of Einsiedln, there faces you on the east side, if orientation has been observed in the Church, the large and famous monastery of Our Lady of the Hermits. The first impression is good and pleasing. It is even something more: it is striking. There is plenty of space in the foreground; and the whole is well kept. In the centre of the extended front is the entrance to the church. To compare what is small with what is great, it reminds you of St. Peter's at Rome, and its Piazza. As the *Place* rises from the point at which you enter it, throughout, up to the monastery, the elevation of the site of the building adds somewhat to its imposing effect. Rows of cell-like stalls, constructed in a stage of the rise, in a curve before the pile, increase its apparent height and size. There is an openness, and a breadth of sky, above, which give a sense of light, and space. As the structure dates from 1719, there is, as might have been expected, nothing in it, architecturally, worthy of notice.

The monastery, and the incidents of the pilgrimage made to its black-faced, and black-handed image of the Virgin, were what we had come to Einsiedln to see; and as there is nothing else in the place to see, we were soon in the church. The interior of the building is less pleasing than the exterior. Whitewash, tawdry tinsel, and pictures, inferior even to what you might have expected, do not produce so good an effect as the space, simplicity, and weather-tinted stone of the outside. No service was then going on; but there were about a hundred people in the church, the greater part of whom were before the shrine of the image.

We again returned for vespers. The church, which is large, was then more than half full; and there was some crowding around the shrine.

We were present once more—the next morning, at mass. The celebrants, if that is the correct appellation, were more than gorgeously vestmented, in vestments which appeared stiff with gold embroidery. These vestments, the screen which separated the priests from the profane laity, the incense, the bell-ringing, the lights, transported me in thought to the old heathen world. I felt as if I were witnessing the celebration, in the style of those times, of some of its sacred mysteries. The material means used, and the motives which prompted their use, that is to say the desire to produce a sense of undefined awe, were the same as they might have been then. I do not say this with any thought that it contains a reason why they should not be reverted to by ourselves: it may be right to aim at producing this effect; and these may be the readiest, the most powerful, and the most inoffensive means for producing it. I am only saying that what I was then witnessing carried my thoughts back to the old mysteries, which Christianity, as a matter of fact and of history, abolished; and which it abolished, because they would have served no purpose but that of obscuring the perception of its simple, intelligible, conscience-originated moral aims. I was told, immediately after the service, by a monk, who was showing me over the library, that in the celebration of the mass, at which I had just been present, a part had been taken by M. Dupanloup, the Bishop of Orleans.

The library, as might have been expected, is rich in folios. Folios, as a general rule, belong, like arquebuses, culverins, and coats of mail, to the past. As far as I saw, the contents of these folios, and of the books generally, were either theological, or classical. The Classics may be so made the instrument, and substance of education, and the study of a life, as quite to preoccupy the mind, and not themselves to suggest, or to allow anything else to suggest, any of the questions of modern controversy. Hence, perhaps, the desire and effort of the Church of Rome to confine education to the Classics. There were also in the library an electrical apparatus, and a cabinet of mineralogical specimens. We were, besides, shown the abbot's private chapel; the guest chambers, most of which make up two beds; and the conference chamber. This last is a large room, on the walls of which, among some other modern portraits, hang those of Napoleon III., and of the Emperor of Germany. If I recollect rightly, these two had been placed where we saw them before the outbreak of the late war.

In the rows of stalls in front of the monastery— there are some of a similar character to the north of the building—and in a great many of the shops of the town, are sold only such objects as pilgrims of the poorest class would purchase, to carry home with them as mementos of their pilgrimage. Among these objects is conspicuous in wood, earthenware, and a variety of other materials, a miniature reproduction of the black-faced image. I thought of the silver shrines of Ephesus; though the precious material of which they were formed, tells us that their purchasers were the wealthy and the educated. The aspect of the locality, in which these mementos are exposed for sale, and the fact that, not the mementos only, but everything else vendible in it, is of the humblest kinds of tinsel, unredeemed by any articles of use or substance, reminded me somewhat of a bazaar, or fair.

What you go to Einsiedln to see is the pilgrims. This is as exclusively the one object there as the Temple of the Sun at Baalbec, or the rock sculptures and excavations at Elephanta. If there were no pilgrims, not only would no one go to see Einsiedln, but there would be no Einsiedln to go to see: for it is supported by pilgrims only, and by nothing else. We are told that about 150,000 visit it yearly. These hosts of pilgrims have built, and maintain, both the monastery and the town. Everything you see of the town shows its origin, purpose, and character. It is a town of pilgrims' inns, and of pilgrims' shops. It is quite a mediæval sight. What is presented to you here enables you to form a picture in your mind of what many a town in those days must have been; as, for instance, Bury St. Edmunds, with its great monastery, and its shrine for pilgrims.

Of course a man does not go a long journey to see some object without a wish to know something about it: that were irrational. If he go to Baalbec to see what remains of it, he would be glad to know how Baalbec came to be placed where he finds its remains; what maintained its population; and what was the kind of life of the place. At Elephanta he desires to know what were the ideas in men's minds, that brought them to expend so much labour on such costly excavations. So at Einsiedln. You may not yourself have come on a pilgrimage to the shrine of the black-faced image: still you are not in every sense an unconcerned outsider. You have come on a pilgrimage of your own sort: its object is to see pilgrims doing a pilgrimage; and to think over the matter with the object, and the doers of the pilgrimage, before your eyes.

Now what is it that brings these tens of thousands of pilgrims here? That is the great question. Several reasons contribute to the explanation of the phenomenon. We will put first the famous Einsiedln inscription, because that is what first meets the eye as we enter the church. This inscription exhibits certain words of Christ's Vicar upon earth—an infallible Pope of Rome. The words are, '*Hic est plena remissio peccatorum a culpâ et a pœnâ.*' No words can be more precise and definite. 'Here,' in Einsiedln, in this Monastery, before this shrine of the black-faced Virgin, 'is plenary remission of sins, from their guilt and from their punishment.' No wonder, then, that the peasants of the Valais, of Bavaria, and of other places, where this statement is known and believed, flock to Einsiedln. This alone would explain their coming. The only wonder is that the whole Romanist world do not make a pilgrimage to Einsiedln the great and paramount object of life. To be sure I had just been told that I had, that morning, seen in the church M. Dupanloup, the Bishop of Orleans. But, during the last five centuries, how many Bishops of Orleans have been there? Was he following the example of his predecessors in being there? or was he there for some other purpose? How many Cardinals have made this pilgrimage? We do not ask how many Popes of Rome have made it; because, if they can give this plenary remission to those who make it, we may suppose that in this matter they do not give away all that they have to give, but reserve of it as much as will be needed for their own requirements.

Another question arises out of this inscription. Who could have expected that this remote, bleak, wild, formerly lonely forest, now open, dank grass-land, would have been so highly favoured? Why is this 'plenary remission of sins both from their guilt, and from their punishment,' to be secured at this out-of-the-way, unhistorical, little-known spot? We might have supposed that, if at any one particular spot upon earth was to be granted this plenary re-mission of sins, it would have been at Bethlehem, or at Nazareth, or at Jerusalem. We, who wish to understand matters of this kind, cannot but ask, why they have been passed over, and why, of all places in the world, Einsiedln has thus been made the gate of heaven? But still in the meantime, as it is the gate of heaven, we cannot be surprised that the peasants of the Valais, of Bavaria, and of other like-minded places, are attracted to it. In them it would be wrong, if they were not so attracted. It would however make the matter a little more intelligible, if the Bishops and the educated neighbours, of these poor people came with them; and showed by accompanying them, that they participated with them in the desire to pass through this wide, and smooth-paved gateway. Can the reason of their not coming be, that they know, that of them, to whom so much more has been given, somewhat more will be required? Can it be at all because they cannot but think that plenary remission is not within their reach on such easy terms?

Another reason for the maintenance of this pilgrimage to the black-faced image of Einsiedln may be the offerings of the pilgrims. The surmise that the latter of these facts stands towards the former, in some way and degree, in the relation of cause to effect, receives a colour of probability from this plenary remission of sins not having been accorded to pilgrimages made to Bethlehem, Nazareth, and Jerusalem; and also from the cessation of pilgrimages to some other places, let us say, for instance, to Canterbury. We all know that pilgrimages to Canterbury were, once upon a time, as common in this country as Einsiedln pilgrimages now are in Switzerland. There are still plenty of Romanists in this country; some remains, at all events, of the shrine of St. Thomas are still at Canterbury; and the Dean and Chapter, we may be sure, would put no difficulties in the way of those who might wish to perform this pilgrimage. Why, then, do we see no parties of pilgrims assembling at, and setting out from, some modern Tabard, or, if Chaucer's shade can forgive the supposition, from Cannon Street Station, for Canterbury? I am afraid we must give as a reason, not that the efficacy of prayers addressed to St. Thomas of Canterbury is less now than it was five centuries ago—any supposition of that kind would be quite inadmissible, for we know of nothing that could have diminished the saint's power: whatever it was five hundred years ago it must be the same at this day, precisely—but that there are none now who can receive the offerings of pilgrims. There is no body of men on the spot who could receive such offerings. And it would hardly do to say to the faithful, make your pilgrimages to Canterbury first; and then make your offerings to some authorized recipients in London, or else remit them by a bill of exchange, or a post office order, to Rome. As nothing of this kind can be done, it comes about that St. Thomas of Canterbury is no longer an object of pilgrimage. If the fact that there is no longer anyone to receive the offerings of pilgrims to Canterbury is, in some way or other, a reason for the cessation of pilgrimages to Canterbury, the fact that there are people to receive the offerings of pilgrims to Einsiedln may, in some way, be a reason for the maintenance of pilgrimages to Einsiedln. This may also throw some light upon the fact, that though the monastery has seven times been destroyed by fire, the black-faced image has, upon every one of these catastrophes, escaped without injury; and that in 1798, though the French carried it away to Paris, it forthwith re-appeared. In short, we may, I think, infer, with some degree of probability, from the nature of the case, and from what we know of such matters, that there would be no monks, no monastery, no black-faced image at Einsiedln, were there no offerings.

One reason more: the peasant of the Valais goes to Einsiedln, because he has not yet arrived at that stage of knowledge which enables men to distinguish between things material and physical on the one side, and things moral and spiritual on the other; and to assign each to its own realm. To do this readily and habitually implies an advance in knowledge which has not yet been reached by the mass of any people in the world. Just as wit is, mainly, the perception of resemblances, so is knowledge the perception of differences; and the differences, which separate the matters we are now speaking of from each other, and which are of their very essence, the peasant of the Valais has not yet been brought to apprehend. He is still in that stage of the perception, or rather of the non-perception, of the differences of these things, which admits of his supposing that, if he drink water from a fountain from which he is told the Saviour drank, he will be thereby spiritually benefited; and that a carved piece of wood, dressed in tinsel, that can neither hear nor see, as was argued of old, but might help him to make a fire to warm himself, or to cook his dinner, is able to intercede with God on his behalf. Having, then, been taught that there is at Einsiedln such a fountain—it stands in front of the monastery, and has fourteen jets—he goes to Einsiedln, and drinks from each of the fourteen jets; to make sure that he has stood on the right spot, and drank from the right jet: though probably all the jets have been replaced many times since the date of the legend; if it have a date. And, having also been taught that there is there such a figure, he goes on a pilgrimage to it, and prostrates himself before it.

As to the poor peasant pilgrim himself: if the wish of his heart is to become a better man, morally and spiritually, then all right-minded people will regard him with sympathy and respect, nothwithstanding his inability to distinguish between things physical and material on the one side and things moral and spiritual on the other. But if the wish of his heart be to purchase, by the means he has been taught to resort to, for the present certain earthly, and for the future certain heavenly advantages, then our sympathy and respect for him will be somewhat diminished. Ammer's common-sense observation on the pilgrims we saw was in the direction of the mark: 'If they really wish to become better men,'—of course he meant morally—'they should try what can be done in that way by honest dealing, industry, and speaking the truth.'

A word or two about the colour of the image of

Our Lady of Einsiedln. Was the Virgin black? If not, why is this image black? As no reason is given, except the authority of the Church, which has received it as a true representation, vouched to be true by the miracles it has worked, and is still working, we are left to what light we ourselves may possess for the elucidation of the difficulty. The blackness is intentional, because it is superimposed on the material, and is repeated in every reproduction of the image. Now we are all aware that blackness of complexion, one of the characteristics of the negroid races, results from the presence in the cuticle of the granules of a kind of pigment, which are not found in the cuticle of the European, and which could not have been present, except to a very inconsiderable degree, in that of a Jewess, especially in one of the house and lineage of David. In the days, however, of Charlemagne, when Ste. Hildegarde of Zurich gave the original black image to the anchorite of the House of Hohenzollern, who retired with it to the spot where Einsiedln now stands, to tend and to serve it, matters of this kind were not thought about; such distinctions were not understood: nor are they at this day understood, or thought about, by the peasants of the Valais; though probably a day will come when it will be otherwise even with them. We, however, cannot help noticing them, and adverting to them, when this image is before us.

The Virgin is here represented as by her complexion of the negroid race. In multitudes of other images, the genuineness and authenticity of which is vouched for by the same authority, she is represented by the same token, that of complexion, as a Caucasian. A Jewess of the house and lineage of David might, possibly, have been as fair as a Caucasian: so that may pass. But she could not have been as swart as the negroid race. That would have been impossible. But the greater impossibility— supposing impossibility to admit of degrees—is that which this authority vouches for, that she was both as fair as a Caucasian and as swart as a negro. Under which colour, then? Infallible authority. Speak, or die. It is not possible to ride off on the assertion that this is a matter of no consequence at all. If the peasant of the Valais is to prostrate himself before this image, let it at all events have some verisimilitude. It is,. however, true that there are some questions of a graver character, which have to be asked, and for which each will have, himself, to find an answer. If authority betrays ignorance in this particular of colour, what guarantee have we that its ignorance stops here? If it be mistaken in this, how can we be sure that it does not make mistakes in other particulars; for instance, in having any image at all of the Virgin, here, or elsewhere; and in addressing prayer to her as a mediator or intercessor, for we have no authority for putting these words into a feminine form? If, in the matter of colour, the authority we had previously been referring to says that black is white; and that white is black; and that there is no difference between them; why may it not rule, in a similar fashion, in other matters? If it is ignorant, mistaken, and contradictory in that which is least, supposing it to affirm that these points are of that category, we have another authority—this time an authority we all defer to—for believing that it may be ignorant, mistaken, and contradictory in that which is greater. If the abbot and his sixty brethren—to say nothing about the infallible head of the Church—are not themselves at all ignorant, or mistaken, in this matter of the black-faced, and black-handed image, their position is not thereby at all improved. From whatever side, then, we look at it, there is about it something ugly.

The world has lately been startled at the manner in which the Church of Rome, after centuries of indifference to pilgrimages, has, all of a sudden, woke up to a sense of their advantages and necessity. They are now being preached up everywhere; but most loudly in France, Italy, and Romanist Germany. Why particularly just now? Why was not this done equally one, or two, hundred years ago? And why, just at this moment, in these countries? Everything has a cause. There was a reason why they were not preached up one, or two, centuries ago; and there is a reason for their being preached up now. And it requires no great amount of sagacity to make out the reason in each case. They are preached up now, because pilgrimages are supposed to be a very good device for stirring up the fanaticism of the ignorant; and it is hoped that, when fanaticism has been stirred up, it may be directed against the Governments of Italy, Germany, and France. *Voila tout.* They are not preached up because they may be profitable to the saving of souls : for, if that were the reason, they ought to have been preached up as much a hundred years ago as to-day. They are preached up now, because it is believed that the spirit they engender may be turned to account in the game the Church of Rome is now playing. Its platform, just at present, is to exasperate the ignorant classes, everywhere, against government. Hence its denunciations of Cæsarism, of which nothing was heard as long as Napoleon III. was acting in conformity to the dictation of the priests. Pilgrimages are a plank of this platform.

Those, who come to this conclusion, will go on to ask, whether that Church is likely to win by these means? We may deem the means both dishonest and insufficient: still it would be unwise for that reason, or for any other, to think lightly of our opponents. Your harpoon may be fixed securely in a whale's vitals; still, if you do not take care what you are about, he may foul your boat with his head, or lash it with his tail, and throw all your hands into the water, and be the death of some of them. He must die: but if you do not keep a good look-out, he will get you into trouble before he dies.

Consider the situation: and you will see that you can afford to wait, and to be calm. Everything in the world that is great, and growing, is on your side: east, north, and west. In the eyes of the great empire of Russia, that will soon number 100,000,000 of subjects, the Church of Rome is regarded, and historically this is not a mistake, as merely an unorthodox and schismatic communion. Germany, the great intellectual and military power of the day, has just crumpled up the political bulwark of the Church of Rome, and is now confronting the machinations of that Church itself; which, by the way, had had no small share in the creation of the animosity that brought its political bulwark to rush upon destruction. Next comes England, the busiest, the wealthiest, and the most prolific of all people, whose empire is greater than that of Rome was of old; and to whom it has been given, as the mother of nations, to occupy the wide waste places of the earth. And then in the New World we have already nearly 50,000,000 of English-speaking people, and these every five and twenty years double their numbers. Russia, then, and Germany, and England, and the United States must all be put into the scale which weighs the opponents of Rome. And what is to be put into the scale in which Rome weighs her resources? Chiefly Italy, France, and Spain—the Latin race. And how do they stand affected to the Church of Rome? And what are they doing for her? They know her best. But the truth is that they know her too well to like her, to trust her, to believe in her, or to do anything for her.

All, of late years, they have done, that has any bearing on her interests, is against her. And how does she meet all this? By the pronunciamento of Infallibility. And what does that mean? It means, looking back, that all the mistakes, and all the crimes of the past are to be maintained; and just now it means the syllabus, and pilgrimages. We can, then, afford to be calm: but we must take care not to be struck by the flap of the tail of the distracted and dying monster.

It is hard, upon this subject, to find anything to say to those who are incapable of understanding that force of mind is rightfully, and, in the long run, practically the greatest force among men; that force of mind is compounded of moral and of intellectual elements; and that neither individuals, nor, and still less, nations who submit alike understanding and conscience to the dictation of Roman Infallibility, which has ever acted with a view to its own supposed interests, can be morally and intellectually strong. Russia, Germany, England, and the United States are not in subjection to this thraldom; and that is a reason, perhaps the chief reason, of their vigour. France is in the unhappy condition of either submitting to it, or of becoming irreligious. At present, therefore, it would almost seem that she can only be strong in proportion as she becomes irreligious. It is the Church of Rome that has brought her into this dilemma. Irreligion, though stronger than thraldom, is weaker than moral and intellectual power animated by religion.

But to go back to our pilgrimages : that to Paray-le-Monial, we have heard so much of lately, has some bearing on the pilgrimage to Einsiedln. There are multitudes of old familiar places of pilgrimage in Italy, France, and Spain. If pilgrimages are to be made, why not to one of them ? The virtue of pilgrimages to them has, in other times, been loudly proclaimed. Why then are they, now, to be set aside, and ignored ? And this in favour of a new place ? Simply, because the world, including the Romanist world, has advanced. If, therefore, in the face of a world that has advanced, and that discusses everything, pilgrimages are to be preached up, something that has the appearance of being more religious, more reasonable, more spiritual, more Christian than the old objects of pilgrimage must be presented in their stead. We can hardly picture to ourselves even the intrepid Archbishop of Westminster preaching up pilgrimages to the black-faced image of Einsiedln. The commonplace visions of the feazy imagination of the nun of Paray-le-Monial, to some extent, met the difficulty. Here was something that might, in a sense, be preached in Paris and in London. True those visions could not bear examination; but few people are disposed, or, should they be, are able to examine such matters thoroughly. And true, also, that what was selected from those visions, to be presented to the Romanist world as the new object of pilgrimages, involves many assumptions: for instance, it assumes that a conception, which is purely spiritual, has a physical, earthly, material form and substance; and then, furthermore, that the heart is the seat and organ of the affections, and that the brain is not. This may, or it may not, be both good physiology, and good psychology: but, as yet, it requires proof. In the meantime it may be suggested that the heart has evidently another duty to perform, which in itself would go some way towards disproving the supposition which supplied the form of the poor nun's hallucinations. And with respect to the lower animals, there is nothing to lead us to believe that the heart is the seat and organ of what affections they possess. The assumption, however, of these points would, for the present, be less damaging than that of those involved in the old objects of pilgrimage.

But in forming our opinions on matters of this kind, we must consider not only our own position, and must regard the points in debate not only from our own point of view, but must also endeavour to understand the position, and the point of view, of the Romanist. Pilgrimages must now be preached up, because the Church of Rome supposes that it wants Crusades. It would be impossible to preach up pilgrimages to the black-faced image of Einsiedln. The object now presented to the devout must be something that admits of open advocacy in the face of the world. Everything must be done now, more or less, in the light of day. The visions of the poor nun of Paray-le-Monial supplied, passably, what was required. It would, too, be in these times very desirable that some new object of this kind should be made, if possible, to supersede the old objects: their day was gone by.

We must also, in endeavouring to understand the policy of the Church of Rome, look at things from the point of view of an Infallible Church. Its Infallibility obliges it to accept, and maintain for ever, everything it ever at any time accepted, or maintained. It cannot disclaim the practice, or the principle, of the Inquisition; nor can it acknowledge that the black-faced image was a mistake. It has bound itself, irrevocably, to the maintenance of everything it ever taught or did. Its assumption of Infallibility obliges it to hold that everything it has taught, and is teaching, rests upon precisely the same ground and authority; that all must stand, or that all must fall, together; and that all must stand, or that all must fall, together with its system: the black-faced image, and the plenary remission, of Einsiedln, belief in the being of God, and in the infallibility of the Pope of Rome, truth of every kind, and the practice of every virtue. Arrogance, disregard for, and distrust of truth, worldliness, unbelief, cowardice can go no further. In this statement they all together culminate in one climax.

Morality and religion, however, do not depend for their being on the Church of Rome. They existed before it, and will exist after it, and notwithstanding it. Even its immorality and irreligion will not, we may be sure, permanently be able to injure morality and religion, even in the Romanist world. France, Italy, and Spain will recover. Morality and religion are eternal; for morality, as we now know by an induction from all kindreds of men, through all ages, in every form and stage of barbarism, and in every form and stage of civilization, is the order of the family, and of society: the very word itself indicates this. And religion is morality, practised not merely with reference to the requirements of the family, and of society, but also with reference to what in these, and in all other, domains of morality is required of us by our conceptions of God, and of a future life. The effect of these conceptions on morality is that they enlarge, elevate, and purify it; and give additional motives for its practice. Morality is eternal, because it is inherent in, and inseparable from domestic, social, political, and individual life. And religion, the principle of the spiritual life, which, of course, is still human life in this world, is the same morality, only regulated, so far as present circumstances admit, by a reference to the unseen world. All this has been obscured; and morality and religion have been corrupted and perverted, by the aims and claims, the policy and the developments, of the Church of Rome. Knock away those aims and claims, that policy and those developments, and then the Romanist world will have a chance of seeing morality and religion in their true forms; and will also see—which the teaching of the Church of Rome has done, and is doing, a great deal to prevent it from seeing—that they are the salt, and the light of life; which have been, for they inhere in the nature of human things, from everlasting, and, for the same reason, must continue to everlasting.

Once more: morality is the right ordering of the life of the individual, and of the family, and of society, and of the state; internally, with a view to his, or its own well-being; and externally, with a view to the well-being of all the rest. And it is not looking too far afield to add what even the old heathen world saw, that it is the right ordering of each with a view to the well-being of mankind, generally; this makes its empire universal, for it advances its dominion to the utmost limits of international law. All its forms are both relative, and related. It is the same ideas and principles applied to different natural units from the individual up to mankind. Religion is the ordering of these forms of morality, when weighed in the balance of the sanctuary. Our quarrel with Rome is that it weighs them all in the balance of ecclesiastical domination. It shapes them all in accordance with the requirements of this low, narrow, class interest; and in every Catholic country these have, hitherto, been found inconsistent with the requirements of the state, and of the home, and of the individual. The perversion of that which is best is, proverbially, the worst thing of all; and the perversions of the Church of Rome have ever been a demonstration of the truth of the proverb. From these perversions, for it is built up with them, and they are of its essence, it can never, except accidentally, deviate. If it were to begin to act upon the principle of the truth, the whole truth, and nothing but the truth, and this for all, it would cease to be the Church of Rome. It lowers to the level of its own worldly interests, for everything must be subordinated to them, the life of the individual, of the family, of society, and of the state; in three words, truth, virtue, and religion : that is to say, all that is best among men, all their dearest interests, all that makes life desirable, and even tolerable. This is the interpretation of every manifesto issued from Rome. We honour the devotion to their Church of the poor peasants of the Valais, and of all others who honestly, and in simplicity of mind, believe in it; be they individuals, or be they nations. But, in respect of that which is best, and highest, and truest, there is, a wide difference—wide as the poles apart—between what it ought to be, to which these good people know their fealty to be due, and that which is only, its corruption and perversion : again, the cause of its corruption and perversion being that those, who lord it over the Church of Rome have, somehow or other, been brought to seek first not that which is truest, and highest, and best, but ecclesiastical domination, and to that to subordinate everything. And hence it is that it has come about, that when men ask for bread the lords of that Church can offer only something very like a stone; when for light, only something very like darkness; when for the highest life, only a low form of life; when for truth, only the infallibility of Mastai Ferretti.

Few things can be more laughable than the threats of social and political cataclysms, the charges of falsehood, unbelief, and other theological abuse, the misrepresentations of facts, of motives, and of history, which are ever on the tongue of the head of the Romanist Church, to be echoed by his subordinate array of Archbishops and Bishops, and their mediæval-minded proselytes, always accompanied, in the name of peace and religion, with earnest deprecations of every kind of controversy, and even of so much as a word in reply: for if a man smite you on the right cheek, ought you not to turn to him the other also? Or if he take away your coat, ought you not to let him have your cloak also? At all events, one profession, and that a legitimate one, would find its occupation gone, and another, but this an illegitimate one, would find its occupation far smoother and more profitable than would be for the general good, were society to allow any such method of proceeding in the management of its worldly affairs, and in the protection of its worldly goods : though, of course, it may be quite different with respect to the higher matters of truth, morality, and religion. The proposal amounts simply to this : 'Just allow us to make whatever accusations, and whatever claims, may suit our purpose. However false and injurious the accusations, and however groundless and injurious the claims, pray do not say a word in reply. Only be silent, and allow judgment to go against you by default. Nothing can be easier and more reasonable. All will then be well. Should you act otherwise, the whole blame, it is clear, will rest with you.'

CHAPTER X.

THE LAKE OF ZURICH—RAPPERSWYL—GLARUS—THE LINTHTHAL—THE PANTENBRÜCKE.

> Sharp-pressing Need, that spurs
> The poor man's wits, and Work that robs from sleep
> And pleasure their due hours, outbraves and beats
> Hard Nature's oppositions.—*Adapted from* VIRGIL.

August 18.—At midday left the mediævalism of Einsiedln to take the rail at Rapperswyl for manufacturing Glarus. Were hardly out of the town when we came upon railway cuttings and viaducts in construction. The iron horse, then, will soon be panting and snorting in, and hurrying into and out of, this great and famous resort of peasant pilgrims. It is not long before you are looking down on the lake of Zurich, and its pleasant, well-peopled shores. At Einsiedln all was damp grass, generally poor enough, with very little wood, and very little variety of outline, and no variety of culture—a dreary, monotonous, saddening scene. But now everything is changed completely. Before us are land and water, mountains and plains, variety of outline, variety of culture, variety of objects, variety of life. You are among orchards and meadows, cornfields and vineyards. You look down over them to the blue lake. Beyond the lake, on its further side, reaching far right and left, is a broad expanse of undulating ground. In this expanse, every here and there, a house is showing, very white and cheery, among the dark green trees and the light green grass—the houses of well-to-do people. You think they have been built, most of them, by professional men, or owners of factories, or shops, in Zurich, Rapperswyl, or some neighbouring town. They are rewards of patient industry, and of well-directed intelligence. All nature is basking in, and absorbing, and being quickened by, the warm sunshine. Grass is growing, grapes are colouring, fruit is ripening, corn maturing. Your mind is stirred. It is full of pictures, and each picture is full of pleasant meanings. But all the meanings of all the pictures, in their simplest expressions, come to this, that, in the charming scene you have before you, there are many indications of much earthly happiness, issuing from the exercise of the earthly virtues of industry, honesty, and frugality; and from the practice of allowing to others what you would wish should be allowed to yourself.

And so you reach the margin of the lake opposite Rapperswyl. Here is a long spit of land projecting into the lake. You drive to the extremity of this, and cross to Rapperswyl by a wooden bridge, three quarters of a mile in length. I do not know whether there is width enough for two carriages to cross each other, but I thought that there was not. It has no side rails to prevent your fancying that you may fall into the water. The planks of the roadway are not fastened; but as they are thick, and set close together, they cannot dance out of their places.

At Rapperswyl took the rail. One does not wish to be much on the rail in Switzerland; and there is not much of it, as yet, in the parts that are worth going to see. But an occasional change in one's mode of locomotion is pleasant; and so is it at times to do a day's work in an hour. Pleasant, too, is it, or you fancy it so, as you sit at ease, to have the mountains passing before you in a moving panorama. To be sure, you cannot act upon the inspiration of the moment, which you hold to be one of the merits of walking; but, then, you make answer to yourself that this does not matter, where one is not particularly desirous of making leisurely inspections. This, however, was not precisely the case to-day, for at Wesen, where from the railway carriage you command a view down the lake of Wallenstadt, and see that the mountains enclosing it are very precipitous, and have a curiously brindled appearance from the colour of their strata, and the fashion in which they are streaked with dark woods; and when you hear of interesting communities with large flocks and herds on their summits; you do wish to stop for a little leisurely inspection. And this wish is real, for it gives rise to a sensation in your feet as if they wanted to be climbing, just as your flesh creeps when your mind is scared in looking over a precipice. But you have in your pocket a ticket for Glarus, and your plans were settled to be there this evening; and so you do not stop for the Wallensee, but go on to Glarus. If there was any loss in this, the moral is not that the railway was bad, but that minute plans, and unchangeable plans, are bad; as must be everything, whether in travelling or in anything else, which curtails advantages, and deprives one of a pleasure.

As soon as your back is turned on the Wallensee, and your face set southward for Glarus, you find that the railway is running in a narrow valley, parallel to and below the embankment of the Linth. Unmistakable factories now begin to appear on the scene: large rectangular buildings, of many storeys; all white, for they are built of undressed stone, which is then plastered smooth, and whitewashed; which whitewash there is no smoke here to tarnish, although you will occasionally see the familiar tall chimney-stalk; for some of these Glarus factories use steam as an auxiliary power. These chimney-stalks, with no accessible coal nearer than the mines of Belgium and of the west bank of the Rhine, invite you to think of the moral causes of national and of individual prosperity. The factories become more numerous. The valley narrows. The mountains increase in steepness and in height. The line terminates in a mountain *cul de sac*; and here is the busy thriving little town of Glarus, the nucleus of a hive of human industry.

From the station to the Glärner Hof is but a few steps. There are in this manufacturing canton some peculiarities in the administration of the Almends, brought about in the Commune of Glarus by the necessity it was under of raising funds for rebuilding the town, after the great fire, which destroyed it in the year 1861; and still more, both here and elsewhere in the canton, from the large increase of the operative population: and it was for the purpose of enquiring into these peculiarities that I had come to Glarus. I had not far to go for the commencement of the enquiry. In the centre of the town is a large open space of ground, of a rudely triangular shape: it is an acute-angled triangle, with a base of 150 yards, or so. This is on the side of the road opposite to the Glärner Hof. The apex of the triangle is about 300 yards, or more, off. This is one of the Almends of Glarus. Ammer paced for me some of the allotments. These, we found, contained, each, as many klafters as would give to each allottee about the tenth of an acre. Hardly any space is lost for paths, which are reduced to a minimum both of fewness and of width. But a practised eye makes out at a glance the extent of each allotment; and infers from its condition, and the way in which it is cropped, something of the character of its occupant. Some were tidy; some were untidy. The latter preponderated. This proportion would have been reversed, if the allotments, instead of being temporarily occupied, had been the private property of their cultivators. Some of the occupiers were rigidly practical. This might, in some cases, mean that they were indisposed to give themselves the trouble of a little thought and arrangement. These devoted their whole space to potatoes. Others, who regarded the *pot au feu* with more of science—though, however, science is the ground of the highest form of practice—or, at all events, with more regard for gastronomy—but gastronomy is a science—assigned little spaces to several kinds of herbs and vegetables; onions, cabbages, haricots, beet, turnips, &c. The general look of the thing was not quite the same as in our labourers' allotments. They run very much on wheat. There was no wheat here. What was most obtruded on the eye, from its height, were the patches of sticked haricots. These our people, not from a difference of climate, but from an ignorance of cookery, know nothing about. Generally there was a far greater variety of cultivation on the land than with us. This indicated a more *savant* cultivation of the stomach, or, at least, of the palate.

This Almend, in the middle of the town, is interesting, not so much for the sake of such observations as I have just been making, as from its being possible to regard it as an element in the lives of operatives, who are successfully competing, under some disadvantages, with the operatives of Mulhouse, Lille, Manchester, and Lowel. I will not say that, in these days of railways, and of education, which we may hope is becoming general, nothing of the kind is possible in the case of the operatives of Manchester; but will here content myself with the remark, that its effect must be good on these Glarus operatives. They work eleven hours a-day, including one for meals; therefore this garden work is not carried on at the expense of their factory work. They are burgers of the commune, and settle for themselves their hours of work, in their yearly assemblies. As, then, the garden work is carried on, with no detriment to the factory work, we may, without having any *per contra* deductions to make, attempt to estimate its advantages. It is a healthy, pleasing, natural, and profitable employment of their spare time. It is a save-all of their odds and ends of time, in which their wives and children can take a part. It is a mental, as well as a bodily, diversion from the uninteresting and monotonous work of the factory. It varies in-door with out-door work, and so lightens it. It prevents their being cut off from the teachings of Nature. Nature teaches those who solicit her bounty in many ways. They discover on what conditions she rewards those who solicit that bounty with knowledge and importunity. They are brought to conform their practice and their feelings to those conditions; to take into consideration the chances that attend their best directed efforts; and to bear the little disappointments, as well as to rejoice over the little successes, incidental to the cultivation of the soil. It is a corrective, to some extent, of some of the bad teaching, and bad effects, incidental to life in a factory.

The occupation of these tenths of an acre is rent-free, because the land is the common property of the burgers of Glarus, that is to say of the operatives themselves; and this is the way in which they decide on using it. But the produce of this small amount of land cannot be so considerable as to enable them to live on wages lower than would be possible without it. We must not, therefore, look to it as in any degree, directly, affecting wages, and so the price of the muslins of Glarus. Besides, the wages of these garden-cultivating operatives of Glarus are the same as the wages of their fellow-operatives, who, not being descendants of old burgers, but immigrants, or descendants of immigrants, have, of course, no share whatever in the Almends, or common lands. The wages of factory hands range for men from two-and-a-half to five francs a day, and for women from one franc. This, of course, is less than with us. And as to their other advantage, the water power, here chiefly used, it is not so cheap as it might appear, for it has, to some extent, to be supplemented with steam-power, the coal for which is brought from a great distance. While on the other side is to be set the expense of bringing the raw cotton from Havre, Antwerp, or Bremen, and of transporting again, by land carriage, down to the coast, the manufactured goods destined for beyond-sea markets in the Levant, and elsewhere. The care I saw the hands bestowing upon what they were engaged on, led me to think that the success of the Glarus manufacturers might in part be attributed to the economical value of moral causes. If so, it might be profitable to enquire how far these moral causes result from these operatives being burgers, and descended from an immemorial line of burgers, that is to say from their having been brought up under the influence of the strongest of all self-acting inducements to self-respect ; and also, though in a minor degree, from the habits of thought, as well as of life, the cultivation of their little bits of land engenders.

It was a bright quiet afternoon, as we walked about the town, taking note of how clean and well-constructed it was ; and what numbers of houses of well-to-do people, what a goodly town hall, what a fine school, built for 700 scholars, what well-furnished shops it had, for a population of 5,000. All this had been done by the public spirit, intelligence, and industry of the little community. Had it remained the capital of a canton, which, in such a situation, was only agricultural and pastoral, it would have been no more than an untidy and insignificant village. The intelligence of its manufacturers, who have had to turn very slender advantages to what account they could, and who have had to overcome many disadvantages, and who are entertaining relations with so many distant parts of the world, must, of course, in a still greater degree be in advance of what would be the mental condition of the place, if agriculture had remained its only employment. It is manufactures that have rebuilt with stone, in a substantial, even imposing, and well-ordered form, the Glarus of wood that was destroyed by the fire of 1861. This improvement of its exterior indicates, for it is the result of it, a corresponding improvement of the inner Glarus of to-day—of the modern manufacturing and commercial city—to that of the old agricultural and pastoral Glarus.

While we were walking over the town, and noting these matters, the atmosphere was in that condition in which a cloud-banner is formed at the summit of lofty mountains. It appears to be set up upon, and to be flying over, their topmost peaks. Both the Glarnish and the Schilt, which look down on this little hive of industry, had, on this afternoon, their cloud-banners flying in the otherwise clear atmosphere. All was quiet when, towards evening, we returned to our hotel; and so it was when we retired to bed. But, soon after midnight, we were roused from sleep by a violent banging of the outer window-shutters, which we heard going on not only in the hotel, but also in the neighbouring houses, and by the sound from the street of hurrying feet, and by the shouting, I suppose, of the night-watchmen. The Föhn, a violent wind, engendered by local causes, that at times sweeps through the valley of the Linth, was rushing by. The laws of Glarus enact, that, when it blows, every fire in the place, for whatever purpose used, is to be extinguished. I rose, and made fast the outer jealousy shutters of the room I was occupying. In the morning all was quiet again. The wind, however, had been succeeded by, or had brought with it, and left behind it, heavy rain, which continued all that day, and till the morning of the following day, for about thirty-six hours.

I mention these matters, because the reader of the narrative of the daily work of an excursion in Switzerland will not be able to feel, at all, as one of the travelling party, or to form any useful conception of what he must expect, when, *in propriâ personâ*, he sets out on such an excursion, if, throughout the narrative, the weather does not form one thread of the yarn. It always has to be consulted, and conformed to. It is the weather that makes the doing of what you have to do pleasant, and even possible ; or, else, unpleasant, and even impossible.

August 19.—As it was a persistently wet day, there was nothing we could do outside of the hotel, except visiting some of the factories I have already referred to. It happened to be a Glarus festival, and so those in the town proper were closed. We had, therefore, to go for what we wanted to see to Ennenda, a manufacturing suburb of Glarus, though quite a distinct commune, on the other side of the Linth. Within the hotel there were people enough to talk to, and plenty of English papers to put one abreast of what was going on at home. At Glarus, on the east of Switzerland, you have the previous day's 'Times' at 4 P.M. It is despatched from London by the morning train; reaches Paris in time to be forwarded to Bâle, or Neuchâtel, that night; and the next day is brought on to Glarus. During the three days we were here, I was surprised each afternoon at having in this way the London papers of the day before. Here, in the centre of Europe, I was only one day, and *in extenso*, behind London. This recalled the sensation of carrying the world about with me, which, some years ago, I had become familiar with at New Orleans. There, every morning, I used to find on my breakfast-table, by the side of the hot rolls, telegraphic intelligence, from all parts of Europe, for the previous day. It seemed to take no more time to collect this intelligence from all parts of Europe, to send it, beneath the Atlantic, to New York, and to forward it to New Orleans, and to set it up in type, than to make the rolls. We look upon the rolls without an emotion of surprise, and upon the telegraphic intelligence as a marvel. But the day was, before the invention of wheat, when the roll would have appeared as unintelligible, or, at all events, as impossible, as the telegraphic intelligence. The telegraphic intelligence will some day stand in the same relation to something not yet dreamt of, in which it is now, itself, standing to the roll.

August 20.—Having a letter to the President of Glarus—I take President to be new style, and that, formerly, the title of the chief magistrate of Glarus was Landamman—I had called at his door yesterday, and found that he was out of town, but would return at night, and be visible early to-day. At 8.30, therefore, this morning I again presented myself at his door ; and was admitted. I knew that at this time a Swiss man of business—everyone here is, of course, a man of business—would not be found still loitering over his breakfast. An English barrister, whose acquaintance I had been so fortunate as to make at the Glärner Hof, and who was familiar with German, had been so good as to offer to accompany me. As the chief object of my visit was to hear, from another Swiss authority, another account of what is meant in these cantons by the word Corporation, I was glad of the assistance of one whose legal training and acumen would keep the enquiry from becoming unprofitably discursive; and who would be quick in detecting inconsistencies and insufficiencies in the replies that might be given to my questions. We found the President engaged with his clerk, or secretary. He, however, immediately dismissed him with his budget of papers, and with the utmost goodnature assured us that he was at our disposal.

By the way, the President's house was perhaps the best in the town. He must, therefore, be one of the wealthiest citizens of Glarus. I found, throughout this tour, that those officials to whom by name my letters introduced me, were, without a single exception, in this position. I mention this because it shows that, in the most democratic country in Europe, wealth carries with it none of the exclusion from office with which we sometimes hear it credited. On the contrary, it appears that long experience in these matters, unwarped by the heat and passions engendered by vice and destitution, has in Switzerland—at all events in these primitive cantons, it may be otherwise in the large cities, though I am not aware that it is—taught the dispensers of power, that is to say the whole community, that self-respect, and the knowledge and the leisure requisite for attention to the affairs of the public, are more likely to be combined in a man who is pretty well off, than in one who ought to be devoting the chief part, if not the whole, of his time to supplying the daily wants of his family.

But to return to the President. No sooner had I told him what was my general, and at that moment, my particular object, than he informed me that I was engaged in an enquiry in which it would be very difficult to reach any conclusion, except that the subject was inexplicable; for the reason that, though the word was the same, the thing it stood for differed in some respects in every commune. Every commune—as we should express it, every parish—having the right to modify these matters in accordance with its own circumstances and ideas, had availed itself of this right; and that hence the divergencies were endless. I told him some of the different definitions of a corporation I had received in Uri and Unterwalden. None of these, he said, would do at Glarus. After half-an-hour's conversation we took our leave, with no distinct impression on our minds, except that the President was very good-natured and clear-headed, and that what he had at first told us was quite right—that the subject was inexplicable. Confusion had become worse confounded.

The conclusion I had been wishing to come to, on account of its simplicity and intelligibility, was that a corporation has no direct political object whatever; that it is a body either of old burgers, or of Beisassen, (originally the Metoeci of the old Greek republics,) endowed with perpetuity, and holding landed property often for some definite object; and that it is distinct from the commune, inasmuch as that is the political entity, which embraces all the old burgers for economical purposes, that is for the administration, and enjoyment of the usufruct, of the communal landed property; and which now embraces both the old and the new burgers for legislative and administrative purposes; with, of course, a great variety of local exceptions and limitations in the different cantons, and in their several communes. This, however, he told us would not be correct for Glarus; but he quite failed in his attempt to show why it would not be correct, or what would be correct.

On the afternoon of this day, as we happened, on our way through Linththal to pass the house of Dr. Bekker, the minister at Linththal of the Reformed Church, who is widely known for his publications on the Swiss Almends, we stopped at his door, and sent in to him the commendatory letter I had received at Berne from M. Cérésole, the President of the Swiss Confederation. The doctor was so good as to admit us, and allow us to confer with him for half-an-hour upon the subject to which he has devoted so much attention. With respect to the Corporation question, I found that he was disposed to accept my conclusions, in the main; at all events, as far as the Commune of Linththal was concerned. I might, he said, take a corporation to mean a section of the burgers, possessed of landed property, held for a definite object. For instance, they had at Linththal a corporation for educational purposes possessed of four alpes, and another for the encouragement of singing. In these there is nothing political in a legislative or administrative sense. The object, in these cases, is intellectual, social, philanthropic, &c.; and it is proposed to effect the object in view by economic means, that is to say, by property held, and used, for the purpose of furthering the object. It may, in these secluded valleys, be in many ways a desirable thing to cultivate singing and to maintain a body of singers. If so, then, a good object is secured by this singing *Verein*, or corporation ; and it is done, in this fashion, at little or no cost ; for the land does not maintain one mouth or one cow the less, because those who have the usufruct of it are obliged to further this object. The only real cost to the individual, and, through the individual, to the community, is the time the members of this corporation give to the object. I found at Stanz that an Orphan Asylum had lately been endowed, in a similar fashion, with land. The objection I, at the moment, suggested to my informant was, that this was throwing on the existing generation, which provided the endowment, the cost of maintaining the orphans of succeeding generations ; and that it would be better that each generation should do its own work. Of course this remark did not dispose of the question of the policy of this particular endowment, and still less of that of endowments generally. It may be wise, where the community is not rich, to place the maintenance of destitute orphans beyond the reach of chance. So of the Linththal singing *Verein*. And as to endowments generally, they may be useful for a particular purpose at a particular time. Our endowments for grammar schools may have done good service three or four centuries ago. But it does not, therefore, follow that they are doing good service now. They may, at this day, contribute to the maintenance of institutions, ideas, and systems unsuitable to the wants of the day. They may hinder people from seeing what is wanted now, and from exerting themselves to provide it. It may be so, at this moment, with respect to our public schools, and even with respect to our universities. The public mind may have been dazzled and misled by a knowledge of what they did well, and usefully, in times when what they taught was the right thing to teach. It may, furthermore, be possible to show that, in such cases as our own public schools and universities, the endowments which originally were intended to act, and did act, in the direction of lessening the cost of education, now act in the direction of increasing its cost; and that they are not so much an aid as a hindrance to them in securing the services of the best men. But be all this as it may, I was glad to find the doctor encouraging me in my supposition, that in these cantons the idea of a corporation must be kept quite distinct from that of a municipality, or of any directly political organization.

This 'interview' of the doctor took place in the afternoon. It had become possible, because at 10 A.M. the rain, that had been falling uninterruptedly for two nights and a day, had shown some disposition to come to an end; and we had then determined to start at once for the chance of being able to see the upper valley of the Linth. What we proposed was to go in a two-horse *char* as far as it could take us, and then to ascend to the Pantenbrücke on foot, returning to Glarus in the evening. Our argument was the old and sound one of nothing venture, nothing get. There was still a little rain. This might continue all day; it might even increase. But, then, on the other hand, it might be dying away; and, if so, then we should have time for what we wished to do. Whereas, if we delayed another hour, to see how the weather was going, we should not have time. Another chance in our favour was that the rain might have become, now that it was feeble, only local, being possibly maintained merely by the lofty mountains that stand round the bowl in the bottom of which Glarus is situated. Our venture turned out favourably. We had not got much more than a mile on our way, when the rain ceased, and gave us a pleasant day. You have seventeen miles of carriage-road up the valley. As you ascend the factories gradually thin-out; and by the time you have got to Linththal there is an end to them altogether. You pass Stachelberg, a place now much frequented for ts mineral waters, and for the numerous excursions, on high ground, that may be made from it. We dined at the Tödi Hotel, a small house at the foot of the ascent to the Pantenbrücke. The way up to the Pantenbrücke is by a good path through pine woods. These abound with, among other ferns, the

Aspleniumviride. The bridge is of one arch over the Linth, here an Alpine torrent, that chafes, and dashes, and forces its way, hoarse and tormented, along the perpendicular-sided channel it has cut for itself, to the depth of nearly 150 feet below the bridge. Having crossed this bridge we went on, still ascending, about three-quarters of a mile further, to the Ueli Alp. It was a strange wild scene—high above the valley we had come from—before us, right and left, only stupendous, sullen, mountain crags, with a glacier in front. About these mountain-high craggy scars, and out of the dark, ruthless chasms between them, were surging up thick masses of cloud; as it were a vast world-storm-factory, where ministers of wrath, themselves unseen, were forging smoking thunderbolts, and uplifting mighty deluges, to affright, and, if need be, to shatter and to sweep away, heedless cities on distant plains.

On our way back to Glarus we stopped at Stachelberg, and again at Diesbach, to look, over the head of the valley, at the summit of the mighty Tödi, the western side of which was in the light of the declining sun. The head of the giant, crowned with unbroken snow, was lifted above the clouds we had seen a few hours before at the Ueli Alp. From that near point of view, they had shown themselves as broken masses in seething, rolling motion. Now looked at from a low and distant point of view, they had become a solid unmoving stratum, pierced only by the head of the

Tödi. At Diesbach we had also a good near view—they were just above us—of the glaciers of the great Glärnish : dark glaciers between darker peaks. Beneath the dark glaciers and darker peaks, Nature's embodiment of hardness, cold, and eternal barrenness, came a green alpe, then a beech wood, then prairies with hay granges, then prairies with fruit-trees and *châlets* down to the road. Below the road potato-patches, and moister prairies along the river side, and here and there a large factory. The glaciers above were supplying the moving power for the factories below; and thus enabling the owners of those factories to supply the wants of people in Italy and the Levant; who thus, again, through an absence of the intelligence and industry, which might have enabled them to turn their own advantages to account, were supporting no small part of the population of this busy Alpine valley.

We should, indeed, have been hard to please had we not been pleased with Glarus—its strange out-of-the-world situation ; its well-deserved prosperity ; its large school ; the little bit of land for each operative, and their self-respecting air. The intelligence, too, and politeness of the proprietor of the Glärner Hof, and of his manager; and the ready and obliging attention of the President to one whom he had never seen before, and would never see again, told for much on the good side. And there was nothing, but the rain, to set down on the other side against all this.

And here it would be discreditable to omit that we had also much reason to be pleased with the man who drove us this day, for thirty-four miles, to the head of the valley and back again, and who to-morrow morning will drive us to Vorauen. He was a tall, well-built, clean-limbed, active man, about forty years of age, smooth-shaved, and tidy in his dress, ready in talk, easy and even in manner, without a suspicion either of self-assertion or of servility, and without any *arrière-pensée* about francs, for his horses and services were to be charged for, according to tariff, in the hotel bill—*tout compris*. He had the genuine Swiss kindliness of manner towards children, and took the little man on the box with him, and putting the reins into his hands, gave him some lessons in driving. He pointed out everything worthy of notice we came in sight of during the day, and in the drive to Vorauen. He showed no impatience at our stopping for half an hour at Dr. Beckker's door, though it was getting late, and he had been out all day. But, then, we must remember that he was a burger of Glarus, as his fathers, before him, ever had been. He had an equal voice with his neighbours in the appointment of the magistrates, and in the management of the affairs of the little community, that maintains a kind of high school, a college it is called in Switzerland, for 700 children, and that assigns a bit of land to each of its humbler members—a community, in which a man is respected because he is a man ; and in which a man thus learns to respect himself.

CHAPTER XI.

THE KLÖNTHAL—VORAUEN—RICHISAU—THE PRAGEL—
MUOTTA—BRUNNEN—THE RIGI KULM.

> Ever charming, ever new,
> When will the landscape tire the view !
> The mountains' fall, the rivers' flow ;
> The wooded valleys, warm and low ;
> The windy summits wild and high,
> Roughly rushing on the sky ;
> Town and village ; tower and farm ;
> Each give to each a double charm.—DYER.

August 21.—From Glarus by the Pragel Pass to Brunnen is thirty-eight miles. As we intended to sleep at Brunnen, we took a *char* for the first nine miles to Vorauen, where the carriage road ends. We were under weigh at 6 A.M. You are now in the Klönthal; so good a valley that it would be better for those to whom walking is not a pain to do it on foot. You enter it as you leave Glarus. The Glärnish is on your left ; on your right steep-sided mountains—ill-clad, but the better for that. On leaving Glarus you do not immediately lose sight of factories. The last of them are at Riedern. Of course you are invited to leave the road, to see, at a few yards' distance, that the torrent of the Klönthal, like other

Swiss torrents, has not forgotten to cut, for the astonishment of tourists, deep into the rock a rugged channel, at the bottom of which, with much dashing and hurrying, it is still continuing its excavations. This, at one point or other of their brief run, all Swiss torrents regard as an imperative duty. In somewhat more than an hour you reach the Klönsee; two miles, or so, in length, and narrow. The lofty, massive Glärnish rises, almost vertically, from its opposite side. The lake is sheltered; and this morning it reflected, as a mirror, the blue sky, and the Glärnish, with its precipices, woods, and snow streaks. You are told that there are still a few chamois on these lofty summits. You think it an illegitimate and cruel use of the rifle to exterminate so agile, graceful, and brave a creature, that only asks, as its portion of the world, for the inaccessible rocks and snowfields. When you reach the head of the lake, you find that what was, once, its upper part is now marsh, passing into meadow. You then come to the inn of Vorauen. Its site has been ill chosen. It seems as if it had dropped out of the clouds upon the open, level, treeless, dank grass. There is an unfinished, untidy, repellent aspect about it, both within and without. You are glad that you are not going to stop at it. Here you leave your carriage; and should you have had the driver we had, you will shake his hand, and say adieu, with a perceptible sense of regret that you are to see his face, his manly good-natured face, no more.

At Richisau, three miles from Vorauen, we engaged a horse for the little man to take him to the top of the Pass. Richisau is a very different kind of place from Vorauen. Instead of being on the damp, naked meadow, it is among woods and mountains. The difference is not unappreciated; for at Vorauen we did not find a soul : here were sixty visitors, many of whom we had passed, strolling about the woods we had just come through. Many more we saw seated, in the shade, under the large, ancient, detached sycamores that surround the inn. I call it an inn, because there were so many people using the little, shed-like structures, which were all that we saw. Had it not been for the visitors we should not have supposed that there was any inn at all. The landlord, however, is now building a large hotel—not quite a monster, still a goodly structure of stone. Any oversights, therefore, or misapprehensions of the kind we might have fallen into, will not, for the future, be possible. Almost all the visitors—all, as far as we saw—were Germans and Swiss ; chiefly the latter. The landlord and his wife are of the simple-minded, smiling, obliging sort; and so we will wish that their new house may be a success. For people intending to do the whole Pass, whether from Glarus, or from Schwyz, of course on foot, the best arrangement would be to go as far as Richisau by the afternoon of the first day. To stop at Vorauen would be in every respect a mistake. To stop at Richisau would, I believe, be in every respect a gain.

As the *Col* is only 5,000 feet above the sea, and as you have at Richisau a good part of the ascent behind you, you will find no stiff work between Richisau and the summit. There are no striking mountain ranges, or masses, in sight as you complete the ascent; nor when you have made the top. A little beyond the *Col* are two summer *châlets* for herdsmen, with a huddling brook in front of them. Here we called a halt for our mid-day cold meats and diluted medoc. For the use of a table brought out, and set for us by the side of the stream, the herdsmen were satisfied with what was left upon it, including a half-franc: it would have been better had it been a whole one. But as, in Switzerland, the price of brandy, except in hotels, is little more than the cost of manufacture, the materials from which it is made being only apples, potatoes, and such-like, which are abundant and cheap, in that half-franc was concentrated an amount of force capable of transmutation into a deep carouse.

We are on our legs again. While gaily making way, apace, down hill, the only effort necessary being that required to prevent our going too fast, we meet three youthful Germans, with, on their large bones, a deal of superfluous flesh, and other matter less solid and more superfluous, painfully toiling up. The two parties salute, as they pass, but with very different feelings. On the way to Muotta we found reason enough for their looking so solemn and dead-beaten. The ascent from that side is at times bad, over long bits of stone-paved pathway: the stones polished by the traffic of centuries to a marvellously smooth surface. One reach of this is through a wood of ancient pine, from the branches of which depend streamers of moss; and on the ground are an abundance of male and female ferns, among which are many fine specimens of *Blecnum spicant*, with the barren fronds spread out in a flat circle on the earth, and the fruitful ones standing erect from the centre of the circle. This indicates much moisture, which makes the polished surface of the pathway very treacherous. The worst bit is on the last descent towards Muotta. There you have a long, broken-up staircase of glass-smooth (and, if there has been any rain, lubricated) blocks of stone. From the summit to Muotta is not impressive as Alpine scenery. But variety is pleasant; and to be passing through these mountain pastures among herds of cows, and cowherds, with somewhat mountainous barriers left and right, over short, smooth turf, and beside clear, lively streams, on a sunny day, with fresh, breezy air, will satisfy many. For those whom it does not satisfy we can only have—well— but imperfect sympathy.

We reached the further end of the scattered village of Muotta, eighteen miles in six hours' walking, the halts deducted. Here at the little inn we made the acquaintance of a Parisian *homme de lettres*. He had come from Brunnen with his wife and another lady for the day. They had a very roomy carriage, and were so good as to offer to give us seats to Brunnen. 'Ammer, having come to a clandestine understanding with the driver, managed to double himself up on the empty baggage board behind. The Muotta is not outdone by the Klön in the ravine matter: so here, too, you must leave your carriage to see what it has to show in this way. It is at the point where the bridge of the old, and now disused, road crosses the river. Its distinguishing feature is that its almost invisible interstices everywhere support a thick growth of shrubs and small trees. They seem to grow out of the rock, and go near towards hiding the water below them. Part of the new road—I believe it is nearly a century old—is grooved out of the mountain-side, two or three hundred feet, in places, above the river. You then pass along the western foot of the Mythen, among innumerable orchards; and so, at last, you reach Brunnen, and the margin of the lake.

It was a lovely evening, with a glorious sunset. The world, in the direction of Stanz, was all ablaze with rapidly changing effects. On the esplanade, in front of the Grand Hotel of the Four Forest Cantons, people of many kindreds and nations had sent their representatives to witness the scene. As I sat on a bench, talking with my new French acquaintance, of course about the future of France and of Europe, he delivered himself, *more Gallico*, of the following epigram : 'You make as many revolutions as we do, but with a difference: yours are all bloodless, and for an object.'

The words magnificent and palatial are hardly inapplicable to this great hotel. And it is only one of a class, of which there are several other specimens around the lake. Another, the Axenstein, is close by, on a spur of the Axenberg, over the Axenstrasse. Another is in sight on the Seelisberg, on the opposite side of the lake. At the foot of the lake, at Lucerne, are others of the same kind. And everywhere, along the shores of its tortuous branches, are multitudes of smaller establishments. You recall this, and think that the hundreds of people, who have just left the esplanade of the Hotel of the Four Forest Cantons, at the summons of the supper-bell, are only a small detachment of the thousands of travellers who at that moment are assembled around that single lake. Perhaps you prefer a cigar to a supper ; at all events the preference may be allowed on so lovely an evening; and, therefore, you remain seated where you are, on the edge of the lake ; and watch the fading, and now white, light above the distant mountains, which have themselves become only black masses. Half-an-hour ago they were purple, and what is now white above them had then been purple-red, which had passed through ruddy orange to pale gold. You will be looking at the last fading traces of departed day:

perhaps, however, you will be thinking of the invading host of travellers, encamped around the lake.

Who are they? They are people, who, formerly, would not have travelled—who, indeed, under the old condition of things would not have existed; for it is new causes, the vast extension, and the rapid profits of trades, manufactures, commerce, and professions, which have called them into existence. This has brought them into the world: railways and steamboats only help them in moving about upon it. And these thousands around you, for the practice of travelling has with this class become general, are merely the contingent it has sent, this year, to this spot. They will all come in their turn. Travelling is a regular part of their education; as much so as what they learn at school, and in their respective callings.

These middle-class throngs have, of late years, taken the place of the few territorial magnates, who, formerly, went what was called then, and was so under the circumstances of those times, the grand tour. They have not ceased to go the grand tour; but they are lost to sight now in these middle-class multitudes. In the days of the grand tour the few, who were on their travels, were somewhat conspicuous, like the large trees in their open parks, standing, detached, here and there; but now a forest has grown up all around these large, detached trees; and they cannot anywhere be seen for the forest.

And you go on to think that it is not merely on

the road, and in the grand hotels, which have been built for them, that this great middle class has made the territorial magnates almost invisible, but that it has also, to a very considerable extent, begun to take their place in Parliament, and as the governing class. Parliament now, and every Government, are largely composed of its members. You are reminded that an old order of things is passing away, and a new coming in its place. These travellers are an indication not only of the existence, but of the numbers and wealth, the power and activity, of the most prominent element in that new order. To it they belong, and here they are to you its representatives. These grand hotels are a gauge of its numbers and wealth.

But the trail of thought does not stop at this point. A mighty element in the new order of things is not at all represented here—that element of modern societies which was so seen and felt in the Paris Commune, that all Europe is now occupied in debating how it is to be dealt with, or rather what place it will achieve for itself in the immediate future. It is the class of the working hands of the vastly-developed trade, manufactures, and commerce of the day. They have remained working hands, because, as things have hitherto been in the world, there has been no way to emerge from that class but that of saving ; and saving requires a combination of favourable circumstances and of suitable qualities, first among the latter of which comes that of a genius for saving. It was the turning to account of this combination, which existed in their own case, or in that of their fathers, that enabled far the larger part of the absolutely many, but, relatively to the number of the working hands, comparatively few, whom we have just been thinking about, to emerge from the working mass; and to become capitalists, that is to say members of the middle class : for capital is the product of saving—of saving only, and of nothing else. And capital, either invested or employed, is the support of the great middle class, and of the various professions, dependent mainly on it, whether they be recruited from above, or from below: capital is its support, just as the rent of land is that of the upper class, and wages that of the lower or working class.

The trail of thought, then, passes on to the unemerged—the vast army of working hands. And the question is asked, What is, and what will be, their relation to the class so largely represented here, before us, by the many more or less wealthy travellers, for whom these grand hotels have been built? One thing is certain : the working hands can no longer be kept down by the middle, capital-supported class, any more than the middle class itself could have been kept down by the upper land-supported class—the territorial magnates. Force was sufficient for such purposes under the old, rude, simple, bygone order of things. Now it is but a broken reed to lean upon ; and will only pierce the hand that would lean upon it. It is the masses, indeed, who now possess the strength of numbers, together with growing intelligence, and means for communicating and combining. You wish to look into the future. It is, to some extent, a clue to its unevolved possibilities, that, under the conditions now establishing themselves, force, in the old significance of the word, will not be the principle, the bond, the dependence, the cement of society. What, then, will be? Nothing can be suggested, but knowledge, intelligence, justice. If they cannot exorcise the evil spirits that may torment modern societies, there is nothing else to turn to. Should, then, an honest attempt be made to spread knowledge, to cultivate intelligence, and to be just to all, we are not without hope. In all changes that come in the natural order of things, what is needed is indicated, and more or less brought about, by the very course of events. Happily, amongst ourselves, the course of events and legislation are working together in the desired direction. All cannot emerge, but all may be raised to a common level. This is what is now being brought about. The artisan now reads the same newspapers, eats the same bread, travels by the same train, interchanges thought by the post on the same terms, and is endowed with the same amount of political power, as the class that was formerly the most favoured. And, now, education, which, because it is the most elevating, is, therefore, the most equalizing, of all agencies, is being provided for his children. We will, therefore, trust that what the travelling middle class see in the many lands they visit, and their meditations on what they see, will bring home to them as a clear conviction, and as of the sort that ought to be acted on, as well as acknowledged, that it will be their wisdom to accept frankly these inevitable changes. And this may be the best way of bringing the working hands on their side to understand, and practically to recognize, the duties of their new position.

August 22.—Our plan had been to climb Pilatus, and having slept at the hotel on the summit, to go down in the morning to Alpnach. The vote, however, which issued in this decision, had been taken in the absence of *le petit caporal.* We now found that the whole question must be reconsidered. On this having been done, the original vote was reversed, unconstitutionally, by the minority. The new decision was, that we must take the railway to the top of the Rigi. This idea had not, in the first consideration of the subject, been lost sight of; but had been rejected from a sense of the cockneyism of going up a Swiss mountain, in a mob of tourists, by rail. It turned out, however,—a result not new to history— that the minority was not wrong.

I am not, though on the Rigi, going into ecstasies, or particulars. You will find plenty of both in the books. Who has not read—perhaps enough—of its sunrises and sunsets; of the eight lakes visible from its summit; of the effects, still uneffaced, and of which you have a near view, of the great mountain-slip of the Rossberg; and of the long range of massive, rugged, snow-topped Alps to the south, from east to west, a world of mountains of many shapes? With all this, and a good deal more, everyone is as familiar as he is with St. Paul's. But however familiar a writer may make his readers with particulars enumerated in this fashion, he will not thereby enable them to reproduce in their minds such a scene and, if he have not enabled them to do this, his ecstasies would be only cold and ridiculous. The question, then, is, How are the particulars of so vast a scene to be so presented, as that it may be adequately and truly reproduced? The most practised describer would, I think, fail. The triumph, however, I believe might be achieved by the aid of two good panoramic maps, drawn for the purpose. One for the northern, and the other for the southern view. The one for the northern view, which, as seen from the Rigi, embraces the apparently level region of northern, and northwestern Switzerland; should be divided, longitudinally, by lines from south to north, into three compartments; a central, a right, and a left one. And then, each of these three should be, again, trisected, latitudinally, by parallel lines from east to west. This would give to each of the three original compartments three distances of its own; its near, its middle, and its further distance. Each of the three distances of each of the three compartments should be made to show the objects conspicuous to the eye from the summit of the Rigi, and those, too, which though not conspicuous, are yet of sufficient interest to be worthy of notice. With such a map before you, you would almost be able to construct, and put together, the view for yourself. He alone understands a scene, who has in his mind distinct images of all its parts, and of the relation of each to its environment. And in a scene of such vast extent, as that of which we are now speaking, the man, who has it actually before him, will not be able to reach this understanding by a glance, or two: effort and study will be required for the purpose; and even he will be much helped by some such artificial arrangement, as I am here suggesting. It would, however, be also, strictly, the natural arrangement; for such a map would only present, in easily comprehensible spaces, what is here presented in one undivided, and almost incomprehensible, expanse, in a marvellously map-like fashion, by Nature herself. What you have spread out before you from the Rigi Kulm is a ¶map: as much a map as one of Keith Johnston's, with the addition, that, though a map, it is also, at the same time, the actual concrete thing to be mapped—in form, substance, colour, detail, life; of all which his paper map would be only a feeble suggestion in symbols. And as to the man, who has not, or who has not had, the scene before him; it would be quite hopeless to attempt to describe it to him without the aid of a map, so constructed as to give separate distinctness to the component parts of the scene. *Qui bene dividit, bene docet*; and the larger the subject, the greater the need of well-planned divisions.

In a similar fashion the world of snow-capped Alps to the south should be divided into three parts; a middle, and two extremities. The general outline of each part should be sketched, and its most conspicuous, and famous summits signalized. And an attempt should be made to give some general ideas of the ground-plan, and character of each range, and of its relations to the contiguous ranges.

With two such panoramic maps before you, your companion in type might then say to you: Look on this picture to the north, and on that to the south. Never were two contiguous scenes—the two parts of an unbroken whole—in more complete and impressive contrast. The picture to the north, and north-west is a bird's-eye view of a fertile, highly-cultivated country. Here is spread out before you the greater part of north-western Switzerland. The view may be roughly spoken of as filling the area of a semicircle, the diameter of the circle being 100 miles. You are, therefore, looking, from the central point, at which you are standing, fifty miles in every direction. This rich cultivated country, while, in the distance, it trends away as far as the eye can follow it, also, as your mountain observatory is precipitous on this side, comes quite up to you—to beneath your feet—for a near inspection. There is a filmy tint of green in everything you look upon, with the exception of the towns, villages, and innumerable detached human habitations, scattered over the whole of it ; but which, of course, as the distance increases, gradually become lost to sight. The grass is, at this season, of a yellowish green ; the trees and woods of a brownish green ; the lakes of a bluish green. I do not know where, from a near point of view, without a particle of intermediate distance, you could look over so wide an expanse of land, that has been, and shows palpably that it has been, brought so thoroughly and successfully into subjection to man. The expanse is vast, but man is everywhere. Everywhere corn-fields, and vineyards, and orchards, and prairies ; maize and potatoes ; hemp and flax ; sheep and cows ; woods for fuel, and streams for irrigation. Who could think of counting the plots of land into which the whole of it is divided ? But that were easier done than to picture, and estimate the sum of the satisfaction and enjoyment, their possession confers on those who own, and cultivate them. From the vast plain—for to the eye, from the height of nearly 6,000 feet, it all appears flattened out—there ascends to the mountain-top, in the air you are breathing, an incense of human happiness, engendered by industry, independence, and contentment. I looked in the direction of Bretzwyl, and hoped that its unsophisticated peasants had had, since I was among them, many more dances and concerts; and that the kindly professor, his pleasing wife, and their rosy, lively children, were still at Sonnen Halle. But there are many Bretzwyls in that broad view. And there is not an acre in the whole of it, but would sell for twice as much—so greatly has it been improved, and so much happiness does its possession yield to its industrious cultivators—as an acre, of equal goodness, in wealthy England.

So is it also with the opposite picture seen from the Rigi Kulm—the other strangely-contrasted half of the wonderful whole—the long range of Alps on the south. It is not their mountain massiveness, and colouring only—unwonted sight to English eyes— that are capable of interesting. They are something more than Nature's architecture in many forms— pyramids, towers, buttresses, pinnacles—appealing merely to the sense of grandeur, of power, and of awe. That is much: but in them there is much more. That is no more than what the eye reports to the mind. There is, besides, what the memory reports, and what the imagination gives body and life to; and which is of still deeper interest. These craggy escarpments, built up from the plain to, and above the clouds, bastioned with horrid precipices, parapeted and battlemented with eternal snow, were, in its early days, the rampart of the cradle of civilization. In its history they played a great and indispensable part.

So was it in early times. And the state of things these Alps aided in bringing about in early times, did, in its turn, contribute to bring about the state, to which we, in these times, belong. Reader, it is demonstrable, that, if these ramparts had not existed, neither should we, who are now contemplating them, have existed. The combinations of human history would, then, have been different from what they are; and in those different combinations we should have had no place.

Again, if that rampart had not been there, what— to let old times alone—would the subsequent history of Italy have been, and where would have been the recent resurrection of united and independent Italy? It could, without that rampart, have been only a province, as it was not far from becoming with it, of France, or of Germany. It would have been so, for the area of nations depends on natural boundaries.

And there is still another train of thought that belongs to the scene before you. All that you are now looking on suggests only nakedness and cold; hardness and barrenness. There is nothing that indicates life. Man can have no dominion or place there. In everything it seems the antithesis of the scene to the north. But this year, and in other years, you have yourself travelled among those mountains. And what did you find among them? A great deal besides nakedness and cold; hardness and barrenness. You found them everywhere intersected and crossed with innumerable valleys; and every valley you found the scene of patient untiring human industry. You found every little plot of corn or garden ground, every rood of grass, every individual tree carefully, nay lovingly tended, and made the most of. You can recall how, not only in the valley, by the streamside, but up the mountain-side also, and even on many mountain-tops, between the crags and the snow-fields, at this moment, man, woman, and child are busy in winning all that can be won from niggard Nature. Here, then, is another order of objects, and other colouring, to be added by the imagination to the scene before you. Now, it is not only the craggy flanks, and the snowy tops of the Eiger and the Jungfrau, the Titlis, the Uri-Rothstock, the St. Gothard, the Glärnish, and the Tödi, that you see. You clothe and people all between them. You are, again, passing through the villages, the prairies, the orchards of Unterwalden and Uri. You are, again, on the Oberalp alpe, and on the long sides of the Surenen, and of the Pragel, among the cows and the cowherds. You are, again, among the looms and the print-works of Glarus. Thought is active in bringing before you the scene as it is; natural details, and human details of many landscapes, set in those mountain-frames; details out of sight, but visible to the mind's eye. Sympathies are awakened. Your understanding and your heart are both, now, admitted to a share in the interest of the scene.

CHAPTER XII.

LUCERNE—ALPNACH—THROUGH UNTERWALDEN—
MEIRINGEN—THE KIRCHET.

′ I could have better spared a better man.—SHAKESPEARE.

August 23.—Yesterday, having spent some hours on the Rigi, we had got to Lucerne with two or three hours of daylight still at our disposal. I here found my *malle* at the post-office, to which I had directed it eight days previously from Altorf: I now redirected it to Lausanne. We walked over the town before dusk, and afterwards took a second stroll to see the tourists sitting out in front of the large hotels. They appeared to be chiefly Germans and Americans. The day had been very warm; and at 8 o'clock it appeared as if those who were remaining indoors could not be many.

There are several churches in Lucerne; and this morning I noticed, as I was walking to and from Tivoli, that the clocks of all these churches were keeping time with wonderful exactness. They went so well together, that, in striking the hours and quarters, the last was but a very few seconds behind the first. Is this uniformity the result of their all being regulated and wound up by one authority? If so, will it be so long? As Lucerne is not a town of poor and ignorant peasants, we may suppose that before many years have passed, many of the better sort, intellectually, will have joined the Old Catholic party, or, at all events, will have refused to join the new church of the Infallibilists ; and will, therefore, have assumed the regulation of, at least, their own church clocks.

I had gone to Tivoli for a swim in the lake. I found the place more than half a mile distant from the town ; and the bath-house inconveniently small and very dilapidated. It seems unaccountable that this should be the only provision of the kind for a population of about 20,000, and for the many thousands of visitors who yearly stay at the place. With this exception—the want, however, appears to be one that is not felt, for at seven this morning I was the only person using the bath-house—the people of Lucerne are doing all that they can for their city. Their quays, bridges, streets, hotels, shops, all show this. They are proud of their city, and have spent much money in making it commodious and handsome. We here, in England, do little or nothing of this kind for our towns ; because with us the owners of the land contiguous to a town do not reside in it, and can take no interest in it. With us, therefore, a town —the exceptions are not many—has become merely an agglomeration of workshops, and retail shops, and public-houses, with the residences of the necessary complement of professional men, everyone, however, of whom is determined to get away from the town as soon as he can. If our system is the best, I am sorry that it is so. I had rather see our towns centres of culture and refinement; with more to please the eye, and with greater resources for amusement.

After another excursion into the city this morning, we left Lucerne at 10 A.M. by boat for Alpnach, which, in turn, we left by diligence at 12. It would have been better to have turned out at 4 A.M., and walked over Pilatus to Alpnach. This might have been done easily, and I had thought of it; but had said nothing about it, knowing that I should not be allowed to do it alone; and so Pilatus now stands over for the chances of another day. The mob of tourists at Alpnach, and the confusion among them, were worth seeing. The post-office had to provide for them all, for they had booked places at Lucerne, or on board the boat, for Interlaken. They were, eventually, provided for by two diligences, and ten *supplementaires*. The senior conductor of the two diligences had to arrange all these good people according to their crotchets and parties, and the nature of the means at his disposal. Some would not be separated from their friends. Some were not averse to separation. Some would not go in a diligence. Some would go in the *coupé*, if they could. Some would not go in a *supplementaire*, supposing that the diligences would go first. In this, however, they were mistaken, for the officer in command was too old a soldier to allow any of his army of carriages to be in his rear, and wisely, therefore, throughout the day, kept them all before him.

On such an occasion, as on many others in travelling, when many people have to struggle, or think they must, for accommodation, it is amusing to observe the diversity of idiosyncrasies. One man knows the world, and is as cool as a cucumber. It is not worth while putting himself out. He knows that, if he did, he would gain nothing by it. Another takes it for granted that the conductor, who has to go through precisely the same scene every day of his life, knows nothing at all about his business. A third announces, with a display of self-command and assumption of profundity, that everybody in the country is in a conspiracy to cheat and plunder travellers. Some are impressively polite, and hope to gain their point by soft words. Others, who have a low opinion of mankind, put their trust in francs. Some wear a look of helpless resignation. Others, who are of the lucifer-match kind, but not of the kind that ignites only on the box—that is to say, in their own homes, where they have a right to be fiery—explode at once. Collision with anything puts them in a flame. And now you amuse yourself with the way in which they are blazing up, if you are not thereby at all scorched yourself.

At last, all these different specimens of humanity having been provided with seats, just as they would have been had not one of them spoken a word, we got under weigh—an imposing procession of twelve carriages. The horses in some of the *supplementaires* had been shockingly overworked. The constant straining up hill had so changed the form of their visage, that it was scarcely equine. On noticing this to the conductor, he was of opinion that it would not have been so had they been Swiss horses; they were French horses that had been left behind by Bourbaki's army; and the effect had resulted from their having been put to work which they had not been used to, and for which they were unfit; but that it was a matter of no great consequence, for the work was killing them fast.

For the two miles beyond Sarnen, there was evidence of how shallow in a Swiss prairie is, generally, the film of good soil. Since I passed by on foot, two or three weeks back, a violent storm-gust had swept over this space, and had thrown down scores of fruit-trees. In every instance their roots, which, it appeared, were quite superficial, had lifted the good black soil, and exposed, beneath, the fragments of white rock, on which the soil, to the depth of nowhere more than two feet, had been superimposed, in great part by the industry of many generations of peasants, who had removed the superficial fragments of rock and levelled the good surface. At

Eywyl my wife and myself left the *diligence*, and walked to Lungern, five miles. I again descended at the foot of the Brünig, and walked to the top.

I here saw a black squirrel, the only living wild quadruped I met with during this excursion. Of wild birds also there is to an English eye a surprising dearth in Switzerland. This results in some measure from everyone being allowed to carry a gun, and to use it at all seasons for the destruction of any feathered, or four-footed wild creature that may come in his way; but chiefly from the length of the winter, and dearth of insects, and of plants bearing such seeds and fruits as, at that season, might supply food for birds. During this excursion the only birds I saw were, on several occasions, on open high ground, a solitary little chirper, probably of the finch kind; one jay in the wood—the Aletschwald—on the west side of the Rieder Alp, just above the Aletsch glacier; one coot in a reedy pool in the Valais; a flock of a dozen, or so, rooks eating grapes in a vineyard near Vevey; some gulls on the lake of Geneva; a small covey of red-legged partridges in the valley of the Tessin; in some few towns a few sparrows; and in some a few swallows: no very long catalogue for the distance travelled over. It is a strange thing that you see bee-hives everywhere, but rarely meet with a bee. The whole of the honey, however, that is consumed by travellers in Switzerland is not the product of this little ill-used hymenopteron; for there is, at all events, one factory in a lofty out-of-the-way retreat in the Canton de Vaud—the Swiss are a very ingenious people—where it is produced without insect aid.

We were to sleep at Meiringen: but we found it necessary to go to Brienz, several miles beyond the point on the Brünig where the road branches off to Meiringen, in order to get a private carriage to take us to Meiringen. Just on this part of our way we had to pass through what to those who are unaccustomed to any but English rain-falls would have appeared a surprisingly dark and heavy storm. While we were leaving the *diligence* at Brienz the darkness and this rain-fall were at their height.

In half-an-hour the rain had ceased, and our carriage came round to the door of the hotel. My engagement with Ammer was now ended. As I took his hand, and expressed a parting wish for his welfare, his last words were, 'Sir, if you write a book, put me into it.' That was not the moment when a man could say no to the harmless request of one who had been his companion for three weeks; and so he returned to Interlaken, to look out for another engagement, in the belief that his request would be complied with. I must, therefore, attempt his portrait. Here it is. He was a tall, bony man, with a long face and grave expression. His talk was that of one who is by nature of an easy simple disposition, but to whom experience has taught that this is a world in which a man must take care of himself. He would rather not have had to do this; but he acquiesced in the necessity of doing it. As to his knowledge of English, he naturally, and allowably enough, overrated it. It was travellers' English only: nothing more; but for that purpose sufficient. For the only purpose I had in view in engaging him, it was of little or no use. Still, notwithstanding, I held him to be worth his eight francs a day. His polyglot, or rather piebald, or, to be precise, his tortoiseshell, of German, French, and English was, at times, an amusing form of speech. The predominant idea in his mind, the mother idea that gave birth to all others, the focal point to which all lines of thought converged, was that there was nothing in the world like francs. As most of us do, he read others by the light of the knowledge he had of himself. He, therefore, always went on the supposition that nothing could so enhance the merit of his services as some scheme for saving me a franc. This, in his ideas of the scale of duty, came first; and he would be overwhelmed with deep disappointment, mingled with humiliation, whenever, in dealing with porters, *voituriers*, hotel-keepers, &c., I took matters into my own hands, and did not allow him to make arrangements for effecting this saving. His uncomfortable feelings, however, on these occasions were quickly dissipated by the offering of a cigar—in extreme cases, of two—which he readily accepted, as implying an amount of general approval, friendliness, and liberality sufficient to salve the wound and kill its smart. If I made some small pecuniary acknowledgment he was disposed to think uncalled for, or did not make a reclamation he thought might have been successful, the light that was within him began to be dimmed with uncertainties and confusion. His accustomed landmarks were disappearing. The scent was being lost. He was off the line: the wheels were revolving, but there was no going forward. When at the Hôtel de Ville at Altorf I gave the official a franc for the few square inches of spongy paper, with a few figures printed upon it, his difficulties of this kind culminated. Was I a lunatic or a millionaire? The easiest conclusion—that to which he came—was that I was something of both. 'There is not,' he said, meditatively, 'a man in Uri who would have given that franc for a large volume.' And then, more confidently, as if he saw, or fancied he saw, a ray of light, 'But the English are very rich.' This solution he frequently, afterwards, reverted to. 'No,' I would always reply, 'not so rich as the Swiss, for they can afford to give twice as much as the English for a thousand klafters of land.' Out of this economical puzzle he could never see his way. The evening before we started he decided that he would draw his pay in one sum, at the conclusion of the engagement. I had proposed to him that he should receive it in weekly payments. He soon, however, began to draw upon me for ten francs at a time. So that, when we had reached Brienz he had, by these payments on account, received a third of the whole. As he knew that I was aware that he must have, originally, taken with him enough for his personal wants, he always gave for these applications, accompanied with many apologies, the reason that he wished to make some additions to his wardrobe. To this, however, I never saw that any additions were made ; for his little water-proof *sac* was always empty ; and he returned home in the same clothes, the same billy-cock felt hat, and the same boots in which he had originally set out—all rather marked objects of their kind. I was obliged, therefore, to come to the conclusion, that these successive draughts on account had no purpose but the satisfaction he would receive from having some of the francs in his own actual keeping. If on any occasion he was charged a few cents more than he had expected, or if his dinner and supper had not, in some way or other, been manipulated into my account, for upon this point he was never sufficiently clear, his solemn denunciations, and feeling reprobation, of this strange form of baseness were invariably concluded with the apothegm—I soon knew when to look for it—'*Il y a des voleurs partout.*' This was always announced in precisely the same tone, and with the same heart-chuckle, as if he were announcing a discovery combining the greatest profundity with the greatest novelty, which had just, at that moment, flashed into his own mind, for the first time in the philosophic observation of mankind.

It was his habit to make the Valaisans, on all occasions where it was possible, and at times, too, when the ground of the remark was not discoverable, a butt for the shaft of a depreciatory comparison. If, for instance, we anywhere saw a boy in a pair of *sabots*, he would say, ' In the Valais the ladies wear *sabots*: they only cost them half-a-franc, and last through a summer and winter.' If he saw the land anywhere ill-cultivated, or a forest ill-managed, or anything done clumsily, wastefully, or neglectfully, he would say, ' That is arranged badly; that is how it is arranged in the Valais.' If I talked to him about schools, he would say, ' We have schools everywhere: but in the Valais they do not teach much.' I would ask him, ' Why?' He would reply, ' You must ask the priests.' If we came up with a flock of goats on a mountain pasture, or by the roadside, he would say, ' The Valaisans keep goats in their forests, to destroy the young trees.'

There was a mystery about his Sunday apparel. On that day his flannel shirt was doffed, and he would appear in a clean hempen shirt, and with a new pair of thick, apparently homespun, woollen trousers, neither of which was it possible for him to have had on the week days, before or afterwards. I must, therefore, suppose that he hired, or borrowed, them for the occasion. When in any little matter I would go my own way, and not his, I was soon prepared for what would come ; and knew, when it came, precisely what it meant ; for, on such conjunctures, he would never fail to announce, with a tone of sorrowful submission, ' It is of your opinion.' When he was utterly in the dark as to some question I was putting to him, and, evidently, knew nothing about the matter, he would assume, suddenly, the air of a man who has, by a happy inspiration of the moment, unriddled some ancient world-puzzle. The whole solution was, in every case, precisely the same, for it was all contained in the never-failing oracular utterance of the single word, 'Infallibly,' accompanied with a fixed look and solemn nod.

I held him at the time to be, and still hold him to have been, cheap at the money. He belongs to a bygone order of things, to the old Swiss world, in which a franc was a large object for contemplation, enough to occupy a man's thoughts, and to satisfy his heart, and most days quite out of reach. He represents a class of guides that was formed before Alpinism had been evolved ; and before streams of travellers had brought into Alpine villages streams of gold —a commodity then only known by report, and which in those valleys no eye had yet beheld. The old and the new experiences are, in his mind, in conflict. No guide on the sunny side of fifty can be like him. Travellers, who are, themselves, on the shady side of those figures, will be reminded by him of the slow and cautious world they once knew; and he will help them to measure how different is the world in which they now are.

We had, then, said our adieux to Ammer, and were now on our way to Meiringen. I observed that the horses we met on the road had dry hoofs; and when we had got a little more than three miles from Brienz the dust was flying; so confined had been the area of the heavy mountain storm, in which we had reached Brienz. We entered Meiringen just as the evening lights were beginning to show through the windows of the village, and of the neighbouring scattered *châlets*. The labours of the day were done, and families were again reunited to talk over its little events, before going to rest. We stopped at the door of the Reichenbach Hotel. We had been there last year, and had been satisfied with our reception. It is about half a mile from the village, near the foot of the mountain. A little stream passes by it; I believe through it. Its *entourage* is of garden-ground, turf, and trees.

I may mention that the manager of this hotel showed me, by reference to his books, that he was paying the commune twenty-five cents a klafter for good garden-ground, and twelve cents for ground of inferior quality. Another Meiringen man told me that good land was letting from twenty to thirty cents a klafter. There are 1,400 klafters in an acre. Twenty-five cents a klafter is, therefore, 14*l*. an acre. These hotels must have vegetables. This high rent, however, does not matter much to those tenants, who are proprietors of hotels, for they can recompense themselves for it through the medium of the little notes they present to their visitors.

August 24.—It was Sunday. We went twice to the English church. It is a new structure; and was erected at the expense of an English clergyman. The services I was glad to see were well attended. As the fashion, in which they were conducted, is a public matter, it is fairly open to comment; I may, therefore, say of them, and which, of course, those who direct them wish should be seen and known, that they were done in the ritualistic style. Those, who are far advanced in the direction of this style, might, perhaps, say of them only, that they showed a tendency towards ritualism. Personally, I am not annoyed at this fashion of conducting the service, any more than I am at witnessing an attempt to create the spiritual excitement, with which the opposite party in the Church has familiarized us; but, as it is presented to us for the very purpose of influencing, or obtruded upon us for the very purpose of challenging, our ideas and opinions, I am quite at liberty to say of it, that I think it, at least, as much of a mistake as the other. Still, as the embodiment of a *bonâ fide* opinion, or theory, it is entitled to be treated as such, that is to say to be met not with outcry and denunciation, but with facts and arguments. Now I am disposed to think, though, indeed, this is not the place for going into the facts and arguments, that neither of these two parties could have helped itself. Each works according to its light, and with the materials, that is to say the amount of knowledge, and kind of ideas, it possesses. And as, too, not far from all of those, to whom each has to address itself, are in the same mental condition as the leaders themselves of these parties, or are ready to be brought into it, little else can, at the moment, be done. We may, therefore, be almost disposed to say, So far well. Still we ought to keep in mind that religion must have, if it be any thing *in rerum naturâ*, a body of absolute truth. Now an induction from all religions appears to demonstrate the fact that the substance and body of religion is morality. And by the same process we come to the conclusion that its morality does not differ specifically from the ordinary forms and divisions of morality, as for instance that which is the regulation of the family, or that which is the regulation of society. Its morality does not differ specifically from these, or from any branches of morality, because it includes them all. Still it has a differentia; otherwise it would be only a synonyme for morality; and that differentia is its motive. It is the moral life, in all its relations, modified by, and practised from, motives drawn from the idea of a future life, or of there being a moral Governor of the world. This is religion in its simplest expression. This it is that makes it something *in rerum naturâ*; gives it existence; and has made it a power in all times, and among all races of men. The more distinctly men see, or even feel this, the more powerfully they are attracted to it; for this it is that reveals to them its nature and its uses, and enlists on its behalf the understanding and the moral sentiments, accompanied with immediate satisfaction, and the hope of better things to come. Anything which obscures the perception of this weakens its power. Now one of the parties, of which we have just made mention, obscures the perception of this simple and mighty truth by a veil of forms, and by what it calls reverence. It thus metamorphoses, and lowers religion. As respects its ministers and exponents; it puts the priest in the place of the prophet. As respects the wealthy, the luxurious, and the self-indulgent; it encourages them in substituting for religion these forms, and this reverence, which are so far from being religion that they may co-exist with that which is its most complete contradiction. And as to the ignorant; it attracts them; though, of course, not morally, but theatrically: for it is delightful to them to find religion so like a stage-play; that is to say something that is pleasant to look at, not something that is to regulate the whole inner and external life. The other party obscures the same great truth by a veil of sentimental excitement, and of exaggerated, factitious spiritualism. These, as they are not the actual things the human soul wants in this matter, cannot, of course, be maintained ; and must, after a time, die away, if not in individuals, yet inevitably in bodies of men. And this accounts for the reaction from the teaching of this party, which is now going on before our eyes ; and which, as it goes on, enables us to see how little, that is substantial and real, it has effected, except in the way of preparing us for what is real and substantial.

Both these parties were, under the circumstances of the times, unavoidable. But the aims and methods of both are, nevertheless, to a great extent, untrue ; and, therefore, to a certain extent, and in a sense, mischievous. They have not sought first the kingdom of God, which is morality shaped and motived by the idea of a future life, or of there being a moral Governor of the world. With respect to the theory, and practice of the ritualistic party, we may be sure that there will be a reaction from them, just as they are themselves an incident of the reaction from the theory and practice of the opposite party. For ten, or even twenty, years we may not see it, but we must see it sooner or later. And those who choose to look at what is now going on will be able to anticipate, probably with some degree of accuracy, the direction the coming reaction will take ; because what is to be, can be produced only by what now is. Those, who resort to this kind of divination, will see that, as both ritualism, and the so-called evangelicalism, so far as they are moral and religious, are efforts, only in unhistoric and unphilosophic minds, to attain to truth and reality; and as even in the outside world, which is neither ritualistic, nor evangelical, the same effort is being vigorously made; therefore the reaction, whenever it may come, will be in the direction of what all are desiring, and in search of, that is to say of truth, and reality. History, and philosophy will not be ignored. On the contrary: their authority will supersede that of men who were unhistoric, and unphilosophic. And, then, perhaps, the idea of religion that underlies, and is embodied in, the Sermon on the Mount, which is neither ritualistic, nor evangelical, will have its turn, again, once more, after so many centuries: and this will be only a reversion to that primitive conception of Christianity, which was what sent it forth conquering, and to conquer.

The source, then, and the forms of the mistakes we have been speaking of, are in our view of these matters, to be ascribed entirely to want of knowledge, both in those who had to lead, and in those who had to be led. We can say this without being disposed in any degree to blame either the one, or the other: for want of knowledge of the kind needed is an ever-recurring phenomenon; because it is an incident of progress. Those, who see this, ought to be satisfied with the faith they may have in knowledge. It must come; and, when it comes, it must have its due effect. There never, in the whole history of the world, has been a time in which, or a people among whom, religion has not been the expression of knowledge which has always, and everywhere, modified it, and necessarily in the direction of lifting it up to its own level. This is its highest, and its main use; for religion is the harmonizing, and the systematizing, of all the knowledge men have at any time attained to, both of nature and of man, for the most practical of all purposes—that of enlightening, guiding, purifying, elevating, and strengthening the moral life.

Before the evening service we walked to the Kirchet, perhaps a mile and a half up the valley, to see the old deserted ravine channel of the Aare. This is well worth a visit, even by those on whose minds such a sight will leave impressions only of strangeness and novelty. The Kirchet is a hill, that, just above Meiringen, runs completely athwart the Haslithal. It is said to be 800 feet high. Above it, therefore, the valley must have been, at some remote period, a lake, as far up as would be requisite for bringing its head to the level of the 800 feet of this bar, which formed its foot. At that time the overflow of the lake, instead of going straight over the Kirchet, when it had reached the summit, somewhere about the middle of it, made an angle on the summit, which is broad and flat, and then took a course along it to the north-east. In this course along the summit, it cut for itself a rapidly descending ravine passage, down to the foot of the lofty mountain that here rises above the Kirchet. At this point, that is to say at the foot of the mountain, the ravine channel made a second sharply defined right angle, and proceeded then almost due north to Meiringen along the line of the junction of the Kirchet and the eastern mountain.

There must, however, in times of floods and freshets, have been in those early days a subsidiary channel all along the foot of the eastern mountain. This was ever deepening itself, as all channels do. Perhaps it could only carry on this work in times of floods and freshets. At last it deepened itself to such a degree as to produce two very notable effects. One was that of draining the lake, and so of laying dry the broad bottom land where Im Hof now stands. The other was that of rendering useless the old channel of the north-eastern half of the axis of the Kirchet. The new channel is straight, and at right angles to the old one. This cutting off of bends and angles is what river channels are constantly engaged in doing. The only difference here is that, the old channel being in hard rock, the lapse of untold centuries has not in the slightest degree obliterated, or defaced, the earlier work of the Aare. The old ravine channel is just as clear, and as sharply defined, as it was on the day upon which the last waning streamlet from the Aare trickled over its bed, and then died away; and the whole outflow of Haslithal took the way of the new channel, which it has retained to this day.

As you go down the steep, narrow, deep descent of this old watercourse, so narrow and so deep that, at times, the rocks completely meet overhead and the sky above is shut out, you read its history more rapidly and more plainly than you can on this page. There are the clear, perpendicular, rock walls, right and left, at most only two or three yards apart; their sides water-worn, with edges here and there rounded off, and in some places hemispherical holes excavated in the rock, where some fracture, or soft spot, had enabled the old torrent to work at an advantage. Beneath your feet, in the long staircase of the ravine— the bed of the old channel—are the loose rocks, just as they were left; some much worn, that had been there, beneath the rushing tumbling torrent, for a long time; some not much worn, that had been brought in not long before the Aare withdrew to the new channel; all worn only on their surface and their upstream side. Everywhere between these rocks is the clean sand, just as it was left, washed clean, thousands of years ago. And when you get to the bottom of the old ravine, there, before you, is the Aare of to-day, thundering by in the new ravine it has cut for itself, exactly at right angles to the old deserted ravine, at the mouth of which you are standing. And here, at this point, down in the bowels of the mountain, is a charming little beach of white sand, two or three yards wide, and a dozen or so yards long, of precisely the same sand as that you have been stepping over in your descent of the old ravine.

Who could stand on this little marge of sand unmoved? It is a point of contact between the distant days—represented by the deserted channel—when the valley above you was a broad and long lake, and your own day—represented by the channel now in use—when, 800 feet below what had been, in the first period, the surface of the old lake, is now the site of the busy and thriving community of Im Hof. Here you are reminded of what was the old, and humanly unrecorded state of things; and are enabled to understand what brought about the existing state of things, and how it brought it about. The old torrent played its part by the slow but unfailing exercise of the rock-eroding power, with which running water had been invested from the beginning of things; and the existing torrent, as it rushes by before you, is, you see, playing the same part in the working of the world-organism—the part it has been playing, without failing or rest, for no one can say how many thousands of years; which, however, only began to run their course, when the thousands of years of the old channel had ended theirs. You are even carried, in the process of thought, beyond the world-organism to the world-Organiser, Who impressed on matter its properties, modes of action, uses, and relations. As these visions pass before you, and these thoughts form themselves, the nerves of your mind are thrilled with an emotion, that will make that little marge of sand, at the juncture of the old with the new ravine, deep down in the bowels of the mountain, ever to you a memorable spot.

CHAPTER XIII.

THE GRIMSEL.—OBERGESTELN.—MUNSTER.—VIESCH.—
THE EGGISCHHORN.

Mind stirs in matter, as a soul,
Not less in atoms than the mighty whole.—VIRGIL.

AUGUST 25.—Were off at 5 A.M. for the longest walk of our excursion, across the Grimsel, down to Obergesteln, and then along the Rhone Valley to Munster, where we were to sleep, and the next morning to go on to the Eggischhorn. The little man was mounted; my wife and myself were on foot. Our *sacs*, somewhat reduced, at Lucerne, from what they had been on the Surenen and the Pragel, where two porters had been required, and this morning again somewhat further lightened by the aid of the little man's horse, were on the back of one Jean Ott, of Im Hof, a good and true man, and eke the father of ten small children. He remained in our service for five days: this enables us to speak of his merits with some confidence.

Our tramp commenced with the Kirchet. As we passed the entrance to the old deserted ravine channel, all we had seen in it yesterday came back to mind; and with the rest the recollection of a tuft of Maidenhair fern I had espied on one of its walls, with some of its fronds erect and some pendant, placed just where it might most charm the eye of the beholder with the contrast of the beautiful fragility of its black thread-stem and tender green spangle-leaflets, to the grey rock, and to the recollection of the dashing angry torrent that had, long ages gone by, excavated for it its little ledge. And I hoped that no thoughtless, unfeeling hand would tear it from the niche, that had been so prepared for it, so long ago.

Im Hof was soon reached, where we walked along the bed of the old lake. This was succeeded by a narrow ascending gorge, where the road is carried through woods, and the opposite mountains are very close. The green meadows of Güttannen came next; and so on to Handeck. I do not dwell on any of these points, for we are now on ground which was passed over in last year's 'Month in Switzerland.' I only note what was not noted then. The difference, however, in the direction in which you are looking, and the difference in the position of the sun, make a great difference in what you see, and in how you see it. The Grimsel, too, is so full of beauty, grandeur, and interest, that I would gladly walk through it, backwards and forwards, day after day, for a week; and should expect to find in it every time something new.

At Handeck, for the sake of the horse, and of Jean Ott, a halt of an hour was called. It was now nearly 10 A.M.; and so far, with a few short breaks, we had carried along with us the morning shade of the eastern mountains. Some bread and cheese, and a bottle of wine which, if not good in itself, was made to appear so by a five hours' brisk walk in the fresh morning air, and by the addition of ice-cold water from the glacier that on the west overhangs the *châlet*, occupied, within the *châlet*, the first half of our time. The remaining half was spent on the rocks and turf outside, in contemplation of the western glacier, and of the eastern mountain, with its fringe of pine along its lower zone, succeeded by a zone of stripes and patches of Pinus Pumilio, on any fissures and coins of vantage they could lay hold of: the rest to the top being naked, dark slate-coloured rock, ending in the broken summit ridge.

Time is up; and we are off again, as gaily as when we started at 5 A.M., over Hellen Platten, then across the mountain flank beyond: a grand scene of naked gneiss, right, left, before, behind, particularly in the last direction, as it presents itself when you turn round and look back while ascending the flank of the mountain, about two miles above Handeck. The form and windings of the sullen desolate ranges that form the valley are here seen to great advantage, and are very impressive. Then the flank of the mountain is rounded, with the Aare beneath you, on your left, far below; buried and bridged, as we passed it, by what still remained of two great avalanches. Then down to and across the Aare, and on to the Grimsel Hospice. Here another halt: this time half-an-hour.

Now up to the Todensee: but this year not taking the left side for the mephitic, fly-plagued Rhone Glacier Hotel, but the right side, straight on to Obergesteln. This, just beyond the Todensee, and for some little way on, is for the pedestrian a very good bit of Switzerland. You are at a height of not far from 7,000 feet, with a grand and varied feast for the eye in every direction. Of course you look first for the great Rhone glacier. That you see, from an admirable point of view, in a grand Alpine picture. Mountains and glaciers have souls; still there can be no Landseer for them. They are too vast and too simple, and the scene, though its objects are so few, is too expanded for the canvas. In the foreground is the dark Todensee, surrounded with its scanty, yellowish, sober herbage, interspersed with granite slabs and rocks. In the middle distance the central object is the great glacier, majestically descending from between the Gerstener snow-fields and rock ridges on the left, and the snow-capped summits of the Galenstock on the right. This majestic descent suddenly passes into the broad, and lofty ice-fall of the glacier—not quite a Niagara of ice, but still very grand and imposing; and the more so to those, who remember that it *is*, while they are looking at it, in motion—an actual ice-fall; and that the majestic descent, too, above it, is flowing—an actual ice-river.

At the point where this is best seen, you get also, by reversing your position, the best view of the Zermatt Alps. There before you, in the south-west, are their multiform summits—Monte Rosa, Weisshorn, Matterhorn, &c. You, who know the whole ground-plan and mountain architecture of that region, recall the relation in which they stand to each other.

Looking straight across the Valais you have a third great sight. Up against the sky, in a gap through the range on the opposite side, is the great glacier over which lies the Pass from the Upper Valais to Domo d'Ossola.

To your right, all along, are the mountain high cliffs, topped with snow-fields, of the Great and Little Sidelhorn.

It is a glorious panorama. Memorable to you, ever after, will be the day, on which you saw it, with a sense of its grandeur and power.

As we went along we made out, with our glasses, a party of Englishmen on the snow of the Sidelhorn, and another party on the Gerstener snow-field, who were searching, as we were told, for the brother of the manager of the Grimsel Hospice, who that morning, while looking for crystals, had fallen into a *crevasse*.

This, by engendering a feeling of awe, added to the interest of the scene. The next day we heard that the poor man having, on the afternoon of this day, been tracked to the point from which he had slipped, had been recovered in a state of insensibility, but not so far gone as not to be brought round again.

The descent to Obergesteln is down mountain pastures, over thymy turf, by hurrying streams, and through a wood of ancient larch. To see this wood to advantage you must go straight down it by a *sentier de speculation*, which will carry you by and under some fine trees.

It had been a part of our original plan for the day to take a *char* at Obergesteln. But, as might have been expected in the height of the season, nothing of the kind was to be had at such a place; every horse and vehicle being on the road, making pecuniary hay whilst the tourist sun was shining. This we thought rather a gain, as there was some good walking in us still; and so, having baited the little man's horse and our porter at Obergesteln, we carried ourselves on to Munster, which we reached at 5.30 P.M. We had been out, including halts, twelve and a half hours: and had done, I suppose, over thirty miles.

Having been from early days something of a pedestrian, and, during this month's tramp, never having once felt fatigued, or had a battered, blistered, or swollen foot, I will venture to say a word here on the great question of walking in Switzerland. A combination of walking with *chars*, when the latter are advisable, of which you must judge yourself, with reference to your own power and objects, and the amount of time at your disposal, is the pleasantest way of conducting an excursion in such a country. To keep yourself in training for a walking expedition, you will find eight miles a day at home quite sufficient. If you are accustomed to this it will be as easy for you to do three times that distance when the whole day is given up to it, as to do the eight miles at home in two hours of the afternoon. But the one primary, indispensable requisite is a proper pair of boots. If they are not what they ought to be, nothing can be done. If they are of the right sort, all that is required may be done with comfort and with pleasure. English shoemakers are the worst and most stupid in the world, except the American; and they are worse because they exaggerate and caricature the stupidity of ours. Crispin, being crassly ignorant of the anatomy and action of the human foot, has come to make it his great object to cripple it, and render it incapable of acting, in the fashion nature intended, as an instrument of locomotion. A moment's consideration will show you that your foot is a piece of mechanism most wonderfully constructed for the work designed it. First, the heel and the toes are so connected by the arch of the instep as practically to give you four feet upon two legs. Of this advantage, by rendering your foot rigid, a tight boot to some extent deprives you. But we will let that pass, though the loss is by no means small. The great point is that nature intended that your foot, as you set it down, and it receives the weight of the body, should expand; and that when you rise upon it to take a step it should expand still further. All depends upon this power of expansion. To enable it to perform this function, it has been constructed of a multitude of bones and of muscles, the interplay of which should be quite free and unimpeded. But to prevent its expanding at all, your shoemaker puts it into a tight case with a narrow sole. It still, however, endeavours to do its work by making all the effort it can to expand. In this tight case it cannot expand. See, then, what ensues: the bones chafe the muscles; the foot swells. Practically the case is screwed up still tighter. The whole machine becomes internally tender and painful, and externally blistered, particularly between the outer toes, where the tight case has been more ignorantly and cruelly constructed than elsewhere. And now you cannot walk any further; and what you did was done with effort and pain. Naturally you become disgusted with walking.

There is a simple, instantaneous, and complete remedy. Measure the sole of the walking boots you have hitherto used, and insist on Crispin making you a pair with soles at least four-eighths, five would be better, wider than you have ever had before. Henceforth, so far from your feet swelling and getting heated by walking, they will, after twenty miles' work, be both cooler and smaller than when you got out of bed in the morning. You will never have another blister. And as to the jar of walking, which affects the whole frame, now that your foot has become elastic instead of rigid, there will be none of that. The width also of the sole will of itself and alone, greatly contribute towards breaking the jar. Nature will thank you for having understood her. And you will thank nature for having taken so much pains to contrive and construct for you so marvellous a machine, if rightly treated, for pleasurable exercise.

Last year, as we were driving through these villages of the Upper Valais, I had inferred their mental condition from the few simple elements, of which, obviously, the lives of their inhabitants were compounded. Now, as we passed through them in more leisurely fashion, I reverted to the same subject, and recalled Ammer's disparagements, and the account of their social and intellectual condition a native of one of them had given me, in a conversation I had chanced to have with him some days back. He had said that 'he was prospering where he was, but would never be able to return with the fruits of his prosperity to his native village in the Upper Valais. The priests would never allow the return of anyone who, while living elsewhere, had acquired some independence of thought as well as of means; and an indisposition to be fed with '—but for his (in English) monosyllable I will substitute—what Infallibility ought to save us all from, at all events the inhabitants of the Upper Valais. 'The priests,' he said, 'still had the power, as they had the inclination, to render return to and residence in their old home, very disagreeable for such people. They were too, the cause of the inhabitants of this part of the Valais being lazy and good for nothing. How could it be otherwise with people who throughout their lives are fed only with '—again what Infallibility should save them from; 'and who are kept in constant subjection? It is bad for men to put themselves into the hands of other men. They should rather be taught to depend upon themselves.'

And so it has come about that an Upper Valaisan who has once seen the world must remain in it, in order that the ignorance in which the priests have a vested interest might be protected against knowledge. If the time is never to be when 'such evil shall on itself back recoil,' then

> The pillared firmament is rottenness,
> And earth's base built on stubble.

But as it has recoiled in Italy, Spain, and France, we may believe that it will in the Upper Valais; and this belief may be accompanied by the hope that the evils of the recoil of the evil may not be long-lived.

August 26.—Our destination was the Eggischhorn Hotel. As far as Viesch we took a carriage. Jean Ott was on the box with the driver. But as it proved to be possible—we should not have supposed it—to squeeze in a third sitter, a bare-headed young lady of Munster, not of the slim order of beauty, took it for granted, without leave asked or offered, that there could be no objection (none was made) to her availing herself of the opportunity: and so she got a lift to Biel. This was like the undoubting confidence with which, in the East, the poorest wayfarer will ask you to allow him to light his cigarette from your cigar. It is a kind of assumption which ought not to be displeasing, as it implies a compliment; for it is an assumption of your good sense and good nature.

For agricultural purposes rain had been abundant wherever else we had been, but here it was evident that none had fallen for a long time. There was no second cut on unirrigated grass land; the potato-haulm was short and withered; so was the hemp. The road was very dusty, and almost in a state of disintegration. On inquiring I was told that these spells of dry weather are here of very frequent occurrence. If so, can they be caused by the ascent of the heated air of the Valais dissipating the clouds that would otherwise have supplied its needs? Such droughts must contribute very considerably towards the impoverishment of the people. I observed, however, that they do not do as much as they might in the way of embanking and draining their low ground, and of irrigating their upper prairies. The appearance of the Valais above Sierre indicates that an insufficiency of moisture is its normal condition.

At 9.30 A.M., our belongings were on Jean Ott's back, and we began the ascent of the Viescher Alp for the Eggischhorn Hotel. The work was warm, for the ascent was steep, and the sun was full on the mountain side; though, in respect of the sun, the forest, as far as it went, befriended us. There was, too, in the air, something of the oppressive closeness which precedes a thunderstorm. The hotel was reached in two hours and a half. We had telegraphed for rooms, but by some *contre-temps*, the two answers the proprietor had despatched to assure us that no accommodation was at present disposable in his house had failed in reaching us. We had, therefore, to take what could be arranged. It was now only mid-day, and the resources available for possible arrangements could not be ascertained till the evening. This caused some hours of suspense. Of what, at last, the good man did for us, as it was the best he could do, it would be ungracious to say more than that it might have been very much worse.

The Eggischhorn Hotel is, doubtless, all things considered, that is to say, the difficulty of access, shelter from wind, water-supply, view, and the objects to be visited in the locality, in the best site that could have been found. Still it may be observed that it is on a spot on the mountain side, from which the eye has no great range, and where, too, standing room had to be constructed for it; which is the same as saying that it is on a little narrow indent, an artificially formed niche, half excavated and half built up from below. This is in keeping with what you might have expected, and so far good. The house is small, but some additions to it, which will more than double its capacity, and very much improve the character of its accommodation, are nearly completed. The number, however, of travellers increases so rapidly that it will probably be, next year, as difficult to obtain a share in the improved and extended, as it has hitherto been in the existing, accommodation.

We had all the afternoon to look about us, and for familiarizing ourselves with the near and the distant objects. Compared with many other well-known localities 7,000 feet high, the distant objects are not numerous. They could hardly, indeed, be fewer. Still what you see of the valley below, its woods, and prairies, and villages, and of the somewhat snowy range opposite, shagged with peaks and precipices of gray rock, will satisfy one who is more disposed to be satisfied with what he has than to be dissatisfied with what he has not. The confined site of the hotel has a kind of novelty, and produces a sense of imprisonment, particularly when you are pacing up and down its miniature esplanade. And then to convince yourself that you are not a prisoner, you will break away from the miniature esplanade, and take little walks above, and to the right and left, on the mountain; and you will sit on the flowery turf, or on a ledge of protruding rock, and meditate till Fancy has had her fill. And you will not be altogether alone, for the quiet-minded kine will be on the hillside around you; and multitudinous grasshoppers will be starting up at your feet, a light-hearted little people, gaily clad in many colours, whose nerves are supple and springy, and sensitive to enjoyment in their short summer.[1] And so there will be enough of the brotherhood of life to attune your heart pleasantly, if it have not been too far enfeebled by the vanities, or ossified by the vexations of life.

Two or three hours after we had reached the hotel, the thunderstorm, from the premonitory

---

[1] I was reminded of the Anacreontic to the Grasshopper, and of Cowley's rendering of it:—

>   Thou dost drink, and dance, and sing,
>   Happier than the happiest king.
>   Thou dost innocently enjoy,
>   Nor does thy luxury destroy.
>   To thee, of all things upon earth,
>   Life is no longer than thy mirth.
>   Happy insect! happy thou,
>   Dost neither age nor winter know.
>   But when thou'st danced, and drunk, and sung
>   Thy fill, the flowery leaves among
>   (Voluptuous, and wise withal,
>   Epicurean animal,)
>   Sated with thy summer feast,
>   Thou retir'st to endless rest.

symptoms of which we had, in ascending, suffered, trailed by. The effects of these mountain storms are always interesting. Immediately below the hotel is a ravine, which widens as it descends towards the main valley. On the whole of the left side of this a pasty cloud, as dark as midnight, settled down for a time. Not a trace of any object could now be seen there but the cloud itself. The mountain side, the woods, the valley, were all equally and utterly obliterated. At short intervals this mass of black cloud below us was rent, and illuminated, by flashes of lightning. It seemed as if it was the bearer of the scarth of doom to all wrapped in it and below it. Then the sun burst out above us, and the broadest, and clearest, and most brilliant rainbow I have ever seen, I do not expect ever again to see another such, rested on the turbid blackness of the cloud. It was its nearness, as well as the contrast of the murky background, that made every band of colour so broad, clear, and brilliant. The air where we were standing was filled with a haze of its colours. It would have been strange, indeed, if man, at the time when he knew nothing of what produced the thunderstorm and the rainbow, had not taken one for the wrath, and the other for the smile of God. Our thoughts they still lift from ourselves, and direct towards the Mind that is in everything, but by another and more excellent way.

August 27.—At 9 A.M. started for the ascent of the Eggischhorn. Reader, if you also have made the same start, let us go over the old ground together. If you have not, then let me endeavour to tell you of something you would be the better for seeing. Jean Ott we took with us for our guide. You must call to mind that we are setting out from a height of 7,000 feet above the level we are accustomed to at home. There are no trees above us, or to the right, or left. Our way is all over the flowery Alpine turf, interspersed with rocks. We shall have to climb not quite 2,000 feet more. After a time we shall lose the flowers and the turf: but of that presently. On this morning there had been scuds of rain, but the weather was evidently clearing for a fine day. When we had got about half a mile from the inn, where the path takes a curve round a depression in the mountain side, there came on a heavy shower. A party of Frenchmen were a little ahead of us. They did not like the rain, and returned to the inn. Just, however, at the point where we were, the rocks, which had rolled down in bygone ages from the summits above the depression, had, as you would have expected, lodged in the axis of the depression. At two or three steps from the path they are so piled up as that some project sufficiently to give shelter from rain. We clambered into one of these chance-formed cavities, and remained in it, quite protected, till the rain was over. While there, we observed how the interstices were being filled up by the decay of mosses and lichens. In about twenty minutes the sun was again bright, and there were no more clouds likely to make showers, and so, without any misgivings, we resumed our ascent over the flowery turf, interspersed with rocks. We soon came to a descending rib of the mountain. From this we first saw ice, that of the Viescher glacier. Upon this we turned our backs, and went up the mountain rib. The turf and flowers now began to die out. The little bright indigo Gentian became scarce. We then came upon loose rocky *débris* from the heights above, with a ravine between us and the summit of the Eggischhorn filled with this loose, naked *débris* and snow. We rounded the top of this ravine by a good path, in places very narrow, and like a rude rock staircase. And now we were close to the summit, which is composed entirely of a pile of clean slabs and blocks of rock, piled up into a steep mountain cone. It did not take us long to climb these clean slabs and blocks. Then we were on the summit— some dozen feet square, surrounded by a rail.

In the last part of the ascent we had seen nothing but the place where, at each step, we were to set our foot. Now the last step of the ascent had been taken, and one step more would carry us down, 2,000 feet, to the Great Aletsch glacier. All the great mountains, and the great ice-field of the Bernese Oberland, are before us. For some moments not a word is spoken. If at that moment we had had anything to say, we should have done as well if we had stayed at home.

Your first glance can only be at the great glacier so far beneath your feet. This, in your previous thoughts, had occupied the chief place in the scene you were coming to look upon, and have now reached. You wish at once to see what it is like, and to ascertain your relation to it. It is a mile wide, and looks precisely like what it is, a river of ice. All inequalities of surface are, from this height, effaced; and it is, to the eye, as level, though not as glassy, as water. And no river could have such clearly defined banks, for here they are mountains escarped as regularly as if the width and grades of the enormous channel had been cut by human hands working by plans and measurements. This is a conspicuous feature: having observed it, you then raise your eyes to make out the relations of the glacier to the mountains on either side of it, and beyond it. If you were to look across it, you would be looking west. But you do not begin by looking across it, because it is itself the great object; and, therefore, you look up it. You see, following it up, that it takes a gentle curve, a point or two to the west of north. For about five miles up it continues of about the same width. It then expands like an open fan. The fan-like expansion is a continuation of about five miles more. This expansion is, in reality, the great snow-field that is the chief feeder of the glacier; and which not only feeds it, but also by its own descent compacts and forces forward the glacier. Around the further side of the expanded fan stand, beginning on the left, the Mittaghorn, the Gletscherhorn, the Jungfrau, the Mönch, the Viescherhorn. These are more than ten miles off, but the distance appears much less, the objects being so large, and the atmosphere, at these heights, so clear. You see many black summits amid the snow, and many long, lofty scars; but of course the snow on the summits that are unpeaked, and on the sides that are not precipitous, preponderates in the scene. As these are the most prominent and interesting objects, you take mental photographs of them first. You then think of the Finsteraarhorn. You soon find him before you, due north: of course, to the right of the great glacier, and some little way back from it. By the air line he is seven miles from you. Between you and him is the Walliser Viescherhorn, and several subordinate peaks. Between the Walliser Viescherhorn and the Finsteraarhorn is the great snow-field that feeds the Viescher glacier we had a passing glimpse of as we were coming up. You now look across to the west side of the Great Aletsch. There you have before you the Aletschhorn, and an archipelago of connected peaks, entirely surrounded, and everywhere permeated, by snow-fields and glaciers. You see the confluence with the Great Aletsch of two of these subsidiary glaciers, the Mittler Aletsch, exactly opposite to you, and the Ober Aletsch, four miles lower down. Of course you see but little of the glacier to the back of this archipelago; that is the Lötschen, the outflow of which passes down the Lötschenthal to join the Rhone at Grampel. Two miles below the junction of the Ober Aletsch, the Great Aletsch itself terminates. You can see almost to its termination.

You have, then, from your lofty observatory, the whole of this marvellous scene spread out before you. No part of it is seen indistinctly. You have a full and clear view of the mountains supporting the snow-fields; the snow-fields feeding the glaciers; the lateral glaciers converging into the main-trunk glacier; the main-trunk glacier flowing by at your feet, a true river. Though the eye does not see the motion, the mind, aided by the eye, does. For you see that it is streaked with the *moraine* lines, which came in with the lateral glaciers, and which it is, obviously, carrying on; and you see the wave-like marks on its surface, more advanced, down stream, in the centre than on the sides, which tell you that the centre is moving faster than the sides. There is nothing to mar the unity, nothing wanting to the completeness, of this grand display of Alpine nature.

In the Märjelensee there is even something *de luxe*. The north side of the Eggischhorn is as precipitous as the west; in fact the north and west sides form a kind of right-angle; and you are standing, up in the air over this angle, at an elevation of 2,000 feet above the glacier, from which the summit takes its last rise—all but a vertical one on these sides. The north side is the south wall of a deep fissure, which connects the channel, the broad valley channel, of the Aletsch with that of the Viescher glacier. This fissure is considerably lower than the surface of the Aletsch glacier; but it is not of sufficient depth, or width, to allow any part of the Aletsch to pass into it, which also appears at this point to have its bearing on the opposite side. It, therefore, flows by this depression in cliffs of ice. Just where it passes the depression or fissure is a little lake, occupying the first part of the depression. Its waters, therefore, wash against the ice-cliffs of the Aletsch, which are its western boundary. The water being slightly warmer than the ice has a tendency to undermine it; and as the glacier has here lost its retaining wall of rock, and is somewhat expanded on the outer side of the curve it here makes, it comes to pass that masses of ice frequently detach themselves from the passing ice-cliffs of the glacier and fall into the lake; and then float off in the form of icebergs to the further end of the lake, from which point issues a little stream, the outflow of the lake, which connects it, when full, with the Viescher glacier. As looked down into from the top of the Eggischhorn, this little lake, with its green glass-smooth water, and white icebergs,— in part the cliffs from which they have fallen are of a tender blue,—and with the sober-coloured Alpine pasture occupying the rest of the depression and reaching down to the Viescher glacier, and with the black mountain on the north of it, is a sight that must be quite unique, and is as charming and interesting as unique.

But if not one of all the near objects we have just been looking at were visible from the Eggischhorn, still it would be worth climbing for the sake of the many distant objects it has to show you. On the north-east you may see the Tödi, and on the southwest Mont Blanc—neither, of course, on account of the distance, and of the intervening heights, very conspicuous. But all between—the many summits of the Zermatt Alps, Monte Leone, overlooking the Simplon, the Galenstock, and the summits of the St. Gothard group, are each grandly distinct; and show—which is what they are—like the nucleus, the ganglion, the structural centre of a Continent.

CHAPTER XIV.

THE RIEDER ALP—THE BELL ALP.

*Minds that have nothing to confer,
Find little to perceive.*—WORDSWORTH.

IN the afternoon we took up our staves for the Rieder Alp. The path runs horizontally along the flank of the range: in its seven miles, from the Eggischhorn Hotel to the hotel at Rieder, you lose about 1,000 feet of altitude. This is a delightful mountain walk, through open pastures and woods, neither of which are without the rose of the Alps, over glancing runnels, by many hay granges and *châlets*, and some small upland villages, and with mountains always in sight at varying distances. It was towards evening, and the cows were loitering along the pastures with heads homewards, and women and children were going out to bring them in.

We reached the Rieder Alp Hotel with still an hour or so of daylight to spare. It is situated on a little rising in the midst of a large irrigated prairie of some hundreds of acres. The hay had just been carried, and we walked straight over the sward to the hotel. The turf was as smooth as that of a garden lawn. There is no waste here. The surface of the prairie is kept quite level, without a stone upon it or a hole in it, in order that every stem and blade of grass might be cut close to the ground : and it is shorn so skilfully and uniformly that you cannot trace the swing of the scythe. We found the hotel full : the proprietor, however, procured for us two apartments in contiguous *châlets*; one for my wife and the small boy about 200 yards from the hotel, in the *châlet* next to the church, and one for me about a third of a mile off, at the head of the valley that lies beyond the hotel.

As it happened, we were in luck at finding the hotel full, for we were well satisfied with our rooms in the village and with their owners. The rooms of course were as clean as those to whom they belonged were proud of them. And as they were proud of them, they did for us all that it was in their power to do. They were very desirous of pleasing, and in turn were ready to be pleased, even with a word. We could not but have been interested with what we saw of their little resources, and of their little contrivances for making the most of them, and of the small matters which naturally were not small to them. There is about the inner life of a humble home a something, one may almost say of sanctity, which is not so apparent, at all events on the surface of things, in splendid mansions. Their splendour, somehow or other, seems a matter of course: it is taken for granted both by those who witness it and by those who possess it. It is transmuted money. There is no poetry in it: if hearts are moved by it it is not in that fashion, or to that issue, that it touches them. Quite different is it with the humble home. There every object seems to have a pleasing history. The care that is taken of it tells you how hard it had been to come by. You read in it a little tale of the labour, the frugality, the self-denial expended on its acquisition. It is a revelation of an inner life which you are the better for contemplating, and for sympathizing with. The Latin text from Holy Writ, carved in ornamented letters on a beam of my wife's room, was a glass window through which you might look into the hearts of this family, secluded from the world, and maintaining bravely and contentedly a hard struggle for existence up here in this lofty Alpine glen.

I did not inquire, but inferred, as I preferred to do, from the aspect of things in the rooms themselves, their stoves, furniture, and ornamentation, setting these by the side of the appearance of the rest of the house, that each of them was the guest chamber, the reception room of the *châlet* to which it belonged; and that in the summer they were hired by the proprietor of the contiguous hotel, to be converted, when his visitors overflowed his own house, into bedrooms. At all events we saw that he had to send bedding to the nearer one; and in the more distant one, that which

I occupied, the bed had to be prepared after my arrival. I guessed that the *châlet* near the church was the house of one of the chief peasants of Rieder. The one I was in evidently did not belong to a peasant. I reached it when daylight was fast fading. The good woman of the house was profuse in reiterating her excuses for things not being better. The good man, taught by experience, bided his time; and, when it came, made the same apologies in fewer words and with more deliberation. He weighed his words. She was more femininely impulsive; he was more masculinely thoughtful and restrained. At last, as far as her resources allowed, things were arranged to her satisfaction, and she left the room. He lighted his pipe. I took a light from him; and a conversation commenced which proved a long one. He was a man not far short of 60 years of age, and not of the hardy, weatherworn, out-of-doors-battling class. He appeared more like one who had been engaged in trade: and this might have been the case, for he told me that he did not live up here, but only came in summer for two or three months for change of air. Nor was he more robust in mind than in body. We talked about the condition and manner of life of the peasants, and about the value of property on Rieder Alp and in the valley below. These things he seemed to contemplate rather from the outside. He did not think that the people were the better morally, not even materially, for the increase that had lately taken place in the value of land and of its produce. He was well-to-do: still his tone was that of a man who feels that he has not been able to turn life and opportunities to so much account as some of his neighbours have done: or who is refusing to accommodate himself to the new conditions of business, though he sees that others are prospering by doing so, and that he is losing ground by not doing it; or who has had losses and disappointments. Night had now settled down on the valley, and no sound broke the stillness outside but the bell occasionally of an unquiet cow or goat that had not yet composed itself to rest in the neighbourhood of the *châlet* where it had been milked. I observed to him that here the goats were of a peculiarly marked breed. Their bodies and hindquarters are white, and their heads, necks, and forequarters black. 'That,' he replied, 'is nothing: merely a fancy.' He was, then, too rigid a utilitarian to have any respect for fancies. No matter what the subject of conversation, or how it might have been dealt with, it always, without fail, by some by-path or other, brought him back to the same conclusion, 'All the world is changing. Everyday there is something new.' In this *châlet* there were no young people —there were in the other—and they it is that create light, and keep alive hope in a house. But for them interest in this world and its concerns might flag. It was past 9 o'clock when our conversation ended, and we wished each other good night.

My room was ceiled and wainscoted with new-varnished deal. On the walls were hanging three maps —of the World, of Europe, and of Switzerland, and half-a-dozen coloured prints of the chase. The series commenced with the hunter receiving, as he sallied forth, fully equipped, the adieux and good wishes of his family. Then came, in separate pieces, the death of the bear, the wild boar, the hare, and the fox—no chamois, our *chasseur* was got up too elaborately for that. The last gave his return, when the family inspect the trophies of his prowess, and offer their congratulations. There were also suspended on the walls two watches. These, from their size were conspicuous objects: probably they had for generations been used only for ornament. They may have belonged to the time when the bear and the wild boar were common in the Valais. There was, too, against the wall, a frame of two shelves for books. Upon this were piles of two weekly papers, one illustrated and one political: both calculated for the meridian of the Valais. They were carefully folded and preserved. Their wisdom, more particularly as it had cost money, ought to be preserved; at all events till it weighed enough for the grocer at Brieg to give something for it. By the side of the hoarded newspapers were some half-dozen very small religious books. On these was the impress of Einsiedln. There was no mirror in the room, and as I saw that the washing-table and its apparatus were brought in, I claim these facts as supports of my theory that the room was really a sitting-room.

August 28.—Rose as early as usual, but, as we were this morning not to breakfast till eight o'clock, had some time to look about me. My *châlet* was charmingly situated. It was above, and out of sight of the hotel—to the left of it, if you turned your back to the hotel. It was at the head of the valley of the Rieder Alp. Above it were the summits of the Riederhorn; a craggy ridge: but immediately behind this house the crags were missing. Probably what had made the valley was what had also removed them. Where they were missing, about a quarter of a mile above the house, was the Pass on the way to the Bell Alp. As I looked out of my window, I looked down a grassy ravine, not of the narrow, deep, rocky, precipitous kind. On the left side of it, as far down as you see, it is all mown smooth. In the central descent, which is that straight before you, are scattered some dozen or so detached *châlets* and hay granges. Each is on some little rocky knob or prominence, a few feet high, to lift it out of the way of the storm water, that in heavy rains comes down the valley. About half a mile down, the valley takes a turn to the right. This prevents your seeing anything more of it; and also shuts out the view, which there, otherwise, would be down into the main valley of the Rhone. To the right is unmown pastured grass, with a dark pine wood below the pasture, and the battlemented crags of the Rieder ridge above it. As you can see nothing of the Rhone valley below, the grassy and wooded slopes of this side meet, to the eye, the flanks of the opposite mountains. In these flanks, just opposite to you, so that you look into them, are some long smooth ravines, or yawning fissures, of naked slate-coloured rock. Above these is a ridge of mountains of the same material and colour. As these opposite ravines and ridges have no vegetation, and are smooth, they look just like the pasteboard mountains one has seen in dioramas, and in the scenery of pantomimes. This is how they show on the upper half. Their lower half is striated, and dotted with dark pine woods and yellowish green prairies. The yellowish tinge was partly the result of the dryness of the season. Behind these scenic pasteboard mountains is Monte Leone, and a little to the right of it the Great Fletschhorn; both more than half covered with snowfields. Between the two you see the zigzags of the Simplon Pass, descending through forests to the cultivated plain of Brieg. Brieg itself is not visible, but some part of the plain is. The view of Brieg is intercepted by the right side of our valley, on which, below the pasture, is the dark pine wood. We have just been looking to the south and right of the pasteboard mountains. If we now turn to the left, we look along the range of the opposite side of the Rhone, streaked and patched with snow, which the sun is now just getting well above, for you were up before he was over their tops; and you see that he is promising, at all events, a fine morning.

There must be some who would find the quiet of a sojourn at Rieder Alp preferable to the crowding of the Eggischhorn, and of the Bell Alp. As to the glacier, the great sight of this neighbourhood, that, of course, is not visible from the Rieder, as it is from the Bell Alp; but then, in compensation, it is more accessible. Nor is the view from the Rieder so good as from the Bell Alp; but still it is good. The Bell Alp, and the Eggischhorn, are both within visiting distance, that is to say, you may go to either of them for an early dinner, and return in the evening. I do not mean that I should like, myself, to stay there. I like staying nowhere, except at home. When I am travelling I like to be moving on. It was for that that I left home. It seems to me insufferable to return in the evening to the place I left in the morning. The same distance in walking would have carried me to some new place: that is to say, I might have had something additional at the same cost of time and exertion. But there are many who, on this point, would not agree with me; and they, I think, might spend a week pleasantly at Rieder Alp.

This quiet place might also be recommended as an experiment to those—on the supposition that they mean what they say—who are in the habit, in season and out of season, of announcing their want of sympathy with the ideas and tone of mind of their travelling fellow-countrymen. It may perhaps be conceded to such fault-finders that they are not quite without materials for getting up a plausible case. Speaking generally, we do not show to advantage when on our travels. What is required for making a traveller agreeable to his fellow-travellers, in their short chance meetings, is versatility, adaptability, *bonhomie*, *savoir faire*, the art of conversation, particularly the power of making anyone you may happen to converse with for a few minutes, believe that you are pleased with him, or, perhaps, and which may be the easier task, of making him pleased with himself. These, however, are qualities for which we are not remarkably conspicuous. For some of them we have not even English expressions. But deficiencies of this kind, though they come out most prominently in the rubs, and collisions, and close contacts of travel, pre-existed at home: our objectors, therefore, ought to have been familiar enough with the thing ; and it is, after all, but a small matter to fash oneself about. Besides, our want of a provision of such small change may not be altogether unbalanced by the possession of some pieces of a coinage which, though not always available at the moment, is yet of sterling value.

Another of their allegations, and it is one on which they lay much stress, is that they find their travelling fellow-countrymen haunted by the idea that they must assert, or maintain, a position. For this, too, there may be some ground, for it is only what might be expected in a state of society such as ours, in which the endeavour is made, illogically, to work the hierarchical principle of rank conjointly with the democratic principle of wealth; and in which, at the moment, that which feeds the democratic principle is rapidly increasing. If wealth and rank were preponderantly found united in the same persons, as was the case some centuries ago, there would be no difficulty in working the two principles simultaneously. In fact they would themselves have entered into combination. But as things are at present, each of the two principles has its own representatives, and these are somewhat in antagonism. They have almost been drawn off into opposing camps. And the representatives of the democratic principle (socially democratic) are, numerically, in the ascendant. From this emanate attempts as naturally as light from the sun, to maintain, or to assert, a position; and as these attempts are made by Englishmen, it is only to be expected that they will very frequently participate rather more of the national *fortiter in re*, than of what should be the traveller's *suaviter in modo*. It is not in us to work the two principles side by side with the ease and smoothness and social dexterity of Italians or Frenchmen. Our objectors then, having, in the close contacts and promiscuous gatherings of travellers such as we fall in with at the Eggischhorn and Bell Alp Hotels, sometimes to witness, perhaps sometimes to deal with, this kind of thing, speak of it as a grievance. But may not its being annoying to them arise from their

S

ideas being too Utopian? They may, from their not having been sufficiently 'tried and tutored in the world,' be expecting impossibilities.

They have, too, imbibed, or affect to have imbibed, the foreign estimate of the ordinary travelling Englishman, which generally assumes the form of an accusation that our ideas are in some way or other narrow, insular, and uncosmopolitan; for example, that we are possessed with the idea that nature has constituted us the moral police of the race, that is to say, a police for enforcing on the race English ideas; and hence our frequent announcements that so much of what we see everywhere is 'lamentable' and 'miserable;' that every foreigner we fall in with is likely to be a rogue —honesty being supposed to be an exclusively English virtue; that people are everywhere dirty—cleanliness also being assumed to be exclusively English; that the rest of the world do not understand their own business—knowledge of this kind being peculiar to this island of ours; that all other people are in a conspiracy against the great English race, and have, to their own loss, wilfully blinded themselves to its merits, and general superiority to the rest of mankind. There is probably some ground for allegations of this kind too, and it would be better if there were not. But larger experience of the world will in such matters teach us what we ought to think, and what we ought, and ought not, to say. In the mean time it will do us no harm to hear how people talk about us : perhaps it may do us some good.

If, then, you are one of those who believe in these multifarious shortcomings and accusations, and are ruffled at what you take to be exhibitions of what is laid to our charge, you will do well to keep clear of such places as the Eggischhorn and Bell Alp Hotels, for in them you will be brought into closest contact with your travelling fellow countrymen. It may, however, be suggested, that if you did yourself possess the good qualities you think ought to be found in others, and were free from the failings you comment on in them, you probably would not notice, as a ground for annoyance, either the absence of the one or the presence of the other in those you meet with in your travels. You would take the world as it comes, and turn it to your own account. What prompts your objections is, perhaps unknown to yourself, the amount of negative electricity in your own system, for from this there are few Englishmen who are wholly exempt. If this be your case to any considerable degree, for your visit to the Great Aletsch glacier try for your head-quarters the Rieder Alp. If you find it dull, then go on to the Eggischhorn, or Bell Alp, taking with you the thought that friendliness and tolerance, like their opposites, are repaid in kind.

August 28.—At 9 A.M. we set out for the Bell Alp.

Having passed my last night's lodging, we were, a few minutes afterwards, on the crest of the ridge. Once on the top, we were soon in sight of the great glacier. To reach it we had to pass through a somewhat dilapidated wood of ancient pines. This is the Aletschwald. Most of the woods of the Valais are dilapidated; and in accordance with Valaisan practice we found here a flock of goats—of the black-jacketed strain—browsing on the undergrowth, and thus preventing a succession of young trees, to take, in their turn, the place of the old ones. As we were passing through the flock, I saw one, reaching over from a rock above, bite off the leader of a thrifty young birch. We were not long in descending to the glacier. As there might be some need of help on the ice, and certainly would be in the ascent on the other side, Ott had asked for an assistant porter. In crossing the ice there are no difficulties; the passage took us a short half-hour. You see no more of crevasses than just about enough to make you think that you had better not, through carelessness, slip into one of them. But as you look up the glacier, you see that half a mile or so above you it is composed entirely of narrow ridges with crevasses between, so that it would be quite impossible, I suppose, either to ascend it or to cross it thereabouts. On the path we took we saw crossing, at the same time, men, women, and children, a flock of goats, a herd of cows, and a horse. It is interesting to observe how unfailingly in travelling over such places, that is, where the way is difficult or dangerous, animals arrange themselves in Indian file. Few people will doubt that there is reasoning in this as well as reason. The motive in the quadruped is the same as in the Indian. Those behind understand that it is likely to be safer for them to go where one of their kind has just passed in safety, than to take the chances of what may lie on the right or left. This is an act of reasoning: it is so in the same sense in which is the choice, made in an instant by a cat, when attacked by a dog, of the best position for defence the locality offers. In both instances there is comparison, and selection for a purpose. That it is done always, instantly, and rightly, does not take the act out of the category of reasoning.

This leads one to ask whether there is any proof that the faculty of reason in man differs specifically from the faculty of reason in the lower animals? If there be no specific difference between the senses, and the vital functions of the two, that alone would, *primâ facie*, be some ground for supposing that there is no specific difference between them as respects the faculty of reason, and this would seem to throw the burden of proof on those who might be disposed to assert that there is such a difference. In reply, however, to their arguments it might be observed that reason in both appears to have the same purpose, and to act in the same way, that of adapting action by the way of deduction from observation and experience to useful ends. The differences in the results are obviously enormous, but perhaps those may be accounted for without supposing any difference in the faculty itself. For instance, the possession of language multiplies and enlarges the uses of reason almost indefinitely. And then, furthermore, the inequalities of condition that exist among mankind determine very largely the degree in which each individual shall use his reason. And, with respect to these inequalities, it is not impossible but that all that exist, and that ever have existed among mankind, may be traced up ultimately to the possession of tools. It may therefore be argued, perhaps with more than plausibility, that if mankind were deprived utterly of language and of tools, the members of any community of men would be reduced among themselves to the same uniformity of level as is seen among the members of a community of any kind of sociable animals; and that then it would be hard to imagine any way in which the reasoning powers exhibited by these dumb, toolless, and among themselves indistinguishable men, would differ from the reasoning powers exhibited by the community of sociable animals. This supposition, if it be well grounded, would not at all lower mankind nor at all elevate the lower animals. It would leave both just where they are. It would only be, as far as it went, a right way of regarding certain phenomena. Upon this subject it ought to be kept in mind that the endless inequalities of condition among mankind oblige every individual to live, more or less, in a way different from others, and that differences of this kind increase as civilization advances; and that this may account for the fact that civilized man has greater powers of adaptation, and is less the child of habit than the savage. If mankind, from want of tools and language, had to spend their lives, like the lower animals, in doing a few simple acts always in the same way, then their way of doing these few simple acts would probably, as is the case with the lower animals, become transmissive, that is, instinctive. Man may be supposed to have the same capacity for forming instincts as the bee and the beaver, but in him the tendency to form them may be counteracted by the consequences of the use of language and of tools, which are incessantly varying human life as respects both its wants and the ways in which they are supplied.

You see a great deal in passing, of the indescribable clear blue of glacier ice—a tender, ethereal blue. Just as pearly pink, fiery red, fresh green, and imperial purple give rise within us to correspondent emotions, almost ideas, so does this glacier-ice blue. You have been admitted to look upon what has in it no smirch, no grossness, no warmth of earth—a purity not of this world. The man who can pass by this blue translucency without emotion, as if he had only looked upon a piece of blue serge, is of a hard heart and of a dull brain. His blood is thick. He is a lumpish Bœotian, a one-eyed Cyclops, a mentally distorted Caliban.

At 11 A.M. we reached the Bell Alp Hotel. It is, I suppose, about 1,500 feet above the glacier, and about a mile back from it. From the seats on the north-east of the house you look up a long reach of it. But now you see no blue. Of that I have just endeavoured to give my impressions: I must now do the same for the glacier as seen from this point. For all the world it looks like a grand highway in a vast mountain cutting. So regular are its surface and its sides, that they appear to have been the engineering, we will not say of man, but of a race of giants that must have once been on the earth. It has, however, the appearance of being still used by their pigmy successors, who never could have constructed it for themselves. They have retained it for their great north road—not the great north road of an island of no very considerable dimensions, but the great north road of a great continent. And it is now winter—for so it appears to be on the road as you are looking upon it—and the great road has been buried for some weeks in snow. And over this snow there has been a great deal of traffic; for it is the mid continental road. And this traffic of a great continent has beaten the snow very hard and much besmudged it. And there had, too, been a previous deep fall of snow, which it had been necessary to heap up in the middle of the road. This heaped up snow shows as a long dirty ridge. This is the great central *moraine*.

After you have seen it at the Eggischhorn much nearer, and much cleaner, and in combination with the snow-fields that feed it, this view, which only gives you a mile or two of the lower part of the glacier, does not much interest you from what is actually before your eyes. It only becomes interesting from what the mind supplies—from the interpretation the mind puts upon the intelligence telegraphed to it through the eye. As to that dirt upon the surface, the mind sees how it came there, and that it is now being carried down before you to aid in forming fruitful valleys. As to the tender ethereal blue below the dirt, that is still visible to the searching mental eye which sees beneath the dirt. The mind asks how far down below the dirt does that blue reach? None can say. There are, however, superficially, twenty miles of it, all of it a mile at least wide, much of it a great deal more, stretching away beyond what the bodily eye is beholding; and all this mass of solid yet ethereal blue was compacted out of little aery-light flakes of snow, and that was constructed out of little globules of floating vapour, and that had been pumped up from the far Atlantic by the sun, acting from a distance of many tens of millions of miles. And as this river of ethereal blue, so solid, so long, so broad, so deep, gravitates from the region of perpetual snow, aided, perhaps, by the irresistible expansion of ever-recurring internal congelation, it will gradually pass into another form, and go to fill Lake Leman, and to feed the Rhine, on its way back to the Atlantic, only to go through again the same process. What a drama of nature passes before the mind as you sit on that bench alongside the hotel, and look upon that Titan-engineered, deep-sunk, snow-buried, traffic-beaten, dirt-streaked road!

And so it is with everything: the mountain, the plain, the city, the *châlet*, the flower, the grasshopper. At first, and to the mechanical bodily eye, they are but unintelligible symbols and figures. It is the mind that enables us to know what the symbols and figures stand for. If your thought has not made out, or endeavoured to make out, with respect to these objects, what they are in themselves, how they came to be what they are, what they do, what is stirring within them, what are their relations to each other and to the great whole, then they are to you so many nothings; no more than so many strokes and dashes and points in nature's notation, not understood. And just so, too, with men and women, than whom there is, after all, nothing better in this world. If we cannot read them—and it is the right reading that enables us to sympathize with them—then they are to us only so much organized matter, consuming so much bread and meat, occupying so much space, and often in our way, standing where we wish to stand; in the eyes indeed of many, organized matter so heinously endowed as to call for only dislike, contempt, and hard words. It is the savant and right, and if savant and right, then kindly, if not always quite pleasing, reading, even when what we have to read is something no better than men and women, than interests, and is good for heart and head. But Worldly Wise, who understands men and women thoroughly, perhaps through what he is able to understand of himself, is of a different way of thinking. 'What if the men and women are good for nothing ? How then ?'

'Flowers are sometimes aberrant : still they ought to have been, and might have been, things of beauty. Their aberrancy is their misfortune, not their fault ; the result of causes in the soil, the atmosphere, the parent plant, or something or other not originally in the flower itself.'

'But how when the aberrancy has obliterated the flower, and nothing remains but unsightly monstrosity ? A plague on such monstrosity.'

'Some, perhaps, of the monstrosity is in your own perverted vision. And what there is of it in aberrant humanity cannot be mended by dislike, contempt, and hard words, but only by setting right the conditions of its growth.'

From this point, your seat near the hotel, you may observe that the glacier, as far as you can see it, is bordered on both sides by a perfectly clean margin of loose stones on the foot of either mountain. This margin appears to reach up from the glacier to the wood or turf or lichen-stained rock above, whichever it may be, for a space of two or three hundred feet. Its line is quite unbroken and uniform in height on both sides. It is a very marked feature when observed from this point. Of course all these are moraine stones and rocks, and are now actually on the marginal ice of the glacier, or have been deposited somewhat above its margin, at times when the glacier, having been flowing at a higher level than at present, was again subsiding.

From another seat, in front of the hotel, you look down on Brieg, 5,000 feet beneath you. Beyond Brieg you have a better view than at Rieder Alp of Monte Leone, and of the Fletschhorn, with the zigzags of the Simplon in the wooded depression between them. If you turn your eye to the right, or south-west, you will have before you, some twenty-five miles off, the Zermatt Alps. This morning, when we first saw them, there was a level sea of unbroken cloud resting on their shoulders, which concealed everything below. The substructure was entirely lost, and the snowy summits were floating on the sea of cloud.

A storm swept by us in the afternoon, at about the same hour as the one we had witnessed two days previously at the Eggischhorn. Its character was different. It came on with so violent a squall of wind, that some ladies who were caught in it found it difficult to get back to the hotel. There was not much rain at our height, or just where we were. The clouds were not dense; so that through them we could see the near mountains, looking indistinct and weird, like the ghosts of mountains. But the most interesting effect of this storm was one that was brought about just opposite to us, and exactly over Brieg. For more than an hour two squadrons of clouds came sailing along, on exactly opposite courses; one down the valley to Brieg, and the other up the valley to Brieg. But over Brieg they never met. They were continuously and unfailingly absorbed and dissipated before they came into collision. This I supposed was caused by a large column of heated air ascending incessantly from the heated plain of Brieg.

A word about these two hotels on the Eggischhorn and Bell Alp. Their hard-beset landlords thoroughly understand their business. They also understand their customers. In your dealings with them it is of no manner of use to put yourself out or to bluster. They are quite familiar with all that kind of thing, and know exactly how to dispose of it. These are just the problems they have to solve every day, for some months every year. How are a score or so of persons more than the house was constructed to hold, some of them very impatient, some of them not very rational, to be accommodated without accommodation, and to be taken in without being imposed upon? All of this score are persons who have come up, either in the teeth of the answers they received to their telegrams; or who dated their telegrams from places they were on the point of leaving, and so could not receive the answers sent to them; or who telegraphed at the moment they were about to commence the ascent; or who had never thought of using, or who had wilfully abstained from using the wires. Some, though they appear to have dropped from the clouds, appear, nevertheless, to be still up in them. Our countrymen, we all know—and we pride ourselves on its being so—like to go where they will find difficulties, and much that will be disagreeable. But then it is not in logical, though it may be in human concatenation, that they should be annoyed at finding what they are in search of. The masters of these two hotels show their knowledge of the world, and their good sense, by the ease with which they dispose of all such cases.

As to charges; if you will only consider the height at which you are up in, or above, the clouds, and that everything you may want—milk is the single exception—has to be brought up on horseback or on men's backs from the valley, and that each journey is a day's work, you will not look upon them as excessive.

The moral of the whole is, that in the case of many, a visit to the Eggischhorn, or Bell Alp, is a dearly bought pleasure, if to them a pleasure at all. Impatient elderly gentlemen, and strong-minded ladies of whatever age, who know what they are entitled to, and will insist on having it, ought to consider beforehand whether, in their cases, the pleasure will be worth the price.

Of course this does not apply to those who can foresee what, under the circumstances, is to be expected ; and who are not in the habit of expecting impossibilities ; and who have imagination enough to see things from other points of view than the single one of what they themselves, at the moment, want ; and who can submit to paying in discomfort, or in any other unavoidable way, the necessary price for what to them will be well worth it. Some even of the *Intransigentes* of travel, whose manner it is to kick against the pricks, will not think that the price was too high, when, at home, they look back to what they saw at the Eggischhorn, and at the Bell Alp.

CHAPTER XV.

BRIEG—THE VALAIS—LAUSANNE AND GIBBON—DETAILS
AND PLAN OF THE EXCURSION—CONCLUSION.

> Accuse not nature ; she hath done her part :
> Do thou but thine ; and be not diffident
> Of wisdom : she deserts thee not, if thou
> Dismiss not her.—MILTON.

AUGUST 29.—We had thought of ascending the Sparrenhorn this morning : but now the aspect of things forbad such an undertaking. The Bell Alp was in the clouds. At such altitudes this means damp, rawness, shivering : nothing to see, and nothing to do. At 10 o'clock things were no better, and there was no prospect of their getting better ; and so we decided to say our adieu to our good host, and to go down to Brieg. He had done for us all he could, having put up for us three beds in what had been intended for the *fumoir* of his hotel, but which cannot, in the height of the season, be afforded for such a purpose.

Brieg was reached in three hours. A descent of so many, it is five thousand, feet must be more or less good, and Alpine in character. Although it may not have anything particularly striking, still it must have upland pastures and pine woods, rills and rocks, prairies, first without and then with orchards : and there must always be mountains in sight, besides the one you are descending.

This was our last walk. In the conclusion of what has for some time been giving pleasure there is sadness : and more so when the pleasure has been of the stirring, and not of the Sybarite kind. If at the moment we had thought of the Sybarite's case, we should have said that he had no business to be a Sybarite, and was rightly served. Certainly the entrance into Brieg, after the Eggischhorn and the Bell Alp, appeared heinously lowland and hatefully alluvial. Within the town the shops, the pavements, the diligences, the churches, the Post Office proclaimed to us that our delightful wanderings had only brought us back again to what seemed for the moment like the pestilent prose of life. For us henceforth would be no more summons from the sun, watched for, and obeyed with a ready mind, to meet him on the mountain side ; no more, the day through, should we walk before him ; no more should we contemplate with contentment the glories of his withdrawal to give the needed rest to man and beast. For us no more trudging on, hour after hour, to see we knew not precisely what, with the feeling that, though it might not be particularly worth seeing when we had come to it, still that it was well worth while going to see it. No more grand views of snow-fields and ice-rivers. No more of nature's battlemented and pinnacled ramparts and castles far above us while the storm was raging far below us. ·No more pleasant halts at mountain *châlets*, or on the turf by the huddling streamlet, in such haste to get down to the valley. No more turning into wayside inns, not knowing what we were to find in them except a welcome. No more hunger and thirst. No more ice-cold draughts from sparkling springs. Our Switzer days and doings had now ended; and we were returning to regular hours, regular work, morning calls, eight o'clock dinners, and the manners and customs of the latter part of the third quarter of the nineteenth century.

In the afternoon, as we walked along the embankment of the Saltine, we cast some longing lingering looks on the Bell Alp and the snow about it; and, too, on the opposite snow fields, right and left of the Simplon. After this, while loafing about the streets, we found ourselves opposite the shop of the Barber of Brieg, whose record is in the 'Month' of last year— the undisputed monarch, in the barber department, of all that he surveys in Brieg. There was no resisting the desire to see him again: at all events he was my only acquaintance in the place. His door, as I opened it, rang his shop-bell, but he was not there to hear it. This was what I had expected. I should have been disappointed had it been otherwise. ·The woman, however, who keeps the little grocery shop opposite, and with whom last year I had had, seated on the bench by her doorside, half an hour's talk, while her bibulous neighbour was being looked for, heard the bell and came out of her shop. There was a smile on her face to imply that the little event of last year was not at all forgotten. Indeed, she looked as if she had been expecting me, and was glad to see me. In anticipation, it must have been, of my turning up that evening, he had told her in which of his resorts he might be found. It was close by, and he was soon unearthed. Of course, I thought it better to be shaved now by my old acquaintance than to have to shave myself early to-morrow morning. The good woman, who had not forgotten that morning of last year, will henceforth be able to add to the weight of metal in her gibes the evening of this day.

August 30.—Were off by the first diligence for Sierre, where we were to take the train *en correspondance* for Lausanne. The day was bright; there was none of the dust of last year; and the drive down the valley was pleasant. Was it not the valley of the Rhone? And were there not the lateral confluent valleys to note, with thoughts of what they led up to and of where their streams came from? And then there was the aspect of things in the valley itself; the evident air of neglect and of waste of opportunity. We could see that we were now in the most improvable and least improved part of Switzerland. We passed through tracts in which every particle of *humus* had been washed out of and floated off from the soil by the permitted overflow of the freshets of the Rhone; and through others which were still willow thickets and marshes. If the Rhone were embanked, as is the Aare, the Linth, and many other Swiss streams, all this land might be reclaimed: the shingle and sand, now naked, might soon be converted into goodly meadows by spreading over them a little earth, and by irrigation, for irrigation in Switzerland will produce good grass anywhere. And besides, if the Rhone were embanked, then there would be everywhere the possibility of utilizing its stream for spinning and weaving. And this will come here, the priests notwithstanding, for it will come in every valley of Switzerland. It is 'the manifest destiny' of the country. The first step will be the continuance of the railway to Brieg, and through the Simplon. This will bring cotton, silk, and wool to be worked up, and will take it to market when worked up. It will bring the machinery, and the iron wanted for repairs, and the coal that will be required both in making the repairs, and for supplementing any deficiency in the water power. All this can be done, and will be done. And then those of the population, as with the land, who are improvable will be improved; and those among the former who are not improvable will be improved from the scene.

Another advantage that will result from the

coming state of things will be that the larger, and busier, and more active-minded population of the future will be better fed than the existing population. In exchange for the fruits of their labour they will then have brought to them good wheaten bread and beef and mutton. At present the staple food here is, as you see, maize and potatoes, somewhat fortified and corrected by their acid wine and rough brandy. This is not the kind of food that such a climate requires. It enfeebles mind as well as body; and these enfeeblements include that of morality.

The history of these matters is instructive, and ought to be noted. Of course there must have been a time, before the advent of maize and potatoes, when wheat was largely cultivated in the Lower Valais. Doubtless the yield was not great, and what there was must have been of very inferior quality. Still home-grown wheat must then have been the mainstay of the people. Maize and potatoes, when time brought them, were found to be more productive, and more to be relied upon in such a locality: and so they have superseded wheat almost entirely. In some other districts, which, while they are more industrious, have also attained to the advantage of easy access to wheat markets, the culture of grass has superseded that of wheat. Their inhabitants, by converting their abundant grass crops into cheese and beef, have obtained the means, from the same extent of ground, and with less labour, for procuring a larger amount of wheat, and of far better quality, than they could have grown at home. This is precisely what was done in the case of the few vineyards which once were cultivated in the south of England. There was a time, when from their immature grapes was produced, at a great cost, very bad wine. It would then, from the deficiencies and uncertainties of transit, have been very difficult to have got wine from beyond sea. Besides, too, there was not much to be given in exchange for it. But the time came when it would cost little to convey from beyond sea what was better than the home produce; and when there were markets for the wheat, and meat, and wool that could be produced at home; and this gave also the means for purchasing the better produce of foreign vineyards. English vineyards, therefore, and their sour, costly, and uncertain produce disappeared. The power of the Rhone at present, like the unutilized powers of an uncultivated and unregulated intellect, not only goes to waste, but also does harm: when it shall have been turned to account it will—railway communication also by that time having come to be more fully carried out, and the principles of free trade more generally understood and acted on—give the millers and bakers of the Valais the means for making their purchases in the corn markets of Germany, France, and Italy: and the people of the Valais will be all the better for it.

In the Valais, as elsewhere, throughout our excursion, I noticed how great had been this year, in Switzerland, the failure of the fruit crop. This had been caused by a very severe late frost, the effect of which we had felt in the same way, almost to an equal extent, in many parts of England: though here, of course, a diminution of that crop is a matter of comparatively little moment. Except in the valley of the Tessin, on the south side of the Alps, I did not see any fruit on the walnut trees, though I looked fo it whenever I passed one. As in Switzerland they are grown largely for the sake of the oil expressed from the nut—the produce of a fair-sized tree is, in average years, worth about six francs—the loss on this item alone of the fruit crop was very considerable. I observed that the foliage of the fruitless trees was unusually luxuriant, and that the foliage of those that had fruit in the valley of the Tessin was not by half so abundant, nor was what they had of so dark a green as that of the barren trees to the north. It was just the reverse with the cherry trees. They also had been smitten by the frost, and they had been hit so hard that many were dead, but nowhere, except on the Rigi, did I see any with healthy foliage. The crop, too, of apples and pears was sadly deficient. Most trees of these kinds were entirely without fruit. Those which had some fruit were, as it was generally easy to see, sheltered in some way or other, frequently by some lofty, partially overhanging walnut tree.

Fruit enters so largely into the total of Swiss industry, that we can readily suppose that the late frosts and snowfalls of 1873 must have cost the peasants some millions of francs.

We reached Lausanne late in the afternoon. Our first care was to get our heavy baggage from the Post Office. I had had mine with me for only so short a time at the commencement of the Month, and had made so little use of any part of it, that I was now almost disposed to think that it would have been as well had I not encumbered myself with it. As, however, one cannot tell what may occur in the way of weather, and of possible mishaps of many kinds, it is as well, to some extent, to be provided with duplicates and supernumeraries. The best limitation perhaps is that of what you can easily lift, and carry yourself, in and out of railway stations.

August 31.—Sunday.—We attended morning service in the chief church of the town. If anything can be inferred from a single sermon, one might suppose, from what we heard this morning, that the Swiss Reformed Church at Lausanne is in the stage in which we were when Blair's Sermons were in high estimation and were passing through many editions. In the afternoon we formed part of an English congregation that was addressed by an English clergyman in the same church.

In the evening we went down to Ouchy to walk,

on the margin of the lake, in the beautiful grounds of the Beaurivage Hotel. We saw in several places the water rising and subsiding through holes it had lately formed in the pavement of the marginal terrace walk. It had been able to effect this in consequence of the level of the lake being this year so much higher than usual that the wash of its waves was able to undermine what had hitherto been out of their reach. Was this elevation of the lake caused by the unusual amount of snow that fell late last spring, at the time when so much injury was done to the fruit trees? There is everywhere this year more snow on the mountains than usual. This must make the streams also, that descend from them, fuller than usual, which must therefore bring more water than usual into the lake. There are, however, in this lake some elevations and subsidences of its level, which cannot be accounted for by such causes as that to which I have just referred.

September 1.—In the forenoon we walked on the fine terrace to the west of the Hotel Gibbon. After a time I took a seat upon a bench on the gravel beneath the lofty elms. Before me was the lake. On the two or three acres of grass behind the trees were some English lads playing at football. I seated myself on the bench, I suppose because I was thinking of Gibbon, and wished to look upon the view he had often looked upon. I repeated, as he gives them in his autobiographical memoirs, two of the most interesting passages in literary history :[1] one being that in which he records that the idea of his great work 'first started to his mind at Rome on the 15th of October, 1764, as he sat musing among the ruins of the Capitol, while the bare-footed fryars were singing vespers in the Temple of Jupiter ;' and the other that in which he describes its completion, within a few months of twenty-three years afterwards, near the spot on which I was seated : ' It was on the day, or rather night of the 27th of June, 1787, between the hours of eleven and twelve, that I wrote the last lines of the last page, in a summer-house in my garden. After laying down my pen I took several turns in a *berceau* or covered walk of acacias, which commands a prospect of the country, the lake, and the mountains. The air was temperate, the sky was serene, the silver orb of the moon was reflected from the waters, and all nature was silent. I will not dissemble the first emotions of joy on the recovery of my freedom, and, perhaps, the establishment of my fame. But my pride was soon humbled, and a sober melancholy was spread over my mind, by the idea that I had taken an everlasting leave of an old and agreeable companion, and that whatsoever might be the future fate of my history, the life of the historian must be short and precarious.' It was a right instinct that led him to

---

[1] Gibbon's Miscellaneous Works, vol. i, pp. 198 and 255.

record both the conception of the idea, and the conclusion, of his great work. M. Guizot, no mean judge of such work, says that it is the only true book in the English language; the only book we have which contains a grand idea worthily worked out. Regarded in this light it almost stands in a class of its own, as the grandest piece of literary work the human mind has ever elaborated. It is great in its subject; human history supplies nothing greater. It is great in the vast amount of labour expended in preparing and shaping the materials requisite for its construction. It is great in its style. It is great in the breadth of view it takes, and in the philosophic spirit with which it is animated. Such a combination of the sources of literary greatness, and each element in so high a degree, are not to be found in any other book. Other books may be named which have given a greater amount of, and more intense pleasure. The Homeric poems doubtless did this, when they formed well-nigh all the intellectual food of the most sensitive-minded of all people. Others may have done more to enrich thought and to humanize hearts. This the dramas of Shakespeare have done: which show, too, the fertility and creative power of the human mind to a degree as far beyond Gibbon's capacity as was the philosophic insight of Aristotle or Bacon. And other historians, as Thucydides, may have had more appreciative sagacity for dealing with the characters of those who cross the scene of their pages. Still there is in

Gibbon's book a comprehensiveness, a massiveness, a grandeur, alike of subject and of treatment, which make it one of the greatest of literary monuments. It is so great a work that the spot on which its last sentence was written, and of which Gibbon records that he penned it there, adding particulars that much enhance the interest of the record, will be regarded, so long as his 'Decline and Fall of the Roman Empire' shall be read, as classical ground in literary history.

How strange that a mind of such capacity for labour, such farness of reach, such power of grasp, should have been encased in, and had to work with so uncouth a body. In my younger days I had an old friend who had known Gibbon well. I often asked him what he recollected of him: but I never got from him anything more than that he was fond of whist, though not a good player; very awkward in his movements; and shockingly ugly. One can imagine that this very ungainliness of form and feature was, in some respects, advantageous to him intellectually. Being physically excluded from those fields of ordinary rivalry in which strength and external beauty win, he was as it were obliged to turn to those in which intellect only can take a part. He almost, to some extent, belonged to that class of men of whom Bacon remarks that they are greatly daring, in order to show that in that respect, at all events, they are the equals of those whose bodily endowments are superior to their own. If he could have taken a part in such vigorous sports as those lads were engaged in who at the moment were struggling and shouting behind me, would his great work ever have been accomplished? Possibly not.

It belonged to Gibbon's age to take a low view of man. But there is a peculiarity in the lowness of the view he took, which may in some degree have received its colouring from the cause I have just referred to. Had he been physically a better man, he would have read men and women with more sympathy and kindliness; and therefore with more sagacity. Some traces there are, I think, of Pope's crooked back, and of Byron's club-foot, in their poetry. So there are, I think, of Gibbon's ugliness and ungainliness in his great history.

But the main point is, what effect has this history had in the world of thought? As its subject, its learning, its style, its length prevent its ever getting into the hands of the generality of readers, on them it can only act at second hand. It must come to them through the minds of the comparatively few who can think, to some extent, for themselves. Now I am disposed to hold that the effect it has on such minds, if at all of the first order, is far from being bad. In them it cannot but deepen the love of truth and virtue, and enlarge the estimate they would otherwise have been disposed to form of the value of comprehensiveness, thoroughness, and honesty in literary work. And may we not say something of the same kind of that other great literary worker also, who was in many respects not wholly unlike Gibbon: at all events in having lived and worked on the shores of this lake, and in this town of Lausanne. As I looked out from this terrace over the blue expanse below, with Gibbon and Voltaire in my mind, I thought it not improbable that the day might come when it will be seen that their faults belonged to their age, and to the conditions under which their work was done. Society, if its regeneration was to be attempted, required then, first of all, the clearance of many inveterate, strong, and poisonous overgrowths. This in a coarse age could hardly have been effected except by coarse means. These workers appeared to be aiming at the destruction both of the noxious overgrowths, and of the soil out of which they grew. Fortunately, however, that was impossible. The soil can support either a noxious or a wholesome growth, but cannot itself be destroyed. It ever remains, ready to support either growth, according to the degree of neglect or care, and the kind of culture applied to it. Under the evil conditions of those times the better culture could hardly have been the prominent idea. The clearance of what was noxious alone appeared either possible or desirable. At all events, in a coarse age those who coarsely assailed hypocrisy and injustice were worlds better than those who coarsely lived in and by hypocrisy and injustice. We must remember this when we shrink from their sneers and scoffs. They did what they could to clear the soil, which is more open now for us to cultivate rightly. Their hatred of hypocrisy and injustice has made it more easy for us to love honesty and justice. When the world shall have come to understand these points, the Lake of Geneva will not be regarded as, in human history, what many now hold it to be, the antithesis of the Sea of Tiberias.

At 1 P.M. I left Lausanne for London. At 4 I was at Neuchâtel. At 6 I crossed, at Verrières, from Switzerland into France. At 5 P.M. the next day I was in London. In these twenty-three hours from the Swiss border to London were included two and a half hours at Paris for breakfast and a bath. When we bring together the magnitude of the events that have recently occurred in the world, the import of the questions now in debate, the facility with which one may now visit whatever scenes of interest or instructiveness the world possesses, and remember that we are now coming to see that all it contains is capable of interesting and instructing, our conclusion I think must be, that there never were such times to live in as these of ours. Almost every object, and every day, has now its interest.

> Prisca juvent alios : ego me nunc denique natum
> Gratulor.

I undertake in my title to give a narrative of a Month in Switzerland. That of course means the narrative of every day in the Month. I have in the foregoing pages attempted to do this. The Month was the August of this year, 1873. I have accounted to the reader for every day separately. He now knows where and how we went, and what we saw each day. The particulars have all been set down; as far as that goes he has been one of the party almost as thoroughly as if he had been with us. All these particulars, however, are to the eye only an alphabet of detached letters, which are precisely the same for all who go over the same ground. Some will leave them as detached letters, unvivified with significance, though full of its elements. Others will spell from them significant words and sentences: some will find in them this series of words and sentences, and another that. Each will extract from them a rendering of his own. None will be able to render them adequately. All the differences, which will be endless, will be in the rendering; the letters, that is, the objects, being the same in every case. I have given one rendering of which they appear to be capable. That also the reader now has presented to him as completely as he might have had it had he been with us and cared to have it.

To the traveller, the weather is to a great extent the frame in which what he does is set. It is sovereign in the disposal of each day. The reader therefore will be unable to form any useful or complete conception of such an excursion as that just described unless the weather also shall have been adequately reported. This too I have done. He knows now when, during the whole month, the sun shone, and when the rain fell. He sees what the weather enabled us to do, and what it hindered us from doing. Here is a summary of it. I have already mentioned that as I was crossing France, and again at Interlaken, there were violent thunderstorms. Both these came at midnight, and therefore by clearing and cooling the air, and by washing away the dust, only aided a pedestrian. I encountered a third storm at Como, but that too came when the day's work was done. At Andermatt I had a wet afternoon, but as it happened that was no hindrance to my forward movements. The most of which it deprived me was some little ascent that might have been made in the immediate neighbourhood. It gave me, however, as much, only in a different kind, as what it deprived me of. We had a wet day at Glarus. This was, for forward movements, the complete loss of a day: but again, a loss not to be regretted. At Brienz, Eggischhorn, and Bell Alp, we had short afternoon storms, but I should have been sorry to have missed them. At Lausanne we had a wet forenoon, but that hindered nothing. All the rest was as bright and fine as could have been desired. There was much luck in this. August of course is a good month. In September the weather generally worsens and begins to break up. It did so this year. From our weather-table two inferences may be drawn. One is, that it is advisable to get your work over early in the day. The other is, that in planning your excursion, as in most things, some margin should be included for possible mishaps and unforeseen hindrances.

And now a word or two on the plan of the excursion just reported. It will have been observed that it was so arranged as to provide for the requirements of two disturbing considerations. First, I had an object: this kept me on a particular line, and sometimes necessitated a short day's march. And then, having been joined in the early part of the excursion by my wife and her little boy, what was best for them had thenceforth to be considered, as well as what was best for myself. This it was that caused my returning through the valleys of Uri and of Unterwalden, over ground I had already traversed. In this there was nothing to be regretted, though of course it would not have been done under other circumstances.

I will now set down the plan upon which I would recommend ordinary pedestrians to take this district. Begin at Lucerne. Go to the Schweizer Hof, and see there the assemblage of people of many nations. Take the boat for Brunnen; for the same reason go to the Hotel of the Four Forest Cantons. From Brunnen begin your walking along the Axenstrasse to Flüelen. Then by Altorf, Am Stag, Wasen, and the Devil's Bridge to Andermatt. From Andermatt by the St.

Gothard, Airolo, Faido, &c., to Bellinzona. Then Lago Maggiore, Lugano, and Como. Up the lake of Como to Colico. From Colico by the Splugen, to Flims, on the Furca-Coire road. From Flims by the Segnes Pass to Glarus.

Alternatives: If you cannot spare the time for the Italian lakes, go from Andermatt to Flims along the Furca-Coire road. Or if you wish for a harder pass than the Segnes, go by the Sand Grat Pass and Stachelberg to Glarus. Or if, whether or no you take the Italian lakes, you do not wish for either of these Passes, then go round by Coire to Glarus.

From Glarus by the Klönthal, and the Pragel Pass and Muotta to Schwyz.

Alternatives: By Rapperswyl and Einsiedln to Schwyz. Or having reached Schwyz by the Pragel, as above, go from Schwyz to Einsiedln by the Hacken, returning to Schwyz by the lakes of Egeri and Lowerz.

From Schwyz, taking the boat at Brunnen, cross the lake to Trieb, for the Sonnenberg Hotel on the Seelisberg. Then down to Beckenried. From Beckenried across the lake to Gersau. Then by Rigi Scheideck to Rigi Kulm. From Rigi Kulm to Küsnacht.

Alternative: To Visnau by the Rigi railway.

From Küsnacht, or Visnau, by steamer to Lucerne. Then Pilatus to Alpnach. Then by Sarnen, Sacheln, Lungern, and the Brünig to Meiringen.

Alternative: From Pilatus to Stanzstad, Stanz, Engelberg, the Surenen Pass, to Klus. From Klus to Wasen. From Wasen by the Susten Pass to Im Hof.

From Meiringen, or Im Hof, by the Grimsel to the Rhone Glacier. From the Rhone Glacier by the Upper Valais to Viesch. From Viesch to Eggischhorn.

Alternative: From the Rhone Glacier Hotel, or the Grimsel Hospice, to the Eggischhorn by the Oberaarjoch.

From Eggischhorn to Rieder Alp. From Rieder Alp to Bell Alp. From Bell Alp to Brieg.

If you want more details than our map supplies, procure the sections for the district of General Dufour's map. It is a map which is almost a picture. It gives the contour of every mountain and valley, and indicates every *chalêt*.

Everything with which we have to do has, or ought to have, its science. So therefore it is, or ought to be, with enjoyment. Anticipation in this science counts for something. The brute only it is who goes straight to the main point first, and at once. Man, endowed with reason, and because he is, looks forward to what will give pleasure. He sees it at the end of a long vista. He dallies with the anticipation, he works up to the supreme fruition. To him there are preparatory stages. And these stages, because they are preparatory, are delightful. This is a privilege of mind. Herein is the philosophy of wooing first and of marrying afterwards. If the course of the wooing have been somewhat prolonged and not quite smooth, so much the better for the marriage. The Turk, who marries without the wooing, is unscientific.

In our science arrangement is well-nigh sovereign. It would not do to begin your dinner with iced pudding and maraschino, taking next venison and champagne, then descending through *entrées* to fish, and concluding with the anticlimax of a plate of *Julienne*. This were what a pig or a Fiji might do. Reason, and a palate, and a human stomach were given us for a better purpose. And as it is with the details of the dinner, so is it with the dinner as a whole. It is too great an event to be placed early in the day. It would not do to have it served at 10 A.M., and then what you would have had for your breakfast served at 8 P.M. On this inverted plan what would in the twenty-four hours be given to the palate and to the stomach would be precisely the same, but as Wordsworth says of another matter, 'Oh, the difference!' The dinner must be looked forward to, for everything after it comes flat. It must be worked up to: in a sense, earned. The labours of the day are lightened, because there is something worthy of them coming at the end of it.

Our science, too, is not one of the rigidly pure order. It is an applied science, and makes the most of its materials and opportunities. For instance, in this same matter of dinner it sees far more than is taken into account in the philosophy of the strong-minded, who say that to assuage hunger is its single object. Certes, it would be so if again we were all of us pigs or Fijis. But we have been evolved into something higher, and so have been enabled to turn dinner to some other accounts. To us the naked, primal purpose is hardly primal, and no longer naked. We have so wreathed it with flowers, so surrounded it with and made it so to minister to other purposes, that the original purpose has long ceased to be all in all, and what is incidental—even so far from the original animal purpose as good-fellowship, society, and conversation—has ostensibly become now the main object. These incidental and secondary objects had no place in the original idea. So far, the strong-minded are right. But now, to their discomfiture, the secondary objects, which are altogether humanizing, and at all events semi-intellectual, have much mitigated the old animalism of the matter, and have become almost the main idea; of course, to those in whom what is humanizing and intellectual has assumed some form and consistency.

And so, to come at last to the matter we have been dealing with in the foregoing pages, is it with a Swiss excursion and its objects and incidents. Arrangement should be studied, and the objects should be taken in an ascending, not in a descending scale. What in its proper place and in a right order is good, sapid, enjoyable, would become in a wrong place, and in an inverted order, bad, insipid, unenjoyable. You must, too, study variety, and light and shade. If you arrange to have things good only in one and the same kind, and all of the highest intensity, everything being grand and striking in the same way, you will soon get tired of what you are about; and deservedly so. Keep the best thing for the end, or for a place towards the end. Look forward to what is best, work up to it, and approach it by an ascending scale. Do not take the Eggischhorn first, and then go to the Lake of Lucerne and the Forest Cantons. So much for anticipation and arrangement.

Understand too that the sources of interest incidentally within your reach are of many kinds. But in these you will find little to interest you if you have not made some progress in those humanities of culture we just now referred to, and this goes some way to prove that if it be not a duty we owe to ourselves, yet at all events it would be wise to make some such acquisitions. Without them some of the highest, and purest, and most accessible enjoyments of life are unattainable. The people then you will be among are interesting, and the different classes in different ways. Every man, woman, and child almost is in some way or other an interesting study. And nature interests in a thousand forms, and in a thousand moods. If bigness only interests you, if nothing less than a mountain moves you, Heaven help you! for then, somehow or other, you have been deprived of infinite sources of enjoyment which have been provided for, or are at all events within the reach of instructed and cultivated perception. Some or other of these are always before you, and should have been to you unpalling and inexhaustible. If it be not so with you, then are you mentally in the state in which Milton was physically, when 'the serene drop had quenched his visual ray.' Your bodily eye sees, but in your inward eye there is no speculation. You are now, instead of 'the book of knowledge fair,'

> Presented with an universal blank
> Of nature's works, for you expunged and razed;
> And wisdom, at one entrance, quite shut out :

and too, together with wisdom, a great part of the enjoyment of life. Endeavour then to note nature's forms, so endlessly varied, and every variation good! Note, too, her garb: again how varied, and again every variation good! Endeavour to note the reciprocal relations of organic and inorganic nature, of life to dead matter. And above all, note the relation of all you see to sovereign man. Think of how what you are beholding informed man's mind and shaped his life in times past, and how it is informing his mind and shaping his life now. Solicit thought to interpret to you what your eye reports. This world belongs to those who understand it. Despise not knowledge. Awaken imagination. Deem none made of meaner clay than yourself.

CHAPTER XVI.

THE SWISS ALLMENDS.

All the realm shall be in common,   *   *   *
And there shall be no money.—SHAKESPEARE.

THE reader will have seen that I was, throughout the excursion recorded in the foregoing pages, paying some attention to the Swiss Allmends. Allmend means land which is held and used, as the word itself indicates, in common. In this general sense it includes common land of all kinds, whether in pasture, under forest, or in cultivation. In ordinary usage, however, it has come, without absolutely excluding the two former kinds, to signify common land under cultivation, with, in fact, almost a further restriction to common land, in which the cultivation is effected by the spade, or at all events, by the hand of man.

It is to the old burgers in any commune that these kinds of land are common. The old burgers are, with but very few exceptions, the lineal descendants of those who were burgers, say 200, it may have been 500, or even 1,000 years ago. New burgers are those, or the descendants of those, who, having come in from other cantons, or communes, settled in the place, and who have no rights of any kind in the common land. Land may be common to all the old burgers of a commune equally : it is then said to belong to the commune. Or it may belong to sections of the old burgers, as, for instance, to those who reside in a particular hamlet ; or to those who belong to a particular class of families ; and these may hold it either simply for their own use, or for the promotion of some defined object : in any such cases it is said to belong to a corporation.

A Swiss commune may be taken as the analogue of an English parish. The difference is that all the burgers, old and new, of a commune have now, generally—the old burgers, according to the old theory of the commune, had always had—an equal voice in the government and administration of the affairs of the commune, with the exception of the management and usufruct of the common property, which belongs, as it always has done, exclusively to the old burgers, either collectively, or sectionally. Residents from other cantons, or communes, are now pretty generally admitted more or less completely to participation in political rights. Formerly this was not the case : they were only tolerated. But with respect to the common property, whether of the commune or of its corporations, they are still rigidly excluded from all participation in it. For instance, there are alien families, that is to say, not descended from old burgers, which have been settled in Schwyz for two centuries, but which at this day have no share in the common lands. In order to bring an English rural parish into the same political condition as a Swiss commune, the humblest day-labourer ought to have, theoretically and practically, an equal voice with the squire in the election of the magistrates and officials of all kinds, and in the management of the Church funds, the schools, the roads, the water supply, the poor, &c., of the parish. To take an extreme supposition, the parochial assembly ought to be competent to enact that the parish should hire or buy so much land as would enable it to allow to each family a quarter, or half, of an acre of garden ground, rent free. If, for the purpose of enabling us to understand the difference, we take the Swiss commune to represent, in the political order, the natural state of things, we must then regard the English rural parish as having lost a part of its rights through the usurpations of the central government, which now appoints the magistrates &c.; and as having had the majority of its inhabitants disfranchised by the usurpations of the rate-payers. Or if we regard the English rural parish as the perfection of local organization, we must say that the Swiss commune has usurped on the one side the legitimate powers of the central government, and on the other deprived the natural parochial depositaries of power, that is to say, the rate-payers, of their rightful privilege of being the exclusive administrators of everything in which the parish is concerned. The governing element in the idea of our parish appears to be the land, in that of the Swiss commune, the individual man.

The commune, then, is not far from being an independent, autonomous entity, both politically and economically. What we have now to consider is one department of its economy; that of its common lands. These, as I have already mentioned, consist of three distinct kinds; summer pastures, forests, and cultivable land. It follows from the fact of its autonomy that each commune will manage its common property very much in its own fashion; and probably there are no two communes which manage it in precisely the same fashion. But it also follows from the general similarity of their circumstances and conditions, that certain general features will pervade their management everywhere. It is with these general features that, in a notice of this kind, we are chiefly concerned. The little I shall have to say, in order to make them understood, will be founded on what I observed in the cantons I visited this summer, and in which I inquired into the system, and saw it at work. Those cantons were Unterwalden, Uri, Schwyz, and Glarus. My observations will, to some extent, be illustrated and checked by facts drawn from other quarters. For there is nothing in the world, whether in human institutions, in physiology, or in anything else, that can be understood if looked at as an isolated phenomenon. There is no such thing

THE ALPES.

as an isolated phenomenon. Not even is the world itself such, any more than anything it contains. Everything is relative, concatenated, dependent ; has causes, a *milieu*, functions, &c. ; all of which so modify it, have so much to do with its being as and what it is, and throw so much light upon it, that if it is to be understood, some reference must be made to them.

We will begin with the common pastures for summering cattle—the alpes. Upon this subject the Statistical Bureau of the Federal Government published, in 1868, a quarto volume of 435 pages, to which I have already referred. It is a work of very comprehensive details, and of much interest. It exhibits completely, and analyzes thoroughly, all the information the office had, up to that date, been able to collect on the subject. I will now extract from this report such leading particulars as will give the reader a general knowledge of this part of the matter, premising the observation, which the Bureau makes, that whatever errors there may be in the figures must always, for obvious reasons, be on the side of their falling short of the truth.

The number of alpes is 4,559. Their aggregate area, in English acres, is somewhere about 2,650,000 ; which about equals the area of the four counties of Middlesex, Surrey, Sussex, and Kent. Their capital value, by the returns made, is 77,186,103 francs. But, as the office remarks, that probably at least a half must be added to this sum to get at the true figures, we may suppose that their aggregate capital value is, in English money, about 4,500,000*l*. Their letting value is returned at 3,362,642 francs. The number of cow-runs is returned as 270,389. The average number of days the alpes are fed at 93. The gross revenue at 10,893,874 francs. The net revenue at 9,545,007 francs. A fairly good cow in Switzerland, I was told, is worth twenty napoleons. We will take the good and the indifferent as averaging fifteen napoleons. This will make the value of the stock yearly put on the alpes, in English money, 3,250,000*l*. If then we put the capital value at 4,500,000*l*., and to this add the value of the stock, and for the sake of round sums, raise the net proceeds, which we may do safely, to 12,500,000 francs, we shall have 500,000*l*. as the net revenue on a capital of 7,750,000*l*. This will give a little less than 7 per cent. profits for this portion of the property of the Swiss people, for 93 days. The Bureau calculates a much higher rate of profit. I say for 93 days, because though this is all they get during the year from the alpes, the cows are earning profits for them elsewhere during the rest of the year.

To this 500,000*l*. of profits we must add, looking at the concern from a national point of view, the support of all those who, as cowherds and cheese-makers, or as engaged in the sale at home of the cheese, or in its transportation to foreign markets, are wholly, or in part, maintained by it. No deductions need be made from this net sum, for the cows replace themselves; and whatever is expended on the pastures has been already deducted.

We now come to the distribution of this property, and of its income. Taking

Francs

	Francs
The capital value at the low and uncorrected figures of	77,186,103
The letting	3,362,642
The total gross revenue	10,893,874

and distributing these several sums according to ownership, we find the respective interests of the several owners to be as follows :—

	Communes	Communes and private owners jointly	Corporations	Private owners	
Capital value	26,226,265	3,851,489	14,565,487	32,542,853	Francs.
Letting value	1,127,355	199,270	443,803	1,592,214	
Gross revenue	4,010,102	624,102	1,788,224	4,471,446	

From this it would appear that the average selling value of a cow-run for an average of 93 days is 287 francs. Its average letting value 12 francs 48 cents. Its gross average revenue 40 francs 45 cents. This is according to the returns, which very much underrate the true figures. Their respective values in the neighbourhood of populous towns rise to several times the amounts of these averages.

The figures given will enable the reader to understand the magnitude of this part of our subject. The population of Switzerland, now somewhat over 2,500,000, has, in proportion to its numbers, a larger share in the manufacture of cotton and silk than any other in the world. Of course this, and the rapid increase in the number of travellers who every year visit the country, must have of late very much augmented the population. If, however, we divide this augmented population into families of 6 souls each, we shall find that the revenue accruing from communal and corporation alpes, excluding those held by private owners, is still sufficient to give yearly, for these 93 days, 10*s.* to every family in the country. The sum required to do the same for every family in the United Kingdom would be 2,666,666*l.* a year. But as we know that in Switzerland the majority of families, from living in towns and from other causes, have no share in the revenue accruing from the use of the common alpes, we must set down the average share of each actual participant as very much more than double this sum. In fact, two would be a low average for the number belonging to those who send up cows to these alpes: but if we take two as the average, this would give about 3*l.* a year as the average net profit of each *usager*.

The next point for consideration is, how has it come about that these common pastures form so large a feature in Swiss agronomy? The probability is that the system was once universal in Switzerland; and not among the Swiss only, but also among all other people when they were in the stage which is intermediate between the pastoral and the agricultural condition. The agricultural condition implies a precedent pastoral condition. Now as long as people are in the pastoral stage, or in the intermediate stage, when the agricultural and the pastoral are in conflict, common pasturage is inevitable. The system now in vogue in our Australian colonies is not a case to the contrary, because that belongs to the era of capital, and takes its form from the action of capital. There is abundant evidence of this conflict, with its necessary condition, common pasturage, having once been the rule in Germany, in France, in this country, and elsewhere. Circumstances, which are absolutely sovereign in a matter of this kind, for there is no possibility of resisting them, carried other countries out of this state of things, while they kept Switzerland in it. If a thousand, or five hundred years ago, some Titans of the race that undertook to set Ossa upon Pelion, and to roll to the top of the pile Olympus with all his forests, had run a mountain-crusher over Switzerland and flattened in its Alps, then the system of common pasturage could no more have existed there down to our time than in the plains of Lombardy or the vale of Aylesbury.

But this is a point there is no understanding without a general acquaintance with the whole subject, which belongs to, and is indeed the main stem in, the growth and evolution of human society. The history of human society is the record of its growth; no particular stage of which can be understood, if disconnected from what preceded it; that is to say, without a knowledge of the precedent history, which was that out of which the subsequent history grew. We ourselves cannot be regarded as having reached the final stage in that evolution. The time of course will come, when it will be seen that the point at which we now are, as respects not the land only but many other things also, was not a permanent resting place, but merely a step in an endlessly ascending series. The evolution, in other words the orderly advance, in harmony with advancing circumstances, of the uses of the land, which has been going on from the beginning, will continue—at all events we have no reason for supposing the contrary—as long as man and the land shall continue. If the past in this matter had been compounded of haphazard progression and retrogression on the same level, or of mingled ascents and descents on haphazard uneven ground, there would probably be no evidence perceptible of plan or design; and then we should not be able to understand how any particular stage—indeed, there would then be no stages—had been reached. Nor, with respect to our own existing position, should we be able to conjecture in what direction things might be tending. Observation and thought would be futile, and action aimless, were everything, in such a fashion, the sport of blind accident. But now, because we see that these matters are subject to a law of growth, we can trace their history, and reason about them, and understand them; and notwithstanding the action of temporarily disturbing causes, even when accompanied with checks and hardships, can rest in the belief that Omnipotent and Beneficent Intelligence directs them, no less than all the other phenomena of the universe.

What, then, we have to determine is, What, as constituted by nature, is the relation of man to the land? What have been the advances in circumstances that bear upon this relation? And how have they affected it, or how has it dealt with them? That is to say, What are the facts, or the principles, that · underlie the history? And what has been their history? It is evident that some general knowledge of this kind must be requisite for the right appreciation of any particular stage. For instance, without it we shall not be able to understand what this Swiss system, about which we are now inquiring, really was? what made it what it was? what is the place it occupies in the great historical series of advances through which man's relation to the land has passed? and what it is that is now rendering it unsuitable to existing circumstances, and so preparing the way for something higher and better?

We must begin at the beginning. What, in the earliest times of all, was the relation of man to the land? What had nature ordained it to be? What was its original purport, form, and character? They will, we can believe, be seen most distinctly under the simplest and léast complicated conditions. The first stage must have been that in which man lived by the chase—by the pursuit and capture of wild animals; and in a less degree by the fruits of the earth produced spontaneously in their season. This must have come first, because if man were placed abruptly in a world, already peopled with wild animals, and with plants that at times bore fruit, these could have been the only means available for supporting life. To this day it continues to be so among many savage tribes; a fact which throws much light upon man's history. We also know that it was so once in parts of the world where it has long ceased to be so. For instance, geological investigations have shown that there was a time when it was so in this island. The relation therefore of the land to primitive man was that it supplied him with the food that was to support his life. That was the substance, the principle, of the relation. Man and the land were two related terms; and the food, which the land produced and the man consumed, was the third term, which brought them into relation. It constituted the relation.

And in the character and purport of this relation there was no difference at all between sovereign man and the lower animals. The relation was precisely the same for everything that breathed. In the first stage, indeed, man's condition was very little in advance of that of the lower animals. His life was passed, and supported very much in the same fashion as theirs.

A coefficient condition of this primæval relation was that of property. Each tribe had its own hunting ground, which was its own property. It was its own property because other tribes were not allowed to hunt over it, to use it, or to encroach upon it in any way. It was jealously guarded for the separate use of the tribe. This was necessary: and therefore, like the relation itself, an ordinance of nature. And it, too, is a condition which exists among and is enforced by, and we cannot but suppose must always have existed among and been enforced by, the lower animals. Each pair of lions, and each pair of redbreasts, has its own hunting ground, from which other lions, or other redbreasts, that attempt to encroach upon it, are violently expelled. But property, among these hunting tribes, must always have been, as we see that it is at this day, of two kinds. There was that which belonged to the whole tribe equally. This applied to the land they hunted over. It was held in common, because, under the circumstances, it was necessary that it should be so held. This was the only way in which the fundamental principle of the relation of the land to man—that its use is to supply man with food—could have been carried out then. Its common use arose out of, and was necessitated by existing circumstances. It could not have been divided into portions for each family, because the wild game, the human food it then produced, was not at all times evenly distributed throughout it, but would sometimes be on one part of the run and sometimes on another. Still the recognition of this necessity, as respected the land, did not exclude either the idea, or the fact, of separate individual property. That form also of property was, in this the lowest stage of human society, understood and acted upon. If a man had fortified a cave against the entrance of wild beasts, or had built a hut, or wigwam, that did not belong to the tribe, but to himself, as much so as the burrow, or lair, or nest, an animal forms for itself, is its own. So with the skins he might have dressed; the stones and bones he might have chipped and pointed; the bows and arrows, the spears and clubs, the slings and throwing sticks he had made; and after a time, too, with the women he had acquired by capture or purchase; and the children they had borne to him.

The necessity of association must also, from the beginning, have been a corollary to the right of property. There never could have been a time when it could have been dispensed with. If each family had dwelt in isolation, it could not have protected itself, or its hunting ground, either against wild beasts, or against encroaching neighbours. Nor could it have hunted so effectually as to have secured a supply of food. Association, therefore, was a necessity. And this, again, we find is resorted to by those animals which are not strong enough to protect themselves, or to capture their food, individually ; or which require for their security more vigilance than could be maintained at all times by an isolated individual. It is not acted on by lions or tigers, because they can do without it, but it is acted on by the herbivorous animals, and even by some of the less swift, or less strong species of carnivors. The herbivors associate because though, notwithstanding their association, many will be destroyed by their natural enemies, still in consequence of their association into large communities, many will escape. And some of the carnivors, which pursue animals stronger or fleeter than themselves, as for instance wild dogs and wolves, associate, because by this means they can best secure their prey. Lions and tigers would associate if their herbivorous prey were to become far stronger than themselves.

Here, then, we have three main facts, a determinate relation, ordained by nature, of the land to man, a coefficient condition of that relation, and a corollary to that condition, which have existed from the beginning ; and which, as far as we can see, must exist to the end. Neither society nor life could be maintained without them. Each of the three, in a sense and degree, the brute also recognizes.[1] The

[1] And may I not be allowed to say here in passing, that our observation of this fact must have a good effect upon our treatment of our dumb fellow-workers, and of every creature that breathes ? Indeed, if they were not dumb, as has been suggested in an earlier part of this volume, they would probably be able to show us, that in the highest

advancing circumstances of human society have in no way abrogated, or weakened them. The only difference is that the constitutive facts themselves, remaining throughout the same, have been suitably applied to the successive advances, whatever their character may have been, that have been made in the circumstances.

To these circumstances, which play so great a part in the history, for they it is that make the matter progressive, and so give it a history, we must now direct our attention. After a time some kinds of animals are domesticated, and society enters on the second, the pastoral stage. This was the first clearly defined advance in the circumstances. We know not where, or when, or how, or by whom were first domesticated the ox, the sheep, the goat, the hog, the horse, the ass, or the camel. The dates of these achievements, pregnant with so vast a series of mighty consequences, lie far back beyond the reach of the dimmest traditions of mankind. Here, however, we are concerned only with the way in which their domestication affected the tenure and the use of the land. The most obvious effects were that the extent of land, which had formerly been required for the maintenance of the tribe

gift also of all, that of reason, their approximation to ourselves is much closer than many of us suppose at present. And may not this eventually prove a new, and very striking instance of the way in which an increase of knowledge enlarges and elevates religion? I say religion rather than the sense of duty, because if such knowledge should bring us to treat the lower animals with kindly interest and consideration, it will not be because we feel in the matter responsibility to them, or to our fellow men, but to the common Author of all.

by the chase, would now maintain a great many more families; and that, in this part of the world, where moisture is continuous, and therefore grass abundant, (it would be different in the dry plains of Asia,) their lives could not possibly be so vagrant as had been the case with their hunting forefathers. Because now, instead of following the migrations of wild animals, and searching for them when sparingly dispersed over large areas, they would have to attend to their flocks and herds. But their flocks and herds would still have to be protected from wild beasts, and from their neighbours. A sufficient number therefore of families must be associated into a village community to enable it to guard its own pasture ground; which in no part of Europe needed to have been of any great extent. Our three great facts, that the object of the land is to produce food; that for this purpose it must be held as property; and that, in order that it may be so held, those to whom it belongs must associate themselves, have in no way been enfeebled. They still remain in force, and govern human life. And we shall see that they will continue to do this under every new combination of circumstances that will arise. We shall never come to a time when men will not remove whatever would, under the circumstances of the day, hinder the land from producing the greatest amount of food; nor when property will cease to exist, or cease to be modified according to circumstances; nor when men will cease to associate for its protection. With respect to the latter, history will show us the village growing into the city, and neighbouring cities associating, and growing, in one way or another, into unions of cities, nations, and empires; but the necessity for, and the object of association will remain the same; for persons and property will always need protection; collectively, against aggressions from without, and, in the case of the individual, against aggressions from within. The need of protection will remain, and will be provided for in just the same way when property shall have become so varied in kind, and the new kinds so vast in amount, that the aboriginal property of land, that once was all in all, shall have become of secondary importance. Neither will the need disappear, or the old means of providing for it become obsolete, when the number of the millions of those who are associated shall exceed the number of families that were associated in the old pastoral or hunting community. The purpose and principle were precisely the same in the village of a score of families, or in the combination of such villages in the primæval German forest, as it is at this day among the forty millions who are now associating themselves into the German Empire.

With respect to the form of private, individual property, that in the pastoral period assumed a great extension: for the flocks and herds—which had now become all in all to the community—were private property; whereas the wild animals, which in the foregoing stage had occupied that position, had been common property. The pasturage, however, still remained common to the flocks and herds of the inhabitants of the village; just as formerly the hunting area had been open to all the members of the old tribe. But the commencement of individual appropriations of land is now becoming visible; for any enclosures, near to the homestead, for the purpose of penning the cattle at night, and for protecting them against wild beasts and bad weather, will belong to those who have themselves constructed them for their own cattle.

In the hunting stage the tribe had ever been on the move, and their whole time had been expended in a hard, and often ineffectual struggle for bare existence. Nothing more was possible. But the inhabitants of the pastoral village have now become stationary; and have, on easy terms, a sufficiency of food. This places some leisure time, during the year, at their disposal. A great advance has been made; and it proves to be one which like all others has in itself the germ of future advances; for it leads on to the culture of the soil, which is the third stage. But this, too, was brought about at so remote a period in the lost history of the race, that there are no traces of traditions of when, or where, or how, or by whom was introduced the culture of any one of the different kinds of cereals. All of the matter that we know for certain is that the fact turns out to be exactly the contrary of what we might have expected. Such improvements, amounting to transformations, of the seeds of some now untraceable natural grasses into our different kinds of grain, we should have felt almost sure were quite beyond the capacities and opportunities of little village aggregations of savages, or at best of semi-savages. First the idea of the possibility of such transformations, and then the thought, care, and patience necessary for effecting them, we should have been disposed to ascribe only to people among whom knowledge had largely accumulated.

Suppositions, however, of this kind, though they would, before the matter had been investigated, have been entertained by almost everybody, are completely contradicted by the facts of the case. These assure us that we are indebted, beyond controversy, not only for the domestication of animals, but also for the existence of our cereals in their present form, to the ideas, and to the patient and thoughtful labour of our remote unnamed barbarian ancestors. And these barbarian inventors of wheat, barley, and oats, and, that we may not ungratefully exclude from their due the natives of the New World, we must add of maize also, were as great benefactors of the race as the inventors of letters, and of the steam-engine. And this ought to awaken within us both a stronger sense than we now have of the continuity and unity of human history, and a greater respect than we have for still existing barbarian races.

A highly interesting illustration and confirmation of the fact now before us has lately been brought to light. In '69 the government of Mauritius sent a commissioner to collect specimens of the different kinds of sugar-cane cultivated by the natives of New Caledonia, and to report on their respective merits. His report was issued only a few months ago. It figures, and describes separately, forty-four kinds he found still in cultivation. In the copy I now have before me each of the forty-four figures is carefully coloured; variation in colour being in this plant an indication of other variations, some of which might be useful. Here, then, are savages of a very low type, for they even practise cannibalism when other means of supporting life have failed, cultivating forty-four varieties of a plant, which probably was not originally indigenous to their island; and of which it is very doubtful whether in their island it ever produced a fertile seed. Every variety therefore which originated among them must have been the result of a sport. And this must have been watched for, and turned to account when it presented itself. Indeed, their method of cultivating the sugar-cane, which is as wonderful as the number of kinds they cultivate, appears to be intelligently directed to the aim of producing sports. But it will be better to allow the commissioner himself to describe to us in his own words what he saw.

He says, 'Besides the sugar-cane the chief alimentary support of the New Caledonians were,' before the French took possession of the island, 'the taro and yam. The former, requiring an abundant supply of water, was usually grown in terraces formed on the slopes of the natural amphitheatres presented by the spurs of the main mountain range, and most ingeniously irrigated by a constant *fillet* of water. The latter, requiring a deep, open, rich, and well-drained soil, was planted on beds formed by heaping up the naturally thin surface soil of a few inches deep into beds of about three feet high by four feet wide, from which only one crop was taken, and the next year fresh ground was broken up for new plantations.

'It was on the edges of these beds, forming, as will be at once evident, a peculiarly rich and deep loose soil, that the natives planted their canes, not in lines near each other, as we do, but twenty or thirty feet apart, and in a single row only. As the detached stools grew they were tied up in a bundle with straw, in order to exclude light and limit the number of shoots, and to force them to lengthen; and likewise to make them tender and juicy, instead of sweet. For a New Caledonian values a cane for the quantity of its juice, not for its saccharine qualities, and has probably never eaten a really ripe cane. No marvel that under such treatment, allowing only three or four canes to a stool, they should grow large and long; so long, in fact, that those which were tabooed, or kept for grand ceremonies, have, after two and a half or three years, attained a length of from twenty-five to

MODERN SAVAGE CULTIVATORS. 319

thirty feet, and a diameter of four inches or more, requiring to be supported on forked sticks as they fell over. Above all it should be noted, that in direct opposition to our system, the cane was never replanted in the same land, thus giving it the best chance of progressive development, and avoiding the chances of degeneracy or disease. Every intelligent cultivator will at once recognize the necessarily practical effect of such a continual principle of selection carried out for perhaps centuries.'

Note the carefulness of these New Caledonians in this matter. The soil is collected and piled up into beds to secure a sufficiency of depth for the descending roots, in order that every root that could be formed might be turned to account. The canes are set in single rows to give to each leaf of each plant all the air and the light possible. The stems are banded up with straw to prevent evaporation. The plants in the single rows are set twenty or thirty feet apart, that there may be no interference of the roots of one plant with the roots of another. That they may have all the stimulation possible, they are never grown in succession on the same spot. Our science can suggest nothing more adapted, were it a seeding plant, to give rise to improved varieties by seed-variation, or to force a plant that does not produce seed into producing varieties by sporting. All this, too, is done under great local disadvantages and discouragements, for the island is most years affected with severe droughts and devastated with swarms of locusts which destroy the leaves of the canes. It is worth noting that the commissioner expresses the surprise he felt at witnessing the wonderful acuteness with which the natives distinguish unerringly, and give the native name to any cane shown to them which may have only an inch or two fully formed; frequently recognizing a still smaller specimen merely by its leaves. He never saw them make a mistake.

In this careful cultivation of the sugar-cane, and preservation of its varieties, we can hardly doubt but that we have an existing instance, *mutatis mutandis*, of the process by which some branch of our remote barbarian ancestors improved some grasses producing small edible seeds, into the kinds of grain we now cultivate. Similar care they had already bestowed on the formation of the races of domestic animals we now possess. And we ought not to forget that they were at the same time rough-hewing our language and morality. With respect to their morality—the parent stock of ours, as was the case with their language—we may, in passing, observe that in all probability they enforced and practised it, as Mr. Wallace, who lived for some years among the savages of these islands, found them practising theirs, much more rigidly than we do ours.

We have now reached a point at which we find that some reconstruction of the agrarian arrangements of the pastoral village community is being forced upon them. Formerly their flocks and herds were their only support. They are so no longer. The cultivated produce of the soil has not taken their place, but has become, to an indispensable degree, a subsidiary means of support. And as time goes on it is becoming so more and more largely, through increasing skill in the cultivation of the soil, and through its consequence, an increase of population. This new means of support has now become necessary; and it cannot be turned to account on land absolutely common. Each crop must be the property of the man who prepared the land for it, sowed, protected, and harvested it. The land therefore upon which it was grown must be his, for at all events the space of time requisite for these operations. This gives rise to the system of property in land limited in respect of time, that is to say, some form of the system of shifting severalties. Of course this must gradually pass into absolute permanent property, because the day will come when that will be necessary for enabling the community to obtain from the land the greatest amount of food. The conditions, however, that will suggest that are still a long way off. As changes become necessary, they will, each in its turn, have to fight for its establishment. The old methods will always have prescription, fact, tradition, custom to support them; the new, utility and necessity.

It is interesting to recall how recently amongst ourselves a stage of this conflict had to be fought out.

From the Saxon times there had been established in this country a form of the agrarian system of village communities, the members of which had defined common rights in the land. It had in the early part of the Middle Ages become general. It was not a survival of, or a reversion to the ideas of the pastoral age. The two main features of that system had been that all the land of the village had been in precisely the same common condition, and that the rights in it also of every member of the village community had been precisely the same. Of this our mediæval agronomic system can be regarded as only a very remote descendant. In the first place it was devised for an agricultural community; and in the next it had to be adapted to a complicated social system of lords of manors, large and small freeholders, peasant cultivators, cotters, &c.; and each of these classes was in a different position from the others for turning to account its commonable rights. It was an attempt, under the social and economic conditions of the times, to make the land support the community. It supplemented the use of land that was more or less appropriated by large and various common rights. In the case of the peasant cultivators this was intended as compensation, just as it was in Russia, for the services exacted from them. The lands of the feudal lord, as of his Saxon predecessor, both of whom were necessary personages in the political system of their times, could not have been cultivated otherwise; for a general arrangement of rents and wages to be paid in money was impossible then. That old system has left in our language some traces of its existence. The words Lammas lands, lot-meadows, shifting severalties, folkland, open time, field-constraint, &c., once stood for some of its details. It was already dying out towards the close of the middle ages. The influx of silver on the discovery of America, by raising the price of wool in foreign markets for manufacturing purposes, at a time when there was no cause in operation to raise the price of wheat, hastened its decay. For it made it profitable to those who were in a position to effect it, to consolidate small holdings, which involved the extinction of the commonable rights that had appertained to their old cultivators. The Enclosure Commissioners of our own day had to deal with the last traces of the system.

For many centuries it did good service. It was workable, when perhaps nothing else could have been with the single exception of the old world form of slavery. But it could not stand after rent and wages had become possible, and when it was seen that by cultivating larger farms, and by the extinction of common rights, the land might be turned to better account for the community generally. New circumstances, possibilities, and requirements necessitated a new system. The object of the land is to provide food for those to whom it belongs, that is to say, for the community to which it belongs. This object has always overridden, and must always override every other consideration. For instance, the practice of Lammas lands (which meant that the members of the agrarian village community must each year cultivate on contiguous pieces of land the same grain crop, in order that the stubbles and succeeding fallow, on the whole space so cultivated, might, after the crops had been carried, be thrown open as common pasture to the cattle of the whole village,) could not possibly have been maintained after the introduction of artificial grasses and turnips; because every one could see that the land might be made to produce a great deal more food by ceasing to be Lammas land, and by being laid down with artificial grasses and cultivated for roots. And this could be done only by enclosing the land, which could not have been enclosed under the old system, and by extinguishing the old common rights. A man would not lay down artificial grasses, and cultivate roots, for the flocks and herds of the parish. If this method of increasing the food supply of an increasing population was to be resorted to, the artificial grasses and roots must be the property of the man who grew them. The land must be enclosed, and his neighbours' flocks must be excluded at all seasons.

Henceforth the number of those who can keep flocks and herds will be much reduced. These will, however, in the aggregate be much larger than in former times. And through the medium of the other forms of industry to which the other members of the community will now be able, and required, to devote themselves, these larger flocks and herds will be in a sense common to all : they certainly will be produced for all. At first, and for a long time, hardships will ensue. But these, and even their long continuance, are no proof that the change does not belong to the natural order of things. Most changes are accompanied by throes and inconveniences ; the use of which is to prevent the introduction of any changes excepting those which circumstances and events have demonstrated to be necessary and inevitable ; and to force men to struggle to accommodate themselves to such as are of this kind. Take as an instance the change we are now speaking of. It was accompanied for some generations with great hardships. But most people will now readily acknowledge that it was both necessary and beneficial ; and that it would be extremely mischievous to attempt to revert to it in any way or degree.

And just as it was with this mediæval system of ours, and with the semi-pastoral, the pastoral, and the hunting stages that went before it, so we may suppose will it be with our present land system, which appears to most of us as an ordinance of nature, that has been from everlasting, and must continue to be to everlasting. It would be to everlasting if the circumstances which gave rise to it were to be everlasting : and the same might have been said of every system that preceded it. But if it should become distinct to men's minds that by the introduction of some change in the system the land of the country could be made, through means that have now become possible, to produce for the people of the country a great deal more food than it does under the present system, then the present system would go as certainly as the Lammas lands, lot-meadows, folklands, &c. of the old system went. To maintain a system which is giving less food, to the exclusion of one which would give more food, would appear as a contravention of the purpose of nature. Its foundations, that upon which it was built, and which upheld it, would be gone. It would have nothing but unsupported prescription to support it. And there would be at the same time events, facts, necessity pushing against it to overturn it, just in the same way as it itself pushed against and overturned what had been before itself. It would be thawed, like snow upon which the sun was shining. The perception by the community of the possibility of turning the land of the country to better account would be the sun that would melt it away; just as it had every system in its turn when its day was done, back to the beginning. For the people have a right to insist that the land shall be allowed to yield for them as much food as it is capable, under the circumstances of the times, of being made to produce.

The new facts would sap, mine, and explode the old and now inadequate arrangements. And it would not be so much reasonings and opinions that would do this, as facts that had established themselves, and upon which reasonings and opinions would be based. Suppose that from actual, unmistakeable instances it were to become manifest to the general comprehension, that the application of capital to the culture of the land, in such amounts as none but owners of the land will apply to it, would vastly increase the amount of food the land of the country could be made to produce for the people of the country; and that what prevented those who might be ready to apply this amount of capital from becoming owners of the land to which they were ready to apply it, was the power the existing landowners have of charging and settling land, then this power in some way or other would disappear as completely as the Lammas lands &c. have disappeared, and for precisely the same reason. It may seem humiliating, but it must be acknowledged that the material interests of mankind have within themselves much more power for enforcing changes by which they may be promoted, than those interests which are moral and intellectual. The fact is that they come first. Man must live. His moral and intellectual interests are not his primary and most pressing concern. In the order of nature they come afterwards. They are, indeed, hardly seen, or even felt, till the material wants have been supplied.

The mass of mankind appreciates these things according to their natural order. What, for instance, can be more truly shocking than the pauperism of this country? The amount of moral and intellectual degradation it implies, and that in the bosom of a society conspicuous not only for wealth, but also for culture, refinement, and philanthropy, is perhaps the most saddening sight on the face of this earth. Its amount baffles calculation, for it is not to be ascertained by counting the numbers of those unhappy persons in the United Kingdom who are at any particular moment receiving relief, but by adding to their number, could it be done, the number of the present generation who have received, and of those who will receive, relief: for the man who received relief yesterday, and the man who will receive it to-morrow, are as much paupers as the man who is receiving it to-day. The total, therefore, of our pauperized population amounts not to one, but to several millions. Many see this and understand it, but no one is shocked at it. At all events, no one calls aloud for inquiry into the causes of so portentous an evil with a view to its mitigation. Why? because the mass of mankind are little affected, as things now are, at the sight of moral and intellectual degradation. Were they, however, only to be brought to see with distinctness, that the land of the country is, as Lord Derby tells us, producing no more than half as much as it might be made to produce; or, as the Lords' Committee for inquiring into the means available for improving the land, tells us, that only one fifth of what requires draining has been drained; then everyone would be shocked, and would clamour loudly for inquiries and remedies. It is the abundance free trade supplies, so long as the highways of the sea are open, that is, in these piping times of peace, blinding our eyes to these facts and to their causes, nature, and consequences, and will probably continue to do so, till a maritime war shall have obliged us, when it will be too late, to understand the everyday wisdom of making the most of our own soil. (By the way, why are such committees as that just referred to exceptionally necessary for the land? Ship-builders, cotton-spinners, iron-masters, &c., do not ask for parliamentary inquiry into means for improving their unfettered industries. No one hears of their languishing for want of skill or capital.)

The foregoing sketch of some of the most prominent facts in the history of man's relation to the land, taking it at the beginning, and bringing it down to the modification of it now existing amongst ourselves, though altogether inadequate as a sketch of the general subject, has occupied more space, I am well aware, than I can claim for anything of the kind here. Still it was quite necessary, for without it we should not be able to assign to the Swiss system its place in the series of advances that have been made in the application and working out of this relation, because without it we should not have had the series before us. Nor without it should we be able to see how honest and successful an attempt the Swiss system was to carry out the substantial purpose of the relation of the land to man, because without it we should not have had our attention directed to the nature of the relation. Nor again, without it, should we be brought to look for the peculiar circumstances upon which the Swiss system had to act, because without it we should not have been brought to see that circumstances are supreme in deciding in what form and fashion the relation itself, and its two efficient conditions of property and association—the three constant quantities in this matter—shall at any time be worked.

As then the substance of the relation is unvarying, and what variation there may be at any time or place can only be in the circumstances, which affect no more than the form of the relation, we have to look in the case now before us for the circumstances which, while other European countries were advancing step after step, in Switzerland, till within a very recent period, prohibited all advance. These, I think, will all be found to be included under two heads, viz., the peculiarities of the physical character of the country, and the absence of accumulations of capital : and the two were, I believe, closely connected. The country had no sources of mineral, nor, under the conditions of former times, of agricultural wealth. It could not maintain a large population on its own resources. Nor could it have any cities, the inhabitants of which, either like those of Flanders, by the easy terms upon which they might get the raw materials, could have manufactured for others, or like those of Venice, Genoa, and of the cities of Holland, might have become common carriers. They could have had no commerce except with their surplus cheese. And the amount of this that could be spared was so small, and the transportation so difficult, that but little could be made of it; and the whole of this little was wanted for the necessaries of labour, such as the useful metals &c. which the Swiss were obliged to procure from abroad. There was therefore no margin for saving, and so there could be no accumulations of capital. For long ages the most assiduous industry could supply the Swiss with only the necessaries of life, and barely with them, even when aided by the surplus cheese. Throughout all this time the system of common pasturage was maintained. It worked well: it saved from perishing a population that was ready to perish.

In these days, however, all this has been changed. By the aid of the new means of transportation and communication, and by the substitution of machinery for manual labour, the motive power for which Switzerland has in abundance, and can now turn to excellent account, the people are becoming rich. Capital has accumulated, and is still further accumulating rapidly. Families, therefore, can be supported without the common use of the land—and in most cases better without it than with it. And besides, if its common use be maintained, it will prove, when capital exists in abundance, a hindrance to the greatest possible production of food for the people. In short, the existence of capital has now brought about conditions which render the system of commonable land no longer the best. That will be its doom. No system that has been assailed by such conditions has ever been able to maintain itself. It will be no defence of it to say that it has hitherto been a good and workable system, and that the long ages of its existence have proved it to be so. This is what might have been said, and doubtless was said, with truth but without effect, of every system, not only of agronomy, but of everything else that was ever established in the world. This is the logic of sentiment, of habit, of custom, of tradition; and of those who think that they have interests distinct from and superior to the interests of the rest of the community; and of those who cannot understand what is understood by the rest of the world. It is, however, no match for the logic of facts, and of the general interest—the public good. That must ever be the strongest logic as well as the highest law. If, then, it is about to be overturned by capital, notwithstanding its long history and all that may be said on its behalf, we may infer that it was the absence of capital which brought it into being and maintained it down to the advent of capital.

Let us take the case of these Forest Cantons. In order to understand their position in respect of this matter, we must not limit our view to their present condition; we must go further back; our survey must include a wider range. Some centuries ago they were much secluded from the world. At that time there was, in comparison with what we now see in them, very little cultivable land reclaimed. Means of communication by wheeled carriages had not yet, in most places, been so much as thought about. The people therefore were thrown almost entirely upon their own scanty local resources. With hardly any means for getting supplies from without, with very little land for cultivating cereals, and in the days before maize and potatoes, their chief reliance was upon their cows. It is very much so even at this day. But in those days the reliance was all but unqualified. Their cows supplied them not only with a great part of their food, but also, through the surplus cheese, with tools, and everything else they were incapable of producing themselves from the singularly limited resources of their secluded valleys. The Switzer was then the parasite of the cow. There were no ways in which money could be made: there were no manufactures, and no travellers, and so there were no innkeepers to supply travellers, nor shopkeepers to supply the wants of operatives, manufacturers, and travellers; and there were none who had been educated up to the point that would enable them to go abroad to make money with which they might return to their old homes: neither they nor the world were then in a condition to admit of this. The adoption of foreign military service for a livelihood, which was a common practice at this period, was a proof of the poverty of the country, and did not at all contribute to enrich it; for the savings from their pay, brought home with them by those who returned, could never have compensated for the cost of bringing up those who through the practice were lost to the country. If the general population had not had the means for keeping cows, they would not have had the means for living. The problem, therefore, for them to solve was, How was every family to be enabled to keep cows? Under the conditions of those times the family that could not have kept cows must have ceased to exist.

The local conditions were very peculiar. Small prairies might be formed in the valley bottoms, and by quarrying the rocks, levelling, surface-soiling, and irrigation, they might in some places be carried a little way up the mountain sides. But if the grass of these prairies were to be consumed by the cattle in the summer, there would be no provision for them in the coming winter. As, then, the prairies could not be fed in summer, what was to be done with the cattle at that season? The mountain pastures, which could not be cut for hay, enabled them to meet this difficulty. The cows of the village community might during the summer be kept on these mountain pastures, and this would admit of the bottom and the irrigated prairies being reserved for making hay, which might support the cows in winter and spring. This, therefore, must be the plan. Everyone must have the right of sending his cows up to these summer pastures. Everyone in summer then would be able to devote himself to keeping up, perhaps to enlarging a little, his prairie land, and to making and storing up hay for winter. But this would depend on a sufficient amount of summer pasturage being kept common. Common property is not generally well looked after, or made the most of: but this is true of Alpine pasturage in a less degree than of other kinds of commonable land, because it does not depend for its produce upon care and labour, as a commonable cornfield or a commonable vineyard would ; nor is it easily exhausted, for it is at rest throughout at least two-thirds of the year. It is very different with prairie, that is to say, made and cultivated grass land: its first formation—it is all made land—and the maintenance of its fertility sufficient for the two or three crops of hay taken yearly from it, and the making and storing up of this hay, require an amount of attention and labour it would be vain to expect as a general rule without the stimulus of private property. If common labour were attempted in a matter of this kind, most men would endeavour to throw as much as possible of the work on their neighbours ; and as to improvements of the common property, what would then in theory be everybody's business, would in practice be nobody's : the labour would be both less in amount, and less enterprising. Clearly the best system with respect to the prairies was that they should be pretty generally private property. The mountain pastures were already formed. They were the gift of nature. They could not be very much improved. Under any treatment they would continue to exist. Not so with the prairies. They could not have been created without a vast amount of labour, and they could not be maintained without its continuance. And so it came to be the established rule, that the natural summer pastures should be common, and that every burger should have as many cows kept upon them in the summer as he had himself kept during the previous winter with the hay he had made from his labour-created and labour-maintained prairies; or, if as yet he had no prairies, with the dried leaves and coarse stuff he had been able to collect from the common forest.

If these mountain pastures had been allowed to become private property in those times when the people were parasites of the cows, the few who had got hold of them would have been very rich, and those who had failed to secure a share in them would have been quite starved out. They would not have been able to have kept cows through the winter, because in the summer they would have been obliged to put them on their little bits of prairie ground, and so could not have reserved their produce for winter.

And in the days anterior to accumulations of capital, this, which is a great point, worked fairly for all. All were placed on about an equal footing.

Whatever differences of condition there might have been then, resulted mainly from differences of industry But these were differences which had play within very restricted limits; for the field for industry had little extent and no variety. The community said to its members: 'Do what you may your struggle for existence must be hard. It cannot possibly be maintained without cows; and you will not be able to keep your cows in the winter without their having been taken off your hands and off your prairies during the summer; for, throughout the whole of that season, you must be attending to your prairies, and to their produce, which must be reserved for winter. In order that this may be done, the mountain pastures shall be treated and used as common property; so that during the summer the cows of all may be kept upon them. Each shall have the right of sending up to them in the summer as many cows as he had kept from the produce of his prairies through the previous winter.' As no family could reclaim and keep up more of this prairie land than was sufficient to provide hay for a few cows—an industrious and prosperous family might do this for five or six, a less industrious and less prosperous for two or three—the people were all placed by this system very much on a footing of equality. The system was both necessary and fair. It originated in the nature of the country, and in its then economical conditions; and, in turn, it created the Swiss life and character. It was evidently a form maintained down to our own times, under peculiar circumstances, of the semi-pastoral stage. The common pasturage was the same in both; and the prairies, held as private property and cultivated for hay, were analogous to the enclosed fields, held as private property and cultivated for grain, of that stage. The shifting severalties also of garden-ground, to which we shall come presently, were genuine incidents of it.

I will show presently how, under the altered conditions of the times, the old system of common pasturage has now become both unnecessary and unfair. To the existing circumstances of the country it is not at all adapted; and so, according to the law which makes them sovereign in human affairs, it must die out: but of that anon.

We now come to the second part of the common property of these Cantons—the forests. Under the conditions of the past it was as necessary that there should have been common forests as it was that there should have been common summer pastures. Wood, with the exception, here and there, of turf, and which followed the same rules, was in Switzerland the only fuel. In times when men did not live much, or at all, on wages, and wood was the only fuel, it was necessary that all the members of the community should have the right of taking so much as would supply their absolute wants from the contiguous forest. This also, therefore, must, at all events so far, remain common property. That it should have been so was quite imperative in Switzerland, on account of the length and the severity of the winter. If any members of the community had been excluded from the right of fuel, they would have died of cold. Suppose that these forests had been allowed to become private property: two evil consequences would have ensued ; a large part of the existing population would forthwith have been deprived of the means of obtaining fuel ; and as a private owner might do with his own what he pleased, his necessities, or greed, or bad judgment, might bring him to cut down, at one time, a large portion of the forest, or might prevent his taking the care necessary for maintaining it in a serviceable condition for the generations that would follow him. These difficulties were overcome by keeping the forest in the hands of the community, and distributing, on a plan which would be fair to all, the amount of fuel that would be necessary for each. It thus became the interest of all to see that the forests were not wastefully used, and were properly maintained ; and a regular supply, which was the great point, of what was indispensable was secured for all.

The rule generally observed in the distribution of the produce of the common forests was, that each family should have an allowance of fuel, and of timber for repairs, in proportion to the size of his dwelling house and byre; so many solid klafters for the former, and so many hewn timber trees, generally fir, for the latter. In the days before accumulations of capital, when, through the condition of each being mainly the result of his own industry and actual manual labour, all were kept pretty much on an equality, this method of distribution was fair enough. Its principle was analogous to that which was observed in the use of the common pastures.

Under the circumstances of time and place the maintenance of common property in the forests was a matter of life and death. In these valleys at that time there were no ways of earning the means for buying fuel. The people had in summer to be attending, each to his little bit of prairie land, to his haymaking, and to his little plot of corn; and in winter he must still be at home, looking after and tending his cows, and doing the many things requisite for the maintenance of his family; and which, under the circumstances of the time and place, would not have been done at all if not done by himself.

What has now been said about the mountain pasture and fuel fully explains the disabilities laid on residents who had come in from other cantons, or communes. They were excluded from political rights, and from participation in the common property, not out of any mean and unreasonable jealousy, but because the common property was barely sufficient for the existing burgers—population always increases up to, it might be more truly said down to, the means of subsistence—and increase of numbers would have destroyed the action and benefits of the system : the only system then and there possible.

We still have to consider a third kind of commonable land—the garden-ground. This was, originally, as necessary as the other two kinds. It would amount for each to shares of an acre or two. It completed the support of the family. It was an indispensable supplement to the cows and the fuel. And even in these times, when money can be earnt in many ways, the quarter, or half, of an acre, in some places still the whole acre, which can be assigned to each member of the commune, has some advantages. It enables the family to secure a sufficient supply of cabbages, onions, haricots, flax, hemp, potatoes, and occasionally, a serviceable amount of wheat or maize. Formerly there was no other way for the household to procure these articles : though, indeed, in these days, this obvious advantage is sometimes counterbalanced by greater, but less obvious disadvantages. The old rule was that every commune should have a certain amount of *terre laborable* ; and that this should, at stated periods, say every year, every five, ten, or twenty years, as might be the local arrangement, be reportioned among those who would themselves cultivate their lots. The community must have hands and hearts to protect it, indeed even to enable it to be a community; and these hands and hearts must have the means of living; and if all the *terre laborable* had been allowed to fall into the condition of private property, many would have been deprived of a necessary ingredient in the means of living. And here again, if *Beisassen* had been admitted to a participation in the communal garden ground, the aim and object of the system would, so far as that went, have been defeated. In many, probably in all communes, it was the rule that new comers might purchase the position and rights of burgers, when, but only when, the old burgers were in favour, unanimously, of their admission. This wise requirement of unanimity upon the question of the admission of a new burger secured the community against the action of a cause, which, if unrestricted, would certainly and rapidly have reduced the severalties of its members in this, and all other kinds of their common property, to insufficiently small dimensions. It is true that they have at last been overtaken by this inconvenience; but it has been brought about by the action of a natural cause which could not have been met and obviated in any way: for it has been the result of an increase of population; and that increase of population has been the result of an increase of wealth; which again, in turn, was the result of an increase of variety in the ways opened for obtaining a living. Our porter from Meiringen to Brieg, Jean Ott, a burger of Im Hof, has ten children. He obtains his livelihood by carrying travellers' knapsacks. Those knapsacks therefore have ultimately been the cause of the existence of the ten children. The boys will all be burgers of Im Hof. Their existence will lessen the value of the severalties of the common property of Im Hof. In this way, everywhere, the severalties are being so reduced as to be no longer sufficient for the support of families. Thus they become only prophylactics, if that, against pauperism.

The four parts then of the system we have been considering, the common summer pastures, the reclaimed appropriated prairies, the common forest for fuel, and for building and repairs, and the common *terre laborable*, hung together inseparably. Each was necessary under the circumstances of the character and natural formation of the country; and of the absence of accumulations of capital, and of anything else to give employment, the existence of which would have meant that there were other sources than land for supporting life. The Switzer—that is the governing fact—was the parasite of the cow. He could not have existed without it. But he could not have kept cows without their having been taken off his hands during the summer by their maintenance on the common mountain pastures. This was necessary for enabling him to form and maintain the prairie land, and to make hay from it. Otherwise the cows could not have been supported in the winter. But these prairies could not, as a general rule, have been formed without the stimulus of private property. Many families could not have existed unless they had had a supply of fuel from the common forest. An assured amount of garden-ground was almost as necessary as an assured amount of fuel.

It will help us to understand how this system acted, and why it acted as it did, if we observe how the introduction of the new conditions has affected it. Switzerland, which was for many ages the poorest country in Europe, is rapidly progressing towards becoming, in proportion to the amount of its population, one of the richest. As I have already reminded the reader, no other country in the world, in proportion to its population, manufactures cotton and silk so largely. Again, it is said that 150,000 travellers pass every year through the single town of Interlaken. We will not take into account any but these; and we will suppose that those who stay in the country some months as well as those who stay some weeks, and those who are careless, as well as those who are careful, about their outgoings, spend each, on an average of the whole, 35*l*. This will amount to 5,250,000*l*. As to Swiss investments in foreign securities, from what inquiries I have been able to make I have come to the conclusion that they are very considerable. This is nothing less than making foreign countries tributary to them. The interest paid on these investments is so much tribute. It is just as much a tribute as that which the Jews paid to the Romans, or which the Khedive is at this day paying to the Porte. How it came about in any one of these cases that the payment had, or has, to be paid, is practically, of no importance: what is essential, as far as the matter before us is concerned, is the fact of the payment. The money goes to Switzerland. Russians, Americans, French, Italians, Germans, are in this way working for, and are being taxed for, the Swiss. English, Dutch, and Danish funds do not pay interest enough for them. There is therefore no longer any point in the Frenchman's sarcasm, 'We fight for honour, but you fight for money.' Nor in the Switzer's rejoinder, 'It is only natural that each of us, like the rest of the world, should fight for what he has not got.' The Swiss have at last come to be so prosperous, and to have so many other means of making money, both at home and abroad, that they would not in these days risk their lives in foreign military service for a franc a day.

What we now have to observe is, that this influx of wealth has, to a great extent, rendered the old system of common pasturage both unnecessary and unfair. While it has been abrogating its necessity, it has been reversing its action. In these days a man keeps an hotel, or a shop; has a bank, or a factory; or in some way or other makes a good deal of money: perhaps it was made abroad, and he has returned home with it. He will now keep a dozen, he may even keep two dozen cows. He will be able to do this, because he will keep them out of the profits of his business, or from the interest of accumulated capital; and not, as was alone possible formerly, by his own labour and that of his family. If he were reduced to that means for keeping them, their number would be reduced to four or five. And this rich man is a burger, and therefore he is entitled to send them all up to the common pastures. If he have more than two dozen, all still may be sent. At the other extremity of society many are called into existence by the existence of the rich. These will be supported by wages. And these wages they will not get unless they work regularly. But if they work regularly for wages, they will not be able to spend the summer in collecting winter provender for cows. Nor in winter, if they had provender, could they devote their time to cows. These men, therefore, though burgers, equally with the rich, will be unable to turn their rights in the common pastures to account. Their rights thus fall into abeyance. And in many places the population has so increased that there is no longer common pasturage enough for those who do keep cows. Some half-dozen rich burgers, then, may alone have more cows than the pastures, which remain common, would be able to maintain, or an increase in the number of burgers who are able to keep a few cows each, may have brought things to the same point. And either of these cases may be coincident with the inability of a large proportion of the burgers to keep any cows at all. Increase, then, of wealth, and consequent increase of population, have altogether altered the action and defeated the purpose of the old system. In those communes in which the rich are in the majority—a state of society which, strange to say, does exist in some—the old rule is rigidly maintained: every burger is still entitled to send up to the common pastures all the cows he kept through the winter. In places, however, where wealth has so increased the number of cows that there is no longer sufficient common pasturage for all, each burger sends up a *pro ratâ* proportion of his herd, say a third, or a half. In such cases, by the very maintenance, as far as possible, of the old, originally fair rule, the poor, some partially, some utterly, are excluded from the use of their property. As Dr. Bekker observed to me, it is the literal application of the saying, that 'to them who have shall be given, and they shall have abundantly; but from them who have not shall be taken away what they appear to have.' In many places it has become the practice, and it is one which the force of circumstances is rapidly extending, to let the common pastures. The question then arises, of what is to be done with the proceeds? In the case of the communal alpes they may be applied to the payment of local rates; or they may be divided among the burgers, who may receive each an equal amount, or an amount proportionate to the number either of his cows, or of his family.

But to each of these methods, and I believe to every conceivable method of appropriating the proceeds, valid objections may be made. If they go in reduction, or whole payment, of rates for schools, roads, churches, fountains, police, &c., then the rich are eased in a far greater degree than the poor; who, according to the original principle of the system have an equal right in the common property with the rich; its use having been, at the time of its institution, so regulated—this was possible under the circumstances of those times—as to enable all to participate in it; and, too, to participate in it pretty equally. Riches have supervened, and have, as things now are, made this impossible. But as those who are now poor may some day become rich, their rights are still, contingently, equal to those of the rich. Or, if the proceeds are divided among the *usagers* in equal amounts, or in proportion to the number of cows owned, or of the family—and these methods of distribution are often resorted to in places where the population has quite outgrown the common pastures—the benefit to each burger will be very small. In the equal *per capita* distributions idleness will always be rewarded, without industry being ever encouraged. And in the proportionate distributions it will generally happen that those who want help most will get the least, and those who want it least will get the most; which difficulty will be further aggravated by the fact, that in these days many of those who want it most are least deserving of it. Again, all these methods of distribution exclude the new burgers; and such exclusions are in direct contradiction to the ideas, the sentiments, and the requirements of modern societies.

In those cases in which common pastures belong to sections of the burgers of a commune, that is to say, to corporations, for instance, to the burgers of a particular hamlet, or to certain families, either with or without a definite object to be promoted by the use, or the proceeds, of the common property, or in some way or other by those who hold it, it is found that the same disturbing action, as in the case of the communal property, though not quite to the same degree, has been introduced by the influx of riches. Some get rich, and some get poor; which in the case of these corporations also, renders the system unmeaning, and even noxious. And riches lead to an increase of population which renders the share of each corporator of little value.

The fact is that the old system is utterly inapplicable to the new conditions into which society has advanced. It was intended for that state of things, modified by the strong peculiarities of Switzerland, in which land is the only means of supporting life. Life may now be supported by capital, either invested or employed, a means which admits of indefinite extension, or by the labour and skill of those whom capital employs. This has deprived the old system of its character and utility; and even in many places made its action prejudicial to the interests both of individuals and of society. Its object—that of supporting life—can now be better attained by other arrangements, and also by other means.

Still the great principle to be dealt with in these days is identical with that which had to be dealt with originally. It must, however, be applied under the circumstances existing now, as it had to be under the circumstances existing then. It is the principle that the land of the country ought to be so held as to ensure the production of the greatest amount of food, possible under the conditions of the time, for the people of the country. Any arrangement which now excludes from the land the application to it of capital, the great modern agent of production, contradicts this principle. The old system therefore of holding the land in common contradicts it. It has also to be considered now; how what must be done for carrying out the paramount principle, can be done on a footing that is fair to all. A system which excludes a large part of the population from the chance of becoming owners of land contradicts this requirement. That is to say, the old system, which was in its day beneficial to the community, and fair to all, is now the reverse of beneficial to all, and the reverse of fair to all. Those who are now under the necessity of attempting to work it are beset with much the same kind of difficulties in which a general would find himself involved, if he were obliged to attempt to carry out a campaign with the commissariat and the tactics of the Homeric age. Much would be lost, much would be hindered, and the attempt, after all, could not be anything but unreal and mischievous; or their antiquated methods and position may be compared to what would be those of a colony of Esquimaux, who, having been settled in the genial climate, and amid the abundant resources, of a temperate region, were endeavouring to maintain inviolate the practices and the ways of living that had been necessary in their old Arctic home.

The administration of the common forests is, under existing circumstances, hampered with similar difficulties, though not quite to the same extent. Their produce for fuel, for building, and for repairs, was distributed in accordance with the size of the house. Now, however, there are 'large mansions, and very small tenements; and, if the old rule of distribution be maintained, the owners of the large mansions, who can very well afford to pay for their fuel, will receive half a dozen or more klafters of fuel, and timber in proportion, while the owners of small tenements may be receiving only one klafter of fuel, and timber in proportion to that. In some places, where the population has largely increased, the produce of the common forests is all sold, and the proceeds are applied to the maintenance of the destitute, or to some other public purpose.

As to the garden-ground, the increase of population has in many places reduced the share of each *usager* to an almost uselessly small plot of ground: the occupation of which must often prove a real detriment, by indisposing him to turn to some trade or employment, by which he might readily obtain the competency, with the hope, or appearance only of which, his few rods of land are now mocking him.

M. Emile de Laveleye, a learned writer, in the *Revue des Deux Mondes*, on the social and political relations of agriculture, thinks that he has discovered in the old Swiss system a remedy for the social and political maladies under which France has long been suffering. He advocates its adoption. Of course the adoption of anything of the kind is impossible. This is a matter in which the arrangements of the time can be engendered only by the circumstances of the time. As well might he advocate a reversion to bows and arrows as a scheme for enabling Europe to get rid of its costly armaments; or to domestic distaffs and looms as a remedy for the evils of the factory system. In these matters there can be no reversions. Even in Switzerland, where exceptional causes, the character of the country, and centuries of dearth of capital, so long maintained the system we have endeavoured to describe, and which he would fain endeavour to reproduce in France, it is seen by the more intelligent part of the nation that now, even in its remote and secluded valleys, in consequence of the increase of population and accumulation of capital, it is going, and must go. The holding of land in common they acknowledge to be, as things now are, an evil, and to be no longer capable of defence. The old ideas cannot now be carried out, the old objects cannot now be secured, by the old methods. Society has now needs, and has assumed a form, and has within it an agent, which renders some other arrangement more conformable to existing conditions, more workable, and more productive of the elements of moral and intellectual, as well as of material well-being; and, too, more fair for all. Those among the Swiss themselves who are in a position to take a view of the whole subject, now recognize what time has established among them—that land is no longer, as formerly, the only means of maintaining a family; that in the case of many it is not the best means; that more can be made of it that is to say, that it can be made to produce more food, which is the equivalent of its being made to support a greater number of families, by its being allowed to pass into the hands of private owners possessed of capital, than by its being kept as the common property of communes, or of corporations; and by its acquisition being made by the way of the results of any kind of industry, equally open and possible to all. They regret the difficulties which stand in the way of the removal of those antiquated shackles which now limit its uses and produce, and which do this mischief, ridiculously, in the name of equality; as if the perfection of equality were to exclude rigidly the majority of the community from all chance of ever acquiring any share in the property of the land. In this matter, the true equality for these days is to make the ownership of the land—the chief instrument of production, and participation in the produce of the land, as far as possible equal to all by the thousand ways of the thousand forms of industry society now requires. What is now wanted is that all should have the chance of such an education as would properly qualify each for some form of industry, and enable him by perseverance, thrift, and cultivated intelligence to turn it to good account. This would enable all, and each according to his merits, which should be the first aims of society in the era of capital, to participate in the produce of the soil. Make the produce as abundant as possible, and at the same time make that, as far as possible, common to all, in proportion to the exertions, which mean the intellectual and moral merits, of each. Of these times these are the requirements, which so far from being promoted, can only be thwarted by the system of common land, or by that of the minute division of the land. Both of these systems carry us in a thoroughly wrong direction.

So soon as facts oblige us to see these points, the

existing system, so far as it is opposed to them, is demonstrated to have become antiquated and false. It begins therefore to be undermined, and to totter to its fall; no matter how unquestioned, varied, and great the services it was capable, under other circumstances, of rendering, and had rendered, to society. It was for the sake of those circumstances that it existed. When they are gone the reasons for its existence have gone with them. As it, itself, formerly superseded some other system, so must some other system now supersede it. This is the law of nature. In such matters gratitude for what once did good service, respect for the past, the charm that memory flings about old arrangements, have nothing to do with the settlement of the questions in debate, except in the way of securing ample time for their complete discussion. The governing consideration must always be, What under existing circumstances will be best for society? That is to say, in this particular case, What, as things now are, will give the community the best supply of food, and in such a manner as will be fairest and best for all, all the wants of society that are affected by the ownership and the produce of the land having been duly attended to? These are the old questions, which, from the beginning, advances in the conditions of society have reopened again and again, and which have been resettled again and again, always in conformity with the existing conditions of the epoch. They are questions that have relative as well as absolute elements, and which therefore, like that of government, and of almost everything belonging to the domain of human affairs, can never be settled once for all by the aid of some abstract theory. The circumstances, however, and events arising out of the circumstances, which are what force them into debate, always, sooner or later, force upon us a corresponding settlement of them.

A word more. Property, which, as we have seen, existed from the beginning, because it is an incident of life, is not theft. On the contrary, the worst theft is that of the highest property. And the highest property a man can have, and that, too, of which, in these days, the political and economical well-being of society requires that he should have as unrestricted use as of his capital and of his labour, is his capacity for moral and intellectual improvement; the point has now been reached at which these ideas are beginning to form themselves in the general mind; and the theft of this capacity is in a sense committed against those who are debarred from the opportunities, now possible, for its culture and development. We are beginning to see that it is a kind of theft to hinder a man from attaining to what, while it would be of advantage to him, is fairly within his reach; and, if this be just what would make him most truly a man, and enable him to discharge his duties to society as well as to himself, the theft is very far from being an insignificant one. It is, in fact, the very theft against which the Christian Church has all along been, or ought to have been, the protest of humanity: this was its *raison d'être*: though very naturally, but quite wrongly, so soon as it came to be an hierarchical organization, that part of the protest that had reference to what was intellectual was hushed, and, from obvious motives, knowledge and reason were thenceforth denounced. But so far it had falsified its purpose, abdicated its position, and ceased to be a Church, having become in its stead only an hierarchical organization. Society it is that is now unconsciously committing this theft, against which it is the highest duty of the true Church to protest. And it is society only, acting in its organized form, and through its accredited agent, the state, that can effectually make the restitution; and so far as the state attempts to do this, that is to say, to make the moral and intellectual improvement of the community its aim, it becomes the ally of the true Church.

The progress of society may be measured by the degree in which it enables larger and larger proportions of its members to enter upon a serviceable possession of this, their highest property. It will have attained a very high degree of progress when it shall have given to every member of the community opportunities and means for doing this: everyone will then have some chance of being able to turn his mental endowments to some account, to stand alone, and to take care of himself. That each should have this chance is now as necessary for society as it is for the individual. When the old Swiss system was established it was the material life only of small, poor, uncommercial communities that had to be thought about. Its originators therefore made such a portion of their land common as would be sufficient for this purpose. That arrangement only, then and there, could give the means for material existence; and no other kind of existence was or could have been at that time taken into consideration. All beyond this the Church took charge of, and attended to in accordance with its own ideas and in its own fashion. But now man can live a higher life; and for the requirements of his material life the possession, or direct participation in the use of land is not necessary: indeed, a better material life can, in many cases, be lived without its possession or use than with it. But these new conditions require that a man should be enabled to turn to good account his moral and intellectual capacities: they it is that must now be so cultivated as to enable him to obtain a livelihood by their exercise in the new world in which his lot has been cast.

This is what the present Swiss system of education aims at doing for every man in the country. Their old agrarian system gave to each, when that was what was necessary, a share in the common land. Life with them has now risen into a higher stage. It has moral and intellectual possibilities, which are also requirements, formerly not needed, nor dreamt of. The Swiss recognize this, and give to each opportunities for participating in the knowledge and moral training, as they conceive it, now possible. Having already freedom and political equality, they were able to rise to the idea of humanity. Their old agrarian system, too (morally it had acted in the very opposite direction to ours with its necessary supplement of a communistic poor law) had made industry, thrift, honesty, and foresight traditional and instinctive among them. There was therefore nothing to obscure their perception of, or weaken their desire for what ought to be done under the altered circumstances of the times. Formerly, in conformity with the possibilities and requirements of the age, the community had made some material provision for all; as much as it could, and as fairly as it could; and which would be enough, if turned to the best account by the industry of the individual, for a competent living in the fashion of those days. Time has rendered those arrangements antiquated and inapplicable. This landed provision cannot any longer be made for all. There are too many people and not enough land for that. But contemporaneously with this increase of numbers, which is the same thing as relative decrease and failure of the old landed means for living, a great variety of other means have been opened on all sides; and the stage upon which these may be turned to account has been expanded in the case of each from a small mountain-locked valley to, practically, the whole world. For these reasons, just as their old agrarian system made land, so their new educational system is making intellectual training, and some amount of moral training (though already they have much of that) common to all. The powers these confer are now in a sense common pastures, upon which all may keep flocks and herds; common forests, from which all may get fuel and building materials ; and common garden ground, by the cultivation of which all may supply their minor wants.

They have endeavoured to apply the old principle to a new, a better, and a higher world. The identity of principle, and the differences of application, are analogous to those that exist between the caterpillar and the butterfly. In both life, with its imperative requirements of food, air, light, warmth, &c., and its essential principles of assimilation, circulation, &c., is the same. But in the caterpillar this life has to be maintained by, and spent upon a leaf. Everything therefore is adapted to this condition. Its powerful jaws, its vigorous stomach, its restricted powers of locomotion, the tenacious hold of its feet, its sluggish disposition, its dull colours, are all referable to the leaf, that is to say, to its habitat and means of living. So with the butterfly. Its life is to be spent in the air, and among the flowers, and upon the honey distilled from the flowers. Hence its large powers of locomotion, its beautiful colours, its lively temperament, its sensitive antennæ, its fastidious stomach, its flexible proboscis. Everything in it has been readapted to the new conditions. So, too, with the Swiss. While they were in the earlier stage of their national existence, what was needed for each was a little bit of land, a cow or two, a spade, a manure basket, and a wife to carry it. This was their caterpillar stage. They are now passing into the butterfly stage. All their arrangements and provisions therefore have now to be reaccommodated to the new conditions in the required fashion. They must now be endowed with the capacity for collecting and turning to account capital, the distilled essence of all property, without which even the land cannot be made much of now. This life does not require the tough hide, the strong sinews, the gross stomach, the adstriction to a single spot, of the old life ; but on the contrary, a vastly enlarged mobility both of body and mind, a readiness for turning anything to account, and for entering on any opening. They must be quick in thought and quick in action. If they cannot find what they want at home, they must be able and disposed to go to seek it elsewhere—here, there, anywhere. They must have scientific and technical knowledge ; must be capable of appreciating new facts, and of taking large views ; must be patient and painstaking ; must have the power of working mentally for distant objects; must have an instinct of submission to law, both to the laws of society, which aim at justice to all, and at order, and to the laws of nature, submission to which enables a man to use effectually his own powers, and to turn to account the powers of nature. These are moral and intellectual qualities. And it is with these that the Swiss school system, like that of their North German neighbours, would fain endow the whole people.

INDEX.

AGR

AGRARIAN evolution, 305. Village community, 322
Agriculture, prehistoric, 315. In New Caledonia, 317
Airolo, 63, 87
Aletsch Glacier, 242, 260, 264, 267
Aletschwald, 260
Allotments, 260
Allmends, 2. Of Stanz, 35. Of Glarus, 165. Of Switzerland, 297. Causes that maintained them, 330. Unsuitable to existing conditions, 345-354
Alpes, at Am Stag, 48. Of Oberalp, 95, Of Waldnacht, 109. Statistics of, 301. Why common, 336. Relation to prairies, 337
Alpbach, 131
Alpnach, 34, 204
Altorf, 43. No bookseller at, 44
American puzzled at Lugano, 78. Medical students, 93. An angler, 104
Ammer, 14, 44, 51, 59, 98. His portrait, 208-213
Am Stag, 46. Intellectual condition of, 47. Common rights at, 48. La Croix Blanche of, 103
Andermatt, 58, 87, 102

BUR

Animal life, scarcity of, 207
Animals, domestication of useful, 312
Association, primæval, 310. Among lower animals, 311, 314

BEISASSEN, Why excluded from common rights, 340, 342
Barber, the, of Brieg, 274
Beckenried, 122-127
Bekker, Dr., 176, 347
Bellaggio, 79
Bell Alp, 264-271. View from, 268
Bellinzona, 68, 85
Berne, 7
Black Virgin of Einsiedln, 147
Blue of glacier ice, 263
Boats, Swiss, 31
Bocketobel, 108
Böningen, Allmends of, 14
Bookseller, none at Altorf, 44
Boots for walking, 232
Bretzwyl, 1-6
Brieg, 272
Brünig, 23, 207
Brunnen, 188
Buochs, 36, 40
Burgers, without cows, 48. Old and new, 297, 340, 342

CAN

CANTERBURY, why no pilgrimages to, 143
Capital incompatible with common land, 349
Carriages at Andermatt, 89. At Am Stag, 104. At Alpnach, 204
Carving in wood, 28
Cenere, view from Monte, 74, 83
Cereals, first culture of, 315
Cheese, its value to the Swiss, 331
Christo in pauperibus, 32
Church of Rome, present position of, 151. The, a protest, 357
Cities, English, 203
Classical studies, why advocated, 138
Climate, favourable to grass and forests, 134
Cloud banner, 114, 170
Common, how produce of land now, 325
Commune, Swiss, 298
Como, Mass at, 81. Shores of Lake, 82
Conversation spoils society, 65
Corporations, 175
Cowley, 238
Culture, moral and intellectual, a means of living, 358-362

DAZIO GRANDE, 64
Delta of Lütschine, 11-14
Deschwanden, M., 122
Devil, Ammer on the, 51. Devil's Bridge, 57. Forms assumed by the, 66
Differences not seen by pilgrims, 145
Diligences, 92
Disappointment, a common, 84

EDUCATION, aims of Swiss' 358-362
Eggischhorn, hotel at, 236.

GRA

Storm at, 239. Ascent of, 240. View from, 242
Einsiedln, 135-160
Endowments, 177
Engelberg, 117-120
Englishman, in Italy, 105
English virtue, 125
Ennetburgen, 36
Enjoyment, science of, 292. Knowledge necessary for, 296
Etruria, perhaps two races in ancient, 20
Evening at Engelberg, 118, 119
Excursion, the kind of, 15. How described, 288. Plan of the, 290. Pleasures of, 295
Exertion, Is—a pleasure, 129
Expression results from mind, 33, 122

FAIDO, 65
Flies, the Devil in the form of, 66
Föhn, the, 171
Forest Cantons, a point in history of, 333
Forest, common, 50, 339. Care of, 133
Forget-me-nots on the Surenen, 111
French *homme de lettres*, 187
Fruit, failure of, 279
Fuel, decrease of, 132

GARDEN, common ground, 341
Gaststube, 29
Geese, about, 90
German anglers, 126
Gersau, 40
Gibbon, 281
Glacier, Rhone, 228. Aletsch, 242, 260
Glarus, 164-182
Göschenen, 55
Grace, decay of female, 19

INDEX. 365

GRA
Grammar, Public School Latin, 65
Grasshoppers, 238
Grimsel, 125

HACKEN PASS, 128-134
   Heusler, Professor, 1
Honey, artificial, 208
Horse, unruly young, 86. End of Bourbaki's, 206
Hotels on Eggischhorn and Bell Alp, 269
Hunting stage, 307

IMPETUOSITY out of place, 117
Infallibility, 152, 155, 234
Intellectual life at Am Stag, 47
Interlaken, 8
Interpretation of what is seen, 265
Inscription at Einsiedln, 141
Instinct, 261
Italian, a cultivated, 16-21
Italy, land in prehistoric, 37. Quick-pulsed, 79

KIRCHET, the, 220-224, 226
   Klönthal, 187
Klus, 107
Knowledge, the perception of differences, 145. Ignorance protected against, 234. Necessary for enjoyment, 266, 295. Advances religion, 312 (note)

LAKE, Thun and Brienz, 10.
   Lungern, 24. Sarnen, 31.
Lucerne, 39. Maggiore, 74.
Lugano, 77. Como, 78-83.
Zurich, 161. Wallenstadt, 163.
Geneva, 281
Land, its object to supply food, 308, 323. Lammas, 324. Affected by circumstances, 326.

PAR
Lords' committee on, 329. What affected tenure of, in Switzerland, 330
Lausanne, 280
Laveleye, M., 352
Liberty, 22. Tree of, 71
Linththal, 179
Locarno, 74
Lombach, 10
Lucerne, 202
Lugano, 76. Lake of, 77
Lungern, 24
Lütschine, 10

MAGGIORE, Lago, view of head of, 74
Maidenhair fern, 126
Manufactures, effects of, 169
Märjelensee, 244
Mass in cathedral of Como, 81
Menaggio, 78
Middle-class travellers, 190
Morality, 73. Relation of, to religion, 156
Munster, young lady of, 235
Muotta, 187
Mysteries, the old, 138

NATURE, a workshop of, 53
   New Caledonians, 317

OBERALP ALPE, 95
   Obergestelen, 230
Object, disadvantage of an, 52
Oleanders in flower, 79
Ott, Jean, 225, 342
Ouchy, 280

PANIER, the Bretzwyl, 6
   Pantenbrücke, 179
Parasite, Switzer the, of the cow, 333
Paray le Monial, why pilgrimage to, urged, 153

PAS

Pass, St. Gothard, 55, 64, 87. Surenen, 107-117. Hacken, 128-134. Pragel, 183-187
Pastoral stage, 313
Pauperism, English, 338
Phenomena not isolated, 300
Phœnicia an autonomous dependency of Egypt, 19
Pilgrimages, 149-160
Pilgrims support Einsiedln, 140. Defect of knowledge in, 145
Pragel, 183-187
Prairies, their history, 334. Relation to alpes, 337
President, letter from the, 7. Of Glarus, 173
Priest's Leap, 51. Of Upper Valais, 233
Progress, a measure of, 357
Property, primæval, 309. Among lower animals, 309, 313. Agriculture implies, 321. Highest form of, 356

RAILWAY under St. Gothard, 56, 63
Rapperswyl, 162
Reason in animals, 261
Religion and morality, 156
Rent at Meiringen, 214
Reverie, a, 53
Rhone Glacier, 228. Valley of the, 275
Richisau, 185
Rieder Alp, 247
Rigi, two views from the, 194-201
Ritualism at Meiringen, 215-220
Rose of the Alps, Ammer's bouquet of, 98

SACHELN, 28
Saint Gothard, 61, 87
Saint Nicholas von der Flüe, 29
Sarnen, 33
Scholarship, 20

VOR

Schöllinen, 56
Schwyz, 128
Science of enjoyment, 292
Scopas, view from Mount, 75
Sidelhorn, 229
Soil, shallowness of, 206
Spider-like, the mind, 56
Stanz, 35, 121
Storms, 8. Effects of, 26, 27, 40. At Como, 79, 80. In the Hacken Pass, 131. At Brienz, 208. At Eggischhorn, 239. At Bell Alp, 268
Sugar-cane, culture of, by New Caledonians, 317-320
Suggestion, a, 255
Surenen, 107-116
Swiss justice, 123. Virtue, 125
Switzerland, wealth of, 344

TICINO, valley of the, 67
Time reckoning lost, 127
Times, possibility of existence without the, 81. At Glarus, 172
Titlis, 116
Todensee, 228
Travellers, a mob of, 205. English, 256
Trieb, 128

URI, Bay of, 42. Census of, 45
Urseren Thal, 58

VALAIS, Upper, priests of, 233. Climate of, 235
Val Tremola, 62, 87
Verriéres, 287
Village, English, community, 322
Vineyards, English, 278
Virgil's good woman, 72
Voiturier, a roguish, 122. A good, 182
Vorauen, 184

INDEX.

WAL

WALDNACHT, 109
Walking in Switzerland, 231
Wallensee, 163
Warped, the Delta of the Lütschine might be, 13
Wasen, 52
Water, 32. Effects of running, 64, 68
Wealth, distribution of, 70. No disqualification for office, 174. In modern Switzerland, 344. Disturbing effects of, 345
Weather-battle, 94. At Glarus, 171. Of the excursion, 288
Wet afternoon at Andermatt, 88-92

ZUR

Women, young, in the Catholic Cantons, 46. Old woman mending road, 54. Good, at Bellinzona, 72. Head-dress of, of Unterwalden, 118. Middle-aged endure fatigue, 135. Strong-minded, 270
Working classes, 192
World, carrying the, about with one, 172. Modern, its interest, 287
Worldly Wise on men and women, 267

ZURICH, museum at, 6

A MONTH
IN
SWITZERLAND.

BY THE REV. F. BARHAM ZINCKE.

Crown 8vo. 5s.

A SELECTION of NOTICES by the PRESS.

'Those who care to read Mr. Barham Zincke's works will gladly welcome another from his hand, and will know pretty well what to expect in it. They will look for occasional pages of vivid and humorous description, interspersed with a much larger allowance of trains of reflection on a great variety of topics, which are always sensible, often new, and never dull. These expectations will be fully realised in reading "A Month in Switzerland."........There is one remarkable chapter of a hundred pages, very well written, which is a little lecture on the various forms of land tenure, and the social and moral results that flow from them. Mr. Barham Zincke, in spite of the attractive aspect which industry wears in the Valley of the Visp, is not in favour of peasant proprietorship. It is not, he thinks, in harmony with the spirit of the age, which recognises capital and not land as king.'

GUARDIAN.

'We part from these results of a month in Switzerland with imperfect sympathy, indeed, in some points, but with satisfaction in most, and with respect in all.'

SATURDAY REVIEW.

'There is quite enough in this little volume to arrest the attention of anybody who cares for an hour's intercourse with the mind of one who has carefully pondered some of the deepest problems which affect the physical well-being of his fellow creatures.'

SPECTATOR.

'The preface to Mr. Barham Zincke's holiday notes on Switzerland warns "those who may have read his 'Egypt of the Pharaohs and of the Khedivé' that this little book belongs to the same family." We are thus prepared for the same features of thought, the same observant eye, the same cast of mind, at once penetrative and receptive, that were displayed so conspicuously in Mr. Zincke's former work; nor are we disappointed.'

EXAMINER.

'Mr. Zincke's dissertation on this most important subject (the land question) deserves careful attention, coming, as it does, from a man whose previous works have thoroughly established his reputation as a thoughtful and original writer. Indeed, Mr. Zincke's book is well worth reading for the fourth chapter alone.'

DAILY TELEGRAPH.

'It is eminently a thoughtful book.'   DAILY NEWS.

London : SMITH, ELDER, & CO., 15 Waterloo Place.

EGYPT OF THE PHARAOHS
AND OF
THE KHEDIVÉ.

By the Rev. F. BARHAM ZINCKE.

Second Edition, much Enlarged. With a Map. Demy 8vo. 16*s*.

SELECTION from NOTICES by the PRESS.

'We have in this volume a thoughtful, almost exhaustive, treatment of a subject too often handled by mere *dilettante* writers, who dismiss as unworthy of notice the problems with which they are unable to cope......We heartily commend Mr. Zincke's delightful book as a fresh pleasure to the thoughtful reader.' SPECTATOR.

'A more independent and original volume of Egyptian travel than at this time of day we should have thought possible. Mr. Zincke has a quickness of eye, a vigour of judgment, and a raciness of style which place him far above the ordinary run of travellers..........Readers will lose much if they do not make some acquaintance with this truly remarkable volume.'
LITERARY CHURCHMAN.

'Each chapter takes some one topic, treats it in sharp piquant style, and generally throws some new light upon it, or makes it reflect some new light upon something else. If these bright and sparkling pages are taken as containing suggestions to be worked out for oneself and accepted or rejected in the light of more mature knowledge, they will be found full of value.'
GUARDIAN.

'Mr. Zincke speaks like a man of rare powers of perception, with an intense love of nature in her various moods, and an intellectual sympathy broad and deep as the truth itself.' SATURDAY REVIEW.

'A very pleasant and interesting book.....Mr. Zincke tells his readers exactly such facts as they would wish to know. The style is captivating.'
WESTMINSTER REVIEW.

'A series of brilliant and suggestive essays.' EXAMINER.

'Mr. Zincke's personal observations, original remarks, and practical views, make him worthy of being consulted by all who desire to have something more than a picturesque and sentimental description of the peculiarities belonging to modern Egypt.' ILLUSTRATED LONDON NEWS.

London : SMITH, ELDER, & CO., 15 Waterloo Place.

www.ingramcontent.com/pod-product-compliance
Lightning Source LLC
Chambersburg PA
CBHW030402230426
43664CB00007BB/706